THE SMITHSONIAN COLLECTION OF RECORDINGS

AMERICAN ★★★★★★★★
MUSICAL THEATER
SHOWS, SONGS, AND STARS

by Dwight Blocker Bowers

Smithsonian Collection of Recordings
Washington, D. C.   1989

The Smithsonian Collection of Recordings
is a division of Smithsonian Press
Felix C. Lowe, Director

Producers: Dwight Blocker Bowers and
      Margaret Robinson
Assistant Producer: Elizabeth Eaton
Mastering Engineer: Jack Towers
Digital transfer by Curt Wittig

Book Editor: Jane Sapp
Graphic Designer: Janice Wheeler
Production Assistant: Tom Dube

ACKNOWLEDGEMENTS

Special thanks to Jack Raymond, whose
generosity, interest, and wisdom proved
invaluable to this project. Thanks also to
the following, for assistance of various
kinds: Charles Bell and the Theatre Arts
Collections staff, University of Texas at
Austin; David Brooks; Sam Brylawski,
Division of Recorded Sound, Library of
Congress; Carol Channing; Theodore S.
Chapin, Rodgers and Hammerstein
Organization; John Franks and Martine
McCarthy, CBS; Dick Gautier; Stanley
Green; Martha Hodges, Labor-Management
Documentation Center, Cornell University;
David Hummel, Institute of the American
Musical Theatre; Larry N. Lash,
PolyGram; Tony Locantro, EMI-UK; Don
McCormick, Rodgers and Hammerstein
Archive of Recorded Sound, New York
Public Library; John McWhorter;
Bernadette Moore, RCA; James R. Morris,
The Production Group; Betty Oakes; Bruce
Resnikoff, MCA; John Salisbury,
Smithsonian Press; Carl Scheele and J. R.
Taylor, National Museum of American
History; William Schurk, Bowling Green
State University; Jim Steinblatt, ASCAP.

TABLE OF CONTENTS

A poster heralding the initial New York engagement of *The Black Crook*.

★ A BRIEF HISTORY

What makes the American musical theater such a unique contribution to world culture? Is it the genre's sheer eclecticism? Surely no other theatrical form encompasses such a breathtaking range of styles. The American musical theater can be as simple as a Jerome Kern ballad or as complex as a Bernstein recitative; it can be a solo tap routine delivered by a self-taught hoofer like Bill Robinson or an Agnes de Mille story ballet performed by a fleet of trained dancers; as carefree as *Lady, Be Good!* and *Hello, Dolly!* or as serious as *Carousel* or *West Side Story*. The medium doesn't even require a linear plot: revues like the *Ziegfeld Follies* and *As Thousands Cheer* have added to the legacy through their songs and staging techniques. It is a genre dependent on stars, either established luminaries or those it creates. Above all, our indigenous musical stage is a flamboyant combination of popular entertainment and inspired art, with commercial considerations often providing the very impetus for its audacious innovations. Its blend of music, lyrics, drama, dance, performance styles, and decor stands as a brilliant model against which other cultures measure their own efforts at creating a popular musical theater.

★

Music has been a vital part of world theater since antiquity. Choral interludes or dithyrambs were important elements in ancient Greek and Roman drama, and in the medieval period the plaintive sounds of the fife and tambour accompanied passages in religious mystery plays. Songs were included in many of Shakespeare's works, often providing a philosophical commentary on the dramatic action. The seventeenth-century Italian *bel canto* operas and the French works of Jean-Baptiste Lully were perhaps the earliest attempts to use music not merely as decoration but as an integral element in developing plot and character. In eighteenth-century France, *operas comiques* came about when spoken dialogue was converted to sung text, thus allowing theater owners to skirt the necessity of obtaining the operating licenses required by the monarchy for legitimate drama.

Broadly speaking, a primordial popular musical theater has existed in America since the eighteenth century, although its earliest manifestations were limited primarily to sporadic activity in the key cities of Philadelphia, New York, and Charleston. Its first and perhaps most enduring influences were British, and its oldest relative may well have been the ballad opera, a comedy interspersed with familiar airs decked out in new, dramatically appropriate lyrics. Ballad opera's most illustrious exemplar, John Gay's *The Beggar's Opera* (1728), inspired our first native, if rudimentary, musical theater work, *The Disappointment* (ca. 1735). Alas, the work lived up to its title, for its thinly veiled satire of contemporary Philadelphia society was deemed unfit for the stage, and it reached audiences only as a published script. By the end of the century, ballad opera had inspired dramatist William Dunlap, "the father of the American stage," to attempt at least six plays with musical interludes. Among these is *The Archers* (1796), a recounting of the William Tell legend with a score by Benjamin Carr, the probable composer of "Yankee Doodle."

With the rise of industrialism and urbanization in the early nineteenth century, various imported forms of musical theater attracted larger and more diverse American audiences. While society's upper crust amused itself with French and Italian grand opera, the business and working classes enjoyed the more distinctly middle-brow European forms of lyric theater. Musical extravaganzas, essentially offshoots of the British and French traditions of court entertainments, first became popular in the 1820s. These series of *tableaux vivantes* ("living pictures"), whose performers were no more than decor, were triumphs of stage machinery over nondescript musical and dramatic content, but the techniques of the extravaganza inspired *The Black Crook* (1866), a legendary milestone in the evolution of the American musical theater. This work came about more by happenstance than artistic vision, when producer William Wheatley decided to use the members of a stranded French ballet troupe to bolster his production of a lunk-headed Gothic melodrama by Charles M. Barras. Its fantasy plot of archfiends and sprites haggling over the soul of a painter was ersatz German romanticism deemed unduly turgid even in its own day, but its combination of story, songs (as with the ballad opera, by a number of hands), elaborate scenery, and ballerinas cavorting scandalously in pink tights delighted Manhattan theatergoers for 475 consecutive performances and confirmed the commercial viability of the born-and-bred American lyric stage. It also established New York City as a major center for the development and production of popular musical theater.

Concurrent with the rise of the extravaganza was a brief vogue for a number of other European musical stage forms: the *opera bouffe,* a melodic French diversion typified by Offenbach's *La Grande Duchess de Gerolstein* (1867); the pantomime, a spectacular, light-hearted British variation of Italian commedia dell'arte promoted in America chiefly by comedian George L. Fox in his 1868 vehicle *Humpty Dumpty;* and the burlesque, an English form that lampooned works of literature and current events in scripts of rhymed couplet and was introduced in the U.S. tours of the formidable Lydia Thompson and her British Blondes. The burlesque inspired the seminal American work *Evangeline* (1874), described by historian Ethan Mordden as a "proto-musical comedy." Derived by Edward E. Rice and J. Cheever Goodwin from Longfellow's poem, the piece had the twin distinctions of being the first American musical with a score created specifically for the occasion and the first to have a run of over 500 consecutive performances.

But the first uniquely *American* form of musical theater had originated nearly fifty years earlier in 1828, in a skit performed by itinerant actor Thomas Dartmouth "Daddy" Rice. His impersonation of an American Negro in a routine built around "Jump Jim Crow," a song derived from slaves' work songs, signaled the birth of minstrelsy. Essentially a variety show of songs and sketches performed by white men in burnt-cork makeup, minstrelsy promoted a sympathetic, though patronizing, view of American life. To its credit, the form promoted a presentational performance style, a direct performer-to-audience relationship that remains an important aspect of our musical theater and contrasts sharply with the pseudo-realism prevalent in the acting techniques of the dramatic stage. Moreover, minstrelsy's colloquial music and lyrics, several of which were composed by Stephen Foster, emerged as the first American commercial songs to be something other than imitations of Old World culture. The medium reached its summit as mass entertainment in the 1840s and 1850s under the influence of Daniel Decatur Emmett's Virginia Minstrels and E. P. Christy's ensemble.

Minstrelsy was eventually superceded in popularity by the entertainments at Tony Pastor's Music Hall, which made variety shows—later known as vaudeville, after their French counterpart—acceptable for family audiences. Pastor's constantly changing bills of specialty acts served as a showcase for such future leading lights as George M. Cohan and Lillian Russell. Futhermore, vaudeville's presentation of acts "in one," "in two," "in three" (referring to the degrees of stage depth, as measured by the portals of curtains) contributed to the organizational pattern of the modern American musical, with its full-stage openings and finales and in-front-of-the-curtain comedy numbers and intimate ballads.

The final quarter of the nineteenth century was a period of great experimentation and exchange between European imports and native innovations. The traditions of a satiric and highly literate comic opera were established with the American premiere of Great Britain's *H.M.S. Pinafore* (1878) by Gilbert and Sullivan. One year later a New York production of von Suppe's *Fantinitza* introduced the romantic styles of Viennese operetta. The mass popularity of these European forms led to the creation of the Boston Ideal Opera Company (later known as the Bostonians), which was dedicated not only to the production of European music theater but also to the sponsorship of American versions. The ensemble was responsible for introducing some of Victor Herbert's earliest works.

The touring ensemble known as Nate Salsbury's Troubadours introduced the techniques of farce-comedy in *The Brook* (1879), which combined popular songs and dances with a thin plot depicting everyday Americans enjoying everyday pastimes. Edward Harrigan, Tony Hart, and David Braham took the tradition several steps further in their *Mulligan Guard* plays (ca. 1873–1885), which celebrated the rising urban immigrant class in extended comedy sketches dotted with colloquial songs. The finest example of the farce-comedy tradition is Charles Hoyt's *A Trip to Chinatown* (1891), a "musical trifle" that produced two of the American theater's first hit songs, "Reuben and Cynthia" and "After the Ball." Beginning in 1894 the importation of George Edwardes's British Gaiety shows, the first entertainments to be known officially as musical comedies, also fostered an interest in contemporary stories and simple tunes, in contrast to the romantic stories and arioso music of comic opera and the star-oriented specialties of the variety stage.

By 1905 the three major subgenres of the modern American musical theater had evolved. The Viennese, English, and French traditions of comic opera had inspired works by Irish-American Victor Herbert; our native forms of minstrelsy and variety entertainment (with a nod to French vaudeville) had matured into the traditions of the revue; and the techniques of English musical comedy and American farce-comedy were in the sure hands of George M. Cohan. In the first six decades of this century, the musically ambitious scores and romantic locales in the comic operas of Herbert and his contemporaries metamorphosed into the quintessential American operetta, *Show Boat,* and eventually into the musical plays of Rodgers and Hammerstein, Lerner and Loewe, and Bock and Harnick. The revue, with its parade of star turns and signature tunes, grew lavish in the 1910s under the influence of producers like Florenz Ziegfeld and the Shuberts, took on sophistication and intimacy during the early 1930s in works devised by Dietz and Schwartz and producer Max Gordon, developed a social conscience in the late 1930s and early 1940s

A period lithograph depicting Edward Harrigan and Tony Hart surrounded by scenes from their theatrical productions.

in the hands of Harold Rome and John Latouche, and became almost extinct by the 1960s. (The form had a brief renaissance in the songologues *Ain't Misbehavin'* [1978] and *Sophisticated Ladies* [1981] and the nostalgic recreation of American burlesque *Sugar Babies* [1980].) The musical comedy, with its hummable songs, everyday characters and naturalistic approach to storytelling, evolved from Cohan's infectious jingoism and Kern's clever Princess Theatre musicals to jazz age versions by Youmans and the Gershwins and eventually to such modern classics as *Finian's Rainbow* and *How to Succeed in Business without Really Trying*. During this period of innovation, there were also brilliant blurrings of these distinctions in such ambitious works as *Of Thee I Sing, Porgy and Bess, The Cradle Will Rock, Street Scene, The Most Happy Fella,* and *Candide*. This golden era in the American musical theater (1898–1964) corresponds with its dominance as a viable form of commercial entertainment, when a hit show meant not only profits from the box office but also income from the sale of sheet music, film versions, radio (and later television) adaptations, and recordings.

★

The rise of our native musical stage coincided, more or less, with that of our recording industry, which had begun in 1877 with the Emile Berliner's introduction of the phonograph. Most of the earliest American recordings of show music, both cylinders and acoustical 78-rpm discs, were performed not by its original stage interpreters but by recording company staff artists, who understood the demands of recording technology, though original cast members occasionally had the opportunity to document their stage performances on disc. Rarely did the orchestrations on these primitive recordings approximate those written for the show; usually, a piece was given a new arrangement played by the recording company's house band. Concurrently, the British recording industry promoted the idea of original cast recordings, beginning in 1900 with 78s of nearly the complete score of Leslie Stuart's operetta *Florodora*. Period documentation of some of the modern American musical

theater's most significant early works lives on only in English cast recordings of productions mounted in London's West End theater district. Among these are excerpts from the musical comedies *Lady, Be Good!* and *No! No! Nanette!* and the operettas *Rose-Marie* and *The Student Prince in Heidelberg*.

In the United States, Brunswick record producer Jack Kapp furthered the idea of recording the sound of the American musical theater with his two pioneering 1932 albums of 78s, which preserved the songs and major star performances of *Blackbirds of 1928* and the first major Broadway revival of *Show Boat*. In 1938 the small Musicraft label issued the entire score of *The Cradle Will Rock* on six ten-inch 78s, the first complete recording of an American musical by its original New York cast. Kapp was also responsible for producing the 1943 Decca original cast album of *Oklahoma!*, and its international popularity established the American tradition of original cast recordings.

Throughout the 1940s most of the major Broadway musicals were recorded either in excerpt, like Ray Bolger's "Once in Love With Amy" from *Where's Charley?* on a Decca 78, or nearly in entirety, as in Columbia's lavish treatment of Kurt Weill's *Street Scene*. The long-playing record, introduced in 1948, provided an ideal medium for documenting the popular musical theater: its 25-minutes-per-side allowed the inclusion of most of the score, an overture, and frequently some of the show's dance music. The phenomenal success of Columbia's cast recording of *South Pacific* convinced record companies that there were riches to be made from show music, not only from cast albums but also from "cover" versions of the show's hit tunes recorded by their own stable of popular singing stars. In the 1950s record companies often invested even more heavily in the theater by backing the production itself. Irving Berlin's *Call Me Madam* and Lerner and Loewe's *My Fair Lady* were two of a number of Broadway musicals financed by major recording companies.

One man who was instrumental in enhancing the quality and style of the original cast recording was Goddard

Lieberson, president of Columbia Records from 1956 to 1966. He instituted the practice of being with a show almost from its inception, accompanying it through rehearsals and out-of-town tryouts to its opening night, in order to find ways to recreate the atmosphere of the theatrical performance without the benefit of its visual elements. To do this, he would often augment the orchestration with additional musicians, eliminate lead-in dialogue, and alter tempos. He also ensured the legacy of important shows that had been produced before the days of original cast recordings by assembling studio casts of some of the theater's finest musical talent to record the scores. One of these efforts, the 1950 recording of Rodgers and Hart's *Pal Joey* with original star Vivienne Segal, led eventually to a successful Broadway revival of the show.

When rock became the predominant form of commercial popular music in the mid-1960s, the cast album and the musical theater itself fell into a period of hard times. Fewer shows were recorded, and often a musical would open without any contract for its cast recordings. In the 1980s, with a resurgence of interest in the golden era of popular music as well as an increasing use of new forms of popular music in the theater, the original cast recording has made a comeback, with new musicals and vintage reissues available on LPs, cassettes, and compact discs.

★ A NOTE ON THE SELECTIONS

These eighty-one recordings reflect the significant trends, authors, and performers in the medium over a period of nearly seven decades—that great blossoming of innovation and achievement that occurred between 1898 and 1964. The significance of the shows themselves determined most of my selections, from the well-remembered title number from *Oklahoma!* to the rediscovered title song from *The Cradle Will Rock*. Both are important to the genre's maturation, for both complementary and vastly different reasons. I also gave generous consideration to memorable recorded performances by major stars. Although *Twirly-Whirly* and *Leave It to Me!*, for example, are largely forgotten musicals, they give us significant recorded milestones in the careers of Lillian Russell and Mary Martin, two entertainers who influenced performance styles in their own eras and for years to come.

Along with the overall importance of the show or the performer, another criterion for the selections was that all, or substantially all, the performers on each recording had to be members of the initial New York production or, barring that, at least a major stage production of a show. In cases where an original cast recording made during a significant show's first New York run proved unavailable or incomplete, I chose a recording from a major New York revival, as in the cases of *Annie Get Your Gun* and *Of Thee I Sing*. If no recording of a revival production existed (or an existing one strayed from the original sound of the show), I looked for a recording of a British production staged during or immediately after the Broadway engagement. (When I found both an American and an English verison by the original Broadway star, invariably the British disc had the edge in preserving the song's theatrical context. For example, the Edith Day recording of "Alice Blue Gown" made during *Irene*'s London run retains the theater orchestration and even the appropriate dialogue from the script in the interlude between the two choruses; the American version, with its bland arrangement, preserves the number simply as a song, not as a souvenir of a memorable moment in the theater.) Finally, my third alternative was to use a studio cast recording made after the demise of the original New York production but featuring the performer who had created the role in the theater. Examples include Vivienne Segal's "Bewitched, Bothered, and Bewildered," Ethel Merman's "I Got Rhythm," and Adolph Green and Cris Alexander's "New York, New York."

Several early and important musicals are missing from this collection because no period recordings by cast members exist. Among them are Victor Herbert's *Naughty Marietta*, Will Marion Cook's *In Dahomey*, and Rodgers and Hart's *Dearest Enemy*. Other important works were ruled out by the absence of a *listenable* recording. My original program included "Play a Simple Melody" sung by Ethel Levey of the London cast of Irving Berlin's *Watch Your Step*, but no suitable source materials could be found; such was also the case with Jules Bledsoe's rendition on British Decca of "Ol' Man River" from *Show Boat*.

The recordings are, for the most part, grouped in chronological order of their shows' New York premieres. Occasionally this varies slightly to achieve a more pointed stylistic organization; for example, the selections from *Oklahoma!, Carousel, Bloomer Girl,* and *St. Louis Woman* appear consecutively because of their thematic similarities, although by strict chronology, selections from *One Touch of Venus* and *On the Town* would separate them. This allows the listener to hear the immediacy of a significant style of theater writing and performance as interpreted by different figures.

Above all, this collection is organized with the aim of being an agreeable listening experience. Combined with the textual commentary and illustrations, the recordings bring us closest to the great past moments in this liveliest of American theatrical forms.

★ SHOWS, SONGS, AND STARS

All selections were recorded in New York City except as noted.

Record Side 1
Cassette Side A
Compact Disc 1

THE FORTUNE TELLER 9/26/98, Wallack's Theatre; 40 performances. Music & orchestrations, Victor Herbert; lyrics & book, Harry B. Smith; producer, Frank L. Perley; director, Julian Mitchell; musical director, Paul Steindorff.
★ Alice Nielsen, Eugene Cowles, Frank Rushworth, Marguerita Sylvia, Joseph Herbert, Joseph Cawthorn, May Boley.
Gypsy Love Song—**Eugene Cowles** Conductor, Walter B. Rodgers. Victor 31544, mx C-3115-3; recorded 5/4/06.

The first edition of the vocal score for *The Fortune Teller* featured photographs of its star, Alice Neilsen, on the cover.

The American musical theater has always thrived on the presence of stars. A number of the medium's finest and most enduring works were created originally to showcase the talents of a particular performer. Although recalled today chiefly for Victor Herbert's enchanting score, *The Fortune Teller* was devised expressly as a vehicle for twenty-one-year-old diva Alice Nielsen (a defector from the influential Boston Ideal Opera Company), who planned the operetta as both her first solo starring effort and the premiere presentation of her own company.

Harry B. Smith's plot is a piece of splendidly romantic nonsense hinging on mistaken identity. Nielsen played the roles of both Irma, a Hungarian heiress in love with a dashing hussar, and Musette, a gypsy fortune teller in love with Sandor, a gypsy musician. The resemblance of the female characters provides narrative intrigue and eventually guides them into the arms of their intended mates. Herbert's score was a striking component of the dramatic action, endowing it with more dignity than it deserved, in a progression of czardases, ballads, and ensemble numbers.

A brief tryout engagement at the Grand Opera House in Toronto preceded the show's limited Broadway run. Like most other musical stage works of the era, it was designed chiefly as a touring production and left Manhattan because of previously committed bookings across the country.

Original cast recordings with Nielsen, Eugene Cowles, the ensemble, and piano accompaniment were made on the pioneering Berliner label during the 1898 production. (These primitive but fascinating documents can be heard on the Smithsonian Collection's *Music of Victor Herbert*.) Six years later Eugene Cowles recreated his original role of Sandor in the 1906 Broadway revival, and during its run he re-recorded "Gypsy Love Song," the most famous number in the score, with full orchestra and greatly improved fidelity. It is one of the earliest American recordings of an excerpt from a native stage work performed by its original interpreter.

8

TWIRLY-WHIRLY 9/11/02, Weber and Fields
Music Hall; 244 performances. Music, John
Stromberg; lyrics, Robert B. Smith; additional
musical material, Wilton Lackaye; producer-di-
rectors, Joe Weber & Lew Fields. ★ Joe Weber,
Lew Fields, De Wolf Hopper, Lillian Russell,
Fay Templeton, Willie Collier, Louise Allen, Will
Archer, John T. Kelly, Peter Dailey, Frankie
Bailey, Bonnie Magginn, Charles A. Bigelow.
***Come Down, Ma Evenin' Star—*Lillian
Russell** Collectors Record Shop 8, no mx; re-
corded 1912.

Beginning in 1896, variety artists Joe Weber
and Lew Fields (né Schanfeld) brought new
dimensions to the fledgling form of the
American musical theater with the unique
entertainments staged at their intimate
Weber and Fields Music Hall. Basically
knockabout "Dutch" (read "Jewish")
dialect comedians with a penchant for
brusque but family-oriented routines, they
offered a strange hybrid of the urban ethnic
humor established in the 1870s by Harrigan
and Hart and the even earlier British
satirical genre of burlesque. Throughout
their eight consecutive seasons of existence,
the Weber and Fields shows kept the same
structure. The first act was pure vaudeville,
with each member of the company having
an opportunity to show off his or her
particular talent. The second half was
devoted to parodies of contemporary stage
hits; for example, Clyde Fitch's Civil War
melodrama *Barbara Frietchie* became
Barbara Fidgety, and Rostand's *Cyrano de
Bergerac* was mercilessly travestied as
Cyranose de Bric-a-Brac. The bills were
changed frequently, and stars and producers
took it as a great compliment when their
shows were parodied.

Weber and Fields's versatile repertory
cast was enhanced in 1899 when famed
soprano beauty Lillian Russell joined its
ranks and proved not just a fine singer but
an able farceuse as well. *Twirly-Whirly,* the
seventh annual edition of the series and the
fourth Weber-Fields outing for Russell, was
the first to identify itself as "a musical
comedy." The burlesque portion lampooned
the season's stage hits, including the
musical comedies *Sally in Our Alley* and
The Defender. Russell portrayed a wealthy
dowager, Mrs. Stockson Bonds, while
Weber and Fields played their stock
characters, Michael and Meyer. The

Lillian Russell

interplay between Russell and the two
comics presages the anarchic schenanigans
of the Marx Brothers and stately Margaret
Dumont. Amid the relentless flow of
unbridled hilarity, the show also had one
greatly touching moment. John Stromberg,
house composer for the Music Hall since its
inception, had committed suicide the
summer before *Twirly-Whirly* opened,
leaving unfinished his score for the show.
On opening night Russell began to sing his

"Come Down, Ma Evenin' Star" but was too overcome with emotion to finish it. Over the years her affection for the song and its composer established it as her signature piece, and she finally recorded it during a reunion with Weber and Fields in the 1912 show *Hokey-Pokey*. Never widely distributed, this represents Russell's only existing recording. Her singing on the disc, though not in its first blush of glory, is pure and unaffected, providing a rare, living document of one of the American musical theater's most legendary figures.

LITTLE JOHNNY JONES 11/7/04, Liberty Theatre; 52 performances. Music, lyrics, book, & direction, George M. Cohan; producer, Sam H. Harris; musical director, Charles Gebest.
★ George M. Cohan, Jerry Cohan, Helen (Nellie) Cohan, Donald Brian, Ethel Levey, Tom Lewis.
Life's a Funny Proposition, After All—
George M. Cohan Conductor, Walter B. Rogers. Victor 60042, mx B-10264-1; recorded 5/4/11.

The modern American musical comedy is rooted in the early works of George M. Cohan. His "plays with music" are unashamed endorsements of the American way, couched in colloquial dialogue and situations and punctuated by songs created for singing actors rather than the full-voiced singers required by operetta.

Little Johnny Jones, his first Broadway hit, is vintage Cohan. Its straightforward plot, about an all-American jockey who is falsely accused of throwing the English Derby and spends the course of the narrative clearing his name, provided a number of outlets for Cohan's patriotism. Unlike so many of its patched-together contemporaries, the libretto is remarkably cohesive, telling its story with a comparatively small ensemble cast and with songs that attempt to function as part of the story line rather than as isolated specialties offering respites from the narrative. Even his use of stage spectacle was well integrated with the action, most notably in the famous "transformation" scene at the end of act 2. Alone on the pier, Johnny has his innocence confirmed by a skyrocket (actually a rudimentary lighting effect) which soars up against a navy blue–painted sky from a miniature boat coursing across the backdrop.

Cohan's score boasts some of his most memorable work. Though the melodies seldom deviate from tried-and-true Tin Pan Alley verse/chorus conventions, the lyrics are remarkably character-oriented and conversational. Curiously, Cohan never commercially recorded the show's big hits, "The Yankee Doodle Boy" and "Give My

George M. Cohan in the "transformation" scene.

Regards to Broadway'' (airchecks from his 1930s radio performances of the songs are too abbreviated to indicate his original stage interpretations). Instead, on his single trip to a recording studio, he chose to document the score's two homespun monologues-set-to-music, ''I'm Mighty Glad I'm Living, That's All'' and ''Life's a Funny Proposition, After All.'' The latter is the more celebrated and, in its unvarnished wisdom, confirms Oscar Hammerstein's observation that ''Cohan's genius was to say simply what everyone else was subconsciously feeling.'' After the supercharged, hyperkinetic portraits of Cohan by James Cagney in the 1942 film *Yankee Doodle Dandy* and Joel Grey in the 1968 stage anthology *George M!,* it is surprising to hear Cohan delivering the number in a pontifical *sprechgesang* more typical of a Chautauqua orator than a Broadway powerhouse.

Dormant for years after its Broadway run and national tours, *Little Johnny Jones* was dusted off, revised (by dramatist Alfred Uhry), and revived in 1982 by Connecticut's Goodspeed Opera House, a Victorian jewel of a theater dedicated to the art of the American musical. In spite of a handsome red, white, and blue production headed by pop singer Donny Osmond (who had succeeded Thomas Hulce and David Cassidy), the revival managed only a single performance in its New York transfer.

THE HONEYMOON EXPRESS 2/6/13, Winter Garden Theatre; 156 performances. Music, Jean Schwartz; lyrics, Harold Atteridge; book, Joseph W. Herbert; producers, Messrs. Shubert; director, J. C. Hufman. ★ Al Jolson, Gaby Deslys, Harry Fox, Fanny Brice, Ernest Glendinning, Ada Lewis, Dixon & Doyle, Harry Pilcer, Melville Ellis, Yansci Dolly.
You Made Me Love You (Monaco-Mc-Carthy)—**Al Jolson** Columbia A-1374, mx 38902; recorded 6/4/13.

Lee, J. J., and Sam Shubert represented a triumph of the American dream. Refugees from Lithuania, as young men they parlayed their claim on two theaters in Syracuse, New York, into a phenomenal national empire of theaters and productions. The Shuberts were notorious for their questionable business practices and shopworn productions, but they were also,

along with Florenz Ziegfeld and Charles Dillingham, the great starmakers of the early twentieth-century American musical theater.

The Honeymoon Express was a lavish but unexceptional vehicle given distinction by two talents in the Shubert stable. One was Gaby Deslys, whom Lee Shubert had discovered during a 1911 visit to France. She was renowned for her beauty, saucy demeanor, and trendsetting wardrobe, and Shubert hoped she would become as popular as Ziegfeld's star and common-law wife, Anna Held. The show's second headliner was Al Jolson, who had skyrocketed to fame two years earlier in the Shubert extravaganza *La Belle Paree.* As Lillian Russell had typified the image of the Broadway prima donna, Jolson projected a more colloquial, high-voltage performance style which grew out of his experience in variety and minstrel shows. In *The Honeymoon Express* he played the part of Gus, a comic valet given to witticisms and antic behavior. Jolson performed the role in

Al Jolson

blackface, which remained an aspect of his onstage persona throughout his career.

Although billed as a "farce with music," the show was really a revue, with its specialty numbers strung together on the most tenuous of story lines about the disrupted honeymoon of Yvonne and Henri Dubonnet, played by Mlle. Deslys and Ernest Glendinning. The free and easy structure allowed Jolson to bolster the workmanlike Schwartz-Atteridge score with interpolations by the cream of Tin Pan Alley tunesmiths. Joseph McCarthy and James Monaco's "You Made Me Love You" gave Jolson his first hit to become a popular standard. His recording of it, made four months after the Broadway opening, reveals all the bravura characteristics that would become his trademark: passionate energy, strong vocal production, and sob-in-the-throat emotionalism.

OH, BOY! 2/20/17, Princess Theatre; 463 performances. Music, Jerome Kern; lyrics, P. G. Wodehouse; book, Wodehouse & Guy Bolton; orchestrations & musical director, Frank Sadler; producers, William Elliott & F. Ray Comstock; directors, Edward Royce & Robert Milton.
★ Anna Wheaton, Tom Powers, Marie Carroll, Hal Forde, Edna May Oliver, Marion Davies, Justine Johnstone.
Till the Clouds Roll By—**Anna Wheaton and James Harrod** Columbia A-2261, mx 47417; recorded 3/13/17.

Jerome Kern led a revolution in musical theater form when he co-authored a series of pre–World War I shows known as the Princess Theatre musicals. Their new, more intimate approach to musical comedy was the brainstorm of literary agent Bessie Marbury, who brought Kern together with her client Guy Bolton on the first two productions in the series, *Nobody Home* and *Very Good Eddie* (both 1915). These works, staged at Manhattan's 299-seat Princess Theatre, effected a breakaway from the elaborate trappings of European operetta. They had modern, farce-oriented plots set in distinctly American locales, songs that evolved from situations and characters rather than being star specialties, small ensemble casts, minimal set changes, and an eleven-piece orchestra. In 1917 lyricist P. G. Wodehouse joined the team, and together they developed the script and score for *Oh, Boy!*, which set a new standard for early musical comedy.

Oh, Boy!'s comic plot hinges on the familiar farce elements of coincidence and mistaken identity. It tells of the misunderstandings that result when hero George Budd tries to keep his marriage to adoring Lou Ellen Carter a secret from his strict, wealthy aunt. His deception is further complicated when madcap actress Jackie Sampson invades his apartment on the lam from a rejected suitor named Tootles. Although the show received rapturous approval from both critics and audiences in its tryout tour, it underwent an almost overwhelming series of alterations in

The Princess Theatre, 1917.

12

both script and cast. The subplot involving the Jackie Sampson character (enchantingly played by comedienne Anna Wheaton) was completely rewritten, the locale was changed from upstate New York to Long Island (which became a favorite setting for musical comedies of the 1910s and 1920s), and the original male leads were replaced by Tom Powers and Hal Forde. When the show reached Broadway in the winter of 1917, the *New York Sun* critic summed up its general reception by hailing it "a masterpiece of musical comedy."

Kern and Wodehouse's delightful score includes such treasures as "You Never Knew about Me," "Nesting Time in Flatbush," and "Rolled into One." The charming "Till the Clouds Roll By," though ignored by virtually all the New York critics, remains the show's loveliest song. It is performed midway in the first act by George and Jackie as a platonic pledge of mutual support. Anna Wheaton recorded it during the Broadway run, with Columbia Records contract vocalist James Harrod singing the role performed onstage by Tom Powers. The intimate orchestration, similar to that heard in the theater, conveys the piquant charm and melodic innocence that were such a vital part of the Princess Theatre musicals. One year later a production was successfully mounted in London with the unexplained new title of *Oh, Joy!*. In its cast was Beatrice Lillie, making her first appearance in a book musical.

IRENE 11/18/19, Vanderbilt Theatre; 670 performances. Music, Harry Tierney; lyrics, Joseph McCarthy; book, James Montgomery; producer, Carle Carlton; director, Edward Royce; musical director, Gene Salzer. ★ Edith Day, Walter Regan, Bobbie Watson, Dorothy Walters, Eva Puck.
Alice Blue Gown—**Edith Day** Frank Tours conducting the Empire Theatre Orchestra. (British) Columbia F-1044, mx 74053; recorded 4/10/20, London

Intimate, colloquial, and uniquely American in tone and setting, *Irene* owed much to the techniques developed by Kern, Bolton, and Wodehouse in the Princess Theatre musicals. It was also something of a throwback to the earlier traditional star vehicle, in that it was designed specifically for petite soprano Edith Day, then at the threshold of fame.

James Montgomery's sentimental story of a poor Irish-American shop girl turned modiste's mannequin, who finds success and happiness among the Long Island smart set, established a vogue for the "Cinderella musical," which remains even today a recurrent narrative type in the American musical theater. Surrounding the spunky heroine are a variety of colorful but believable characters, including her salty mavourneen of a mother, an eccentric male couturier known as Madame Lucy, and the rich Long Islander Donald Marshall, who becomes the object of Irene's affections. The Harry Tierney–Joseph McCarthy score was praised for its tuneful songs, which evolved naturally from plot and character. Though the romantic ballad "Castle of My Dreams" borrowed its melody from a theme by Chopin, the show's hit, "Alice Blue Gown," was a complete original. Occurring early in the first act, it establishes Irene's double virtues of frugality and tenderness as she wistfully recalls an "almost new" dress, given to her by a friend, that she wore "till it wilted." The song's Irish-tinged melodic simplicity and dramatic lyric place it among the best of American show music. Edith Day recorded it twice, first for Victor during *Irene's* Broadway run and then for (British) Columbia while she was appearing in the West End production. The latter version, included here, reproduced the number exactly as it was heard in the theater, and Day's completely charming performance demonstrates why she became the reigning diva of the 1920s British musical stage.

For eighteen years *Irene* held the record as Broadway's longest-running musical. In 1973 producer Harry Rigby, the man behind the successful 1971 revival of *No! No! Nanette!*, refashioned *Irene* as a vehicle for Debbie Reynolds's Broadway debut. Although the new production had its own merits (primarily the dynamic Miss Reynolds), it bore little resemblance to the original. Its book was completely rewritten by Rigby, Hugh Wheeler, and Joseph Stein, and its score, with interpolations by Charles Gaynor, Otis Clements, and Wally Harper, retained only five of the Tierney-McCarthy songs, including "Alice Blue Gown."

Irving Berlin and a bevy of *Follies* chorines.

ZIEGFELD FOLLIES 6/16/19, New Amster-
dam Theatre; 171 performances. Music, Irving
Berlin, Harry Tierney, Dave Stamper, Victor
Herbert, Albert Von Tilzer; lyrics, Berlin, Gene
Buck, Joseph McCarthy, Lew Brown; sketches,
Buck, Rennold Wolf, George Lemaire, Eddie
Cantor; producer, Florenz Ziegfeld; director-cho-
reographer, Ned Wayburn; musical director,
Frank Darling. ★ Eddie Dowling, Eddie Cantor,
Marilyn Miller, Mary Hay, Ray Dooley, Bert
Williams, Gus Van & Joe Schenck, George Le-
maire, John Steel.
A Pretty Girl Is Like a Melody (Berlin)—
John Steel Victor 18588, mx 18588-A; recorded
6/30/19.

Today the lavish tradition of songs,
sketches, and showgirls known as the revue
is at best a quaint and faded memory, but in
the early decades of this century it was a
vibrant part of every theatrical season, as
much a social event as a show business
phenomenon. Unquestionably, the form
reached its pinnacle in the regular editions
of the legendary *Ziegfeld Follies*.

The idea for the series originated in 1906
when Ziegfeld's wife, the hour-glass-figured
Anna Held, suggested that he adapt the
style of French cabaret performances for
Broadway audiences. The first Ziegfeld-
supervised revue was actually produced by
Theatrical Syndicate members Klaw and
Erlanger at the Manhattan rooftop theater
Jardin de Paris on 8 July 1907. Librettist-
lyricist Harry B. Smith contributed its title,
after the name of his newspaper column,
"Follies of the Day."
Edition thirteen (Ziegfeld's favorite
number) of the series, produced in 1919, was
the finest of the twenty-two installments.
Opulent in cast, material, and visual
splendor, it also displayed a healthy taste for
social satire, most notably in its running
commentary about the onset of Prohibition.
Although the score was the collective work
of a number of Tin Pan Alley tunesmiths,
many of its most popular pieces were written
by Irving Berlin, whose first theatrical songs

had been heard eleven years earlier in *The Boys and Betty* (1908). Along with specialties for stars Marilyn Miller ("A Syncopated Cocktail"), Bert Williams ("You Cannot Make Your Shimmy Shake on Tea"), and Van and Schenck ("Mandy"), Berlin contributed the revue genre's song of songs, "A Pretty Girl Is Like a Melody." Sung by tenor John Steel, the number prefaced a procession of show girls fancifully attired as classical compositions, such as Dvořák's "Humoresque," Mendelssohn's "Spring Song," and Schumann's "Traumerei." The piece was then reprised orchestrally as underscoring for Ben Ali Haggin's extravagant living tableau, "Melody Fantasy and the Folly of Years Gone By," with show girl Simone D'Herlys astride a pâpiér mache horse as Lady Godiva surrounded by her courtiers.

After Ziegfeld's death in 1932 his widow, Billie Burke, sold the rights for the series title to the Shuberts, who produced their own editions of the *Ziegfeld Follies* in 1934, '36, and '43. The final edition to date was a shoddy 1956 production starring Beatrice Lillie.

Noble Sissle and ladies of the *Shuffle Along* chorus.

SHUFFLE ALONG 5/23/21, 63rd Street Music Hall; 504 performances. Music & musical direction, Eubie Blake; lyrics; Noble Sissle; book, Flournoy Miller & Aubrey Lyles; orchestrations, Will Vodery; producer, Nikko Producing Co. (Al Mayer); director, Walter Brooks; choreographer, Lawrence Deas. ★ Flournoy Miller, Aubrey Lyles, Noble Sissle, Gertrude Saunders, Lottie Gee, Roger Matthews.
***Baltimore Buzz*—Noble Sissle and His Sizzling Syncopators** Emerson 10385, mx 41783-2-3; recorded ca. 5/21.

Along with Herbert, Kern, Berlin, and others of European descent, a number of African-Americans have enriched the legacy of the American musical theater. The short-lived *A Trip to Coontown* (1898) was the first full-length musical composed and performed by blacks. Will Marion Cook and Paul Lawrence Dunbar's *In Dahomey* (1903), starring the great Bert Williams, was the first black musical performed at a major, previously whites-only, Broadway theater. One of the most illustrious descendants of these pioneering works was

Shuffle Along, which evolved from a vaudeville routine written by Flournoy Miller of the comedy team Miller and Lyles. Miller hoped to expand the sketch, a satire on small town politics, into a two-act musical comedy to be called *The Mayor of Jimtown*. Early in 1920 at a Philadelphia NAACP benefit, he and Lyles shared the bill with songwriter-entertainers Eubie Blake and Noble Sissle and were impressed with their original, rhythmic songs. Some months later, in a chance encounter on a New York street, the four men vowed to devote themselves to turning Miller's idea into a reality.

Their greatest problem in getting *Shuffle Along* on the boards was one of money. They financed the entire show out of their weekly vaudeville salaries and salvaged its sets and costumes from the shows *Roly-Boly Eyes* and *Frank Fay's Fables,* both of which had foundered earlier in the season. Many of the production numbers that Sissle and Blake designed were first made to correspond to the available wardrobe and then worked into the plot. Instead of aiming for big-name stars, they took a chance on a bunch of young hopefuls, with Sissle, Miller, and Lyles assuming major roles while Blake conducted the orchestra.

Following a series of tryout stops in Washington and Philadelphia, *Shuffle Along* came back to New York with promising reviews but no advance ticket sales to speak of and precious little reserve funds. Business finally took off when the show instituted a policy of Wednesday midnight performances, which became *the* social event of the season.

Blake and Sissle's score is remembered today for the lively "I'm Just Wild About Harry," which, strangely enough, was one of the few numbers from the show not recorded as a vocal by the original cast. Upon re-examination, the score boasts a number of fine songs, including the romantic ballad "Love Will Find a Way" and the torchy "I'm Craving That Kind of Love," both introduced and recorded by soubrette Gertrude Saunders. The selection included here, "Baltimore Buzz," is performed by its lyricist and original interpreter, Noble Sissle, as the show's comic bon vivant Tom Sharper. With its insistent, devil-may-care rhythms, it was perfect as the show's final big production number, sung and danced by Sissle backed by the ladies of the chorus.

Sissle and Blake revised and revived the show in 1928, '32, and '52, but none of these subsequent editions captured the original's artistry and commercial success.

Record Side 2

LADY, BE GOOD! 12/1/24, Liberty Theatre; 330 performances. Music, George Gershwin; lyrics, Ira Gershwin; book, Guy Bolton & Fred Thompson; orchestrations, Stephen Jones; producers, Alex A. Aarons & Vinton Freedley; director, Felix Edwardes; choreographer, Sammy Lee; musical director, Paul Lannin. ★ Fred & Adele Astaire, Walter Catlett, Cliff Edwards,

Alan Edwards, Gerard Oliver Smith.
***Fascinating Rhythm*—Fred and Adele Astaire** Pianist, George Gershwin. (British) Columbia 3969, mx WA-3184-1; recorded 4/19/26, London.

Alex Aarons and Vinton Freedley formed a producing partnership in 1924 with the goal of developing jazz-age equivalents to the superlative Princess Theatre musicals of a decade earlier. For their first effort they selected a Guy Bolton–Fred Thompson concoction called *Black-Eyed Susan,* a contemporary farce with the leading roles designed for Fred and Adele Astaire. Its loose-jointed plot related the exploits of brother-and-sister vaudeville team Dick and Susie Trevor. When they become dispossessed, they embark on a series of adventures that eventually lead to wealth and popularity among the Long Island *haut monde.* The authors provided frequent outlets for Adele's comedic flair, Fred's guise of sophisticated straight man, and the duo's incomparable skill as singing dancers. Aarons and Freedley assigned the responsibility for the songs to another talented pair of siblings, George and Ira Gershwin. The show marked the team's first complete score to be produced on Broadway. Among George's contributions to the production was the inclusion of duo-pianists Phil Ohman and Victor Arden in the pit orchestra, thus establishing a trend that would come to typify the sound of 1920s theater orchestration.

Shortly before the tryout tour began in late November, the librettists changed the title to *Lady, Be Good!,* after one of the show's songs. Relatively few changes were made on the road, with the now-famous "The Man I Love" being one of the few musical casualties. The Manhattan opening was warmly received, and after a ten-month run on Broadway, the show had a successful national tour and West End edition. The Astaires remained its stars in all the immediate incarnations of the original production.

While in London, they joined George Gershwin at a Columbia Records studio to record the show's hit, "Fascinating Rhythm." The rendition is definitive, even without the lively syncopations of Stephen Jones's theater orchestration. Gershwin had gotten the idea for the melody early in 1924, when he was putting the finishing touches on his first British musical, *Primrose*. The song was included in *Lady, Be Good!* simply as a divertissement for the Astaires and ex-vaudevillian Cliff "Ukelele Ike" Edwards near the end of the first act. The Gershwins' angular tempos and colloquial lyrics set a new standard of freshness and modernity for theater songs.

OH, KAY! 11/8/26, Imperial Theatre; 256 performances. Music, George Gershwin; lyrics, Ira Gershwin & Howard Dietz; book, Guy Bolton & P. G. Wodehouse; orchestrations, Hilding Anderson; producers, Alex A. Aarons & Vinton Freedley; director, John Harwood; choreographer, Sammy Lee; musical director, William Daly. ★ Gertrude Lawrence, Oscar Shaw, Victor Moore, Harland Dixon, Marion & Madeleine Fairbanks, Sascha Beaumont, Gerard Oliver Smith.
***Someone to Watch over Me*—Gertrude Lawrence** Arthur Wood conducting His Majesty's Theatre Orchestra. (British) Columbia 4618, mx WA-6326-4; recorded 10/25/27, London.

When a Manhattan journalist asked Gertrude Lawrence why she had elected to appear in *Oh, Kay!,* she replied simply, "Because George Gershwin wrote it for me." Actually, the idea of starring the British actress in her first American-made musical comedy had originated not with Gershwin but with librettists Bolton and Wodehouse, who several years earlier had been entranced by her performance in the West End revue *Rats.* Bolton dashed off a complimentary note to Lawrence, promising to create a Broadway vehicle expressly tailored for her talents. After fulfilling a two-year commitment as a featured player in the New York company of the imported *Charlot's Revue,* she was eager to accept their offer.

Although written in England, the libretto centered on Long Island rum-running, a timely topic for Prohibition-era audiences. Lawrence portrayed Lady Kay Durham, a down-at-heels peer of the realm who falls in love with millionaire playboy Jimmy Winter (Oscar Shaw), whose beach-front mansion has been the secret site of her bootlegging operation. Victor Moore, a Broadway resident since his 1904 debut in Cohan's *Forty-Five Minutes from Broadway,*

Gertrude Lawrence as Lady Kay Durham.

appeared as her bumbling assistant Shorty McGee. The large supporting cast included eccentric dancer Harland Dixon, the Fairbanks Twins, and Betty Compton, the girlfriend of New York mayor Jimmy Walker. In the Gershwins' fourth complete Broadway score together, they created yet another superior collection of songs in the angular patterns of the jazz age. During the writing of the score, Ira underwent an emergency appendectomy and, at George's request, was spelled on several lyrics by Howard Dietz. As Lawrence recalled in her autobiography, *A Star Danced,* "The piece had lots of humor and that undefinable thing called spirit."

In rehearsals the musical was known variously as *Mayfair, Miss Mayfair,* and *Cheerio!.* Just before the Philadelphia tryouts, Bolton and Wodehouse gave it the title of *Oh, Kay!,* recalling their earlier exclamatory success, *Oh, Boy!*. Following the Broadway unveiling, Brooks Atkinson pronounced the show "an excellent blending of all the creative arts of musical entertainment."

The score contains several Gershwin standards: the bubbling "Do, Do, Do," the revivalistic "Clap Yo' Hands," and the infectious title number. But the most endearing excerpt is the ballad "Someone to Watch over Me." George Gershwin first conceived the melody as a lively dance number for the ensemble but then realized it was more effective at a slower tempo. Howard Dietz supplied the title and Ira Gershwin wrote the touching lyrics. In the original production Lawrence, masquerading as a maid to conceal her identity, sang the number to a doll—a directorial suggestion from George Gershwin. Of the many recordings of the song Lawrence made during her career, that closest to her stage interpretation was recorded for (British) Columbia during the show's London production. It reveals a star at the peak of her interpretive powers.

NO! NO! NANETTE! 9/16/25, Globe Theatre; 321 performances. Music, Vincent Youmans; lyrics, Irving Caesar & Otto Harbach; book, Harbach & Frank Mandel; producer, H. H. Frazee; directors, Frazee & Edward Royce (uncredited); choreographer, Sammy Lee; musical director, Niclas Kemper. ★ Louise Groody, Charles Winninger, Josephine Whittell, Wellington Cross, Eleanor Dawn, Jack Baker, Georgia O'Ramey.
I Want to Be Happy—**Joseph Coyne and Binnie Hale** Percival Mackay conducting the Palace Theatre Orchestra. (British) Columbia 3630, mx A-1870; recorded 3/18/25, London.

With its giddy procession of flappers, philanderers, and farcical situations, *No! No! Nanette!* is the quintessential 1920s musical comedy. Producer H. H. Frazee, an entrepreneur in both the sports and theatrical worlds, commissioned the work as a song-and-dance version of Frank Mandel's play *His Lady Friends* (based on a novel by May Edgington), which Frazee had originally presented on Broadway in 1919. Mandel's and Otto Harbach's adaptation retains the comic plot and the three-act structure of its source, centering on Jimmy Smith, a meek, married Bible

publisher who has innocently become involved with three gold diggers, and his teenage ward Nanette, who longs for romantic adventure. As naively beguiling as the tissue-thin plot seems today, the show's chief attribute is Vincent Youmans's gaily syncopated score. Ironically, Youmans was not Frazee's first choice as composer; he won the assignment only after his wealthy mother agreed to finance the production.

No! No! Nanette! underwent an astounding number of changes in its year-long pre-Broadway tryout tour. When a lukewarm response greeted its world premiere at Detroit's Garrick Theatre, Frazee gave Youmans and co-lyricist Irving Caesar just twenty-four hours to come up with new material or be replaced by *Irene* co-authors Harry Tierney and Joseph McCarthy. Youmans and Caesar responded to his threat by writing the two songs that became the show's greatest hits: "Tea for Two," a second act ensemble number for the heroine, her boyfriend Tom Trainor, and the "maids, marrieds, and bachelors" of the chorus; and "I Want to Be Happy," a sunny duet in the first act for the warm-hearted Jimmy and Nanette. During the eleven-month Chicago engagement, Frazee himself took over the directorial reins and replaced all the principal cast members except one, comedienne Georgia O'Ramey, who held onto the role of the long-suffering maid Pauline throughout the tryout tour and the Broadway run.

Even before the New York opening, *No! No! Nanette!* was an international hit, having already spawned two road companies, a raft of popular recordings by the era's best dance bands, and a West End production starring Joseph Coyne, Binnie Hale, and George Grossmith that ran more than twice as long as the Broadway edition. Once again, only the London cast had the opportunity to record its performances. Coyne and Hale's delightful rendition of "I Want to Be Happy," although flavored with unmistakable British accents, is a treasured souvenir of 1920s musical theater, conjuring up the innocent insouciance of both Youmans's score and the show itself.

No! No! Nanette!, minus its exclamation points, received a surprisingly stylish and successful Broadway revival in 1971. Under the supervision of co-directors Busby Berkeley and Bert Shevelove and co-producer Harry Rigby, the cast was headed by Ruby Keeler, Patsy Kelly, Jack Gilford, Helen Gallagher, Bobby Van, and the perennial ingenue Susan Watson. The revival ran for over 800 performances on Broadway, and its satellite touring productions were greeted enthusiastically both here and abroad.

Cassette Side B

ROSE-MARIE 9/2/24, Imperial Theatre; 557 performances. Music, Rudolf Friml & Herbert Stothart; lyrics & book, Oscar Hammerstein II & Otto Harbach; orchestrations, Robert Russell Bennett; producer, Arthur Hammerstein; director, Paul Dickey; choreographer, David Bennett; musical director, Stothart. ★ Mary Ellis, Dennis King, William Kent, Dorothy Mackaye, Arthur Deagon, Edward Cianelli, Pearl Regay.
Indian Love Call (Friml-Harbach-Hammerstein)—**Edith Day and Derek Oldham** Herman Finck conducting the Drury Lane Theatre Orchestra. (British) Columbia 9038, mx AX-982; recorded 4/25, London.

With *Rose-Marie,* Oscar Hammerstein II took his first step toward writing the kind of operetta cum romantic musical play that would reach full maturity in his best collaborations with Richard Rodgers. Still working in partnership with his mentor Otto Harbach, he experimented with forging a closer, more natural relationship between plot and song elements; in fact, in *Rose-Marie*'s program notes he asserted, "The musical numbers of this play are such an integral part of the action that we do not think we should list them as separate episodes." If his claim was not entirely true, it affirmed his desire to expand the boundaries of the conventional musical theater.

Hammerstein's libretto was inspired by his brother Arthur's interest in producing an operetta about a winter carnival in Toronto that ended with the ritual melting of a mammoth ice sculpture of a castle. Although Hammerstein's research proved the story false, it sparked his interest in writing a script with a Canadian locale. The plot that resulted is a melodramatic tale of French Canadian singer Rose-Marie LaFlamme and her love for rugged fur trapper Jim Kenyon. Their romance is threatened when Jim is falsely accused of

Friml, Harbach, and Hammerstein's "Totem Tom-Tom" inspired one of choreographer David Bennett's most spectacular dance numbers for *Rose-Marie.*

killing Indian chief Black Eagle, but they are reunited at the finale when the real culprit is discovered to be the victim's squaw, Wanda. The authors embellished the narrative with colorful subsidiary characters, such as the comic Lady Jane and "Hard-Boiled" Herman. Several episodes in the story, particularly the murder scene, were enacted in pantomime with musical accompaniment, like the tableaux vivantes in silent movies.

Although recalled today as Rudolf Friml's masterwork for the American musical theater, the score for *Rose-Marie* was actually a joint effort with Herbert Stothart. The latter's work, chiefly a collection of comedy numbers, was unremarkable when new and has worn the years rather badly, but Friml's contributions, particularly the justly famous "Indian Love Call," brought new rhythms to the operetta genre and provided the basis for countless parodies.

In addition to lavish scenic decor by Gates and Morange, the original production featured stellar performances by soon-to-be matinee idol Dennis King and former Metropolitan opera star Mary Ellis. When Ellis declined to star in producer Alfred Butt's West End production, her role was taken by Edith Day, Broadway's original *Irene*. It is Day's recording with co-star

Derek Oldham that preserves the original theatrical context of Friml's classic love duet.

Rose-Marie has enjoyed international success, especially in Paris, where it holds a record of over 1,200 consecutive performances. Today, it is perhaps most widely remembered in the greatly altered 1936 film version starring Jeanette MacDonald and Nelson Eddy.

THE STUDENT PRINCE IN HEIDELBERG

12/2/24, Al Jolson Theatre; 608 performances. Music, Sigmund Romberg; lyrics & book, Dorothy Donnelly; producers, Messrs. Shubert; director, J. C. Huffman; choreographer, Max Scheck; musical director, Oscar Bradley. ★ Howard Marsh, Greek Evans, George Hassell, Roberta Beatty, John Coast.
Deep in My Heart, Dear—**Harry Welchman and Rose Hignell** (British) Columbia 9057, mx WAX-6689-1; recorded 7/25/25, London.

The Student Prince in Heidelberg may well be the ultimate American operetta; at least, it is the most wildly and widely successful of its unashamedly romantic genre. It was the longest-running musical play of the 1920s and generated nine national touring companies, which continued with various cast replacements for over twenty-five years. It came about more because of

"Stupendous, enthralling," boasted the Shubert brothers in a promotional brochure for the original Broadway production.

business than artistic impulses on the part of its producers, Lee and J.J. Shubert. As owners of the performance rights for the turn-of-the-century play *Old Heidelberg,* they were eager to mine for additional profits by sponsoring its conversion into an operetta. To write the score, they selected Sigmund Romberg, who had become mired in the easy money to be made in churning out special material for Shubert-sponsored revues. Dorothy Donnelly, Romberg's collaborator in the 1921 operetta *Blossom Time,* was hired to provide the script. Her adaptation was remarkably faithful to its source, centering on the tender but doomed romance between Prince Karl Franz and beer-garden waitress Kathie, set against the student high life in Heidelberg in the 1860s.

Following the world premiere performance in Atlantic City, the Shuberts threatened to close the show. They detested the unhappy ending, found Romberg's score "too highbrow," and were bewildered by both the absence of glamorous showgirls and the omnipresence of a forty-member male chorus. Donnelly and Romberg held to their convictions and refused to make any concessions to jeopardize the integrity of their work, and when the show was met with near-ecstasy by critics and audiences at the New York opening, the canny producers changed their tune and revelled in what would obviously be one of their biggest hits.

Along with his score for *Maytime,* Romberg composed some of his most beautiful melodies for *The Student Prince.* For the large male chorus he wrote the lusty, full-throated anthems "To the Inn We're Marching" and "The Drinking Song." The heroine is introduced with a delightful ensemble number, "Come Boys," and is wooed by the royal hero's rapturous tenor solo "Serenade" ("Overhead the Moon Is Beaming"). The principal duet, "Deep in My Heart, Dear," allows the lovers to swear their eternal allegiance to each other with a waltz that would not have been out of place in old Vienna.

Although the original production made stars out of Howard Marsh (later of *Show Boat* fame) and Ilse Marvenga, neither ever recorded any of its songs. The recording heard in this collection features Harry

Welchman and Rose Hignell, the stars of a popular English production that toured the provinces a year after the Broadway premiere. In its meticulous preservation of both the song and its dramatic context, this version reaffirms the importance of the British recording industry in documenting the formative years of the American musical theater.

SHOW BOAT 12/27/27, Ziegfeld Theatre; 572 performances. Music, Jerome Kern; book & lyrics, Oscar Hammerstein II; orchestrations, Robert Russell Bennett; producer, Florenz Ziegfeld; directors, Hammerstein & Zeke Colvan; musical director, Victor Baravalle. ★ Charles Winninger, Norma Terris, Howard Marsh, Helen Morgan, Jules Bledsoe, Edna May Oliver, Sammy White, Eva Puck, Charles Ellis.
Can't Help Lovin' Dat Man—**Helen Morgan** Conductor, Victor Baravalle. Victor 21238, mx BVE-42442-1; recorded 2/14/28.
Ol' Man River—**Paul Robeson** Conductor, Victor Young. Brunswick 20114, mx BX-12096-A; recorded 7/21/32.

One evening in the autumn of 1926, Jerome Kern picked up a copy of Edna Ferber's current best-seller *Show Boat,* a sprawling saga of forty years of American social history as viewed from the perspective of a show boat family. Kern was immediately captured by the novel's bold treatment of such controversial issues as racial bigotry, miscegenation, unhappy marriage, and compulsive gambling, and he began to envision an unconventional musical play based on the work. Thirty-one-year-old Oscar Hammerstein II, who had recently teamed with Kern on the hit *Sunny* (1925), shared his enthusiasm for the novel and joined him as collaborator, building on the romantic musical play tradition Hammerstein had begun in 1924 with *Rose-Marie.*

At first Edna Ferber found the idea of converting *Show Boat* into a musical preposterous. She feared that the integrity of her prose would be undone by a medium with a propensity for high-kicking chorines, extraneous specialty turns, and contrived happy endings. But on the strength of Kern's achievements with the Princess Theatre musicals and the power of the song "Ol' Man River," she relented and gave permission for the adaptation.

Kern and Hammerstein lavished fourteen

Scenes from *Show Boat*:
(Top) A climactic moment occurs in act 1, scene 4, when Julie's racially mixed parentage is revealed; from left, Allan Campbell, Charles Ellis, Helen Morgan, Norma Terris, Charles Winninger, and Edna May Oliver.
(Bottom) The wedding of Magnolia Hawks and Gaylord Ravenal provides the first-act finale. Pictured center are Charles Winninger, Howard Marsh, Norma Terris, Sammy White, Eva Puck, and Edna May Oliver.

months on the creation of *Show Boat,* a gestation period unprecedented in that era of swift and often slapdash assembly of musical shows. As Hammerstein later recalled, "We had fallen hopelessly in love with it. We sang to each other. We had ourselves swooning." During the development process "the Great Glorifier," Florenz Ziegfeld, agreed to produce. In his haste to capitalize on the novel's success, he announced that the premiere of the musical was set for April 1927 and its stars would be Elizabeth Hines, Guy Robertson, and Paul Robeson. When the work proved unready to meet the deadline, Ziegfeld postponed the production until the fall and cancelled the performers' contracts. (Hines tried unsuccessfully to sue Ziegfeld for breach of contract.)

Show Boat finally entered rehearsals in September 1927 with comedian Charles Winninger heading the cast as show boat captain Andy Hawks and Howard Marsh (Broadway's first Student Prince) and Norma Terris as the romantic leads Gaylord Ravenal and Magnolia Hawks. In important secondary roles were prune-visaged Edna May Oliver as the heroine's mother, singer Helen Morgan as a tragic mulatto actress, and Jules Bledsoe as Joe, the black stevedore who functions as an omniscient chorus figure commenting on the actions of the principal characters.

Show Boat had its world premiere in Washington, D.C., on 15 November 1927. Its extraordinary length of $4\frac{1}{2}$ hours required extensive cutting, which took place there and in the subsequent tryouts in Pittsburgh, Cleveland, and Philadelphia. Upon its Broadway opening in late December, it was hailed as a major breakthrough in a lyric theater that had been dominated by tried-and-true conventions. *New York Herald Tribune* reporter Percy Hammond summed up the critical consensus when he proclaimed it "the most distinguished light opera of its generation." After its initial Broadway run, *Show Boat* was given major New York revivals in 1932, '46, '66, and '80.

Kern's remarkable score, a significant advance from the light-hearted charm songs of his Princess Theatre days, contains no fewer than seven songs that became standards: "Ol' Man River," "Make Believe," "Can't Help Lovin' Dat Man," "Why Do I Love You?," "You Are Love," and "Life upon the Wicked Stage." "Ol' Man River," which functions as an eloquent leitmotif throughout the work, is Kern and Hammerstein's musico-dramatic correlative for Ferber's use of the Mississippi River as a recurrent narrative device. Paul Robeson eventually got his chance at the song when he played Joe, the role written for him, in both the 1928 London production and the 1932 Broadway revival. His 1932 recording (part of Jack Kapp's earliest effort to document the American musical theater on disc) preserves his commanding performance and confirms the song as his own. In later recordings Robeson would alter Hammerstein's lyrics, increasing the song's inherent qualities as an anthem of racial protest. Helen Morgan recorded "Can't Help Lovin' Dat Man" twice during her all-too-brief career: first during the initial New York run and again in 1932 at the time of the revival. The former (heard here), conducted by the show's musical director Victor Baravalle, preserves much of Robert Russell Bennett's theater orchestration and captures the waif-like persona that Morgan brought to the role of the fragile, doomed Julie. Curiously, she prefaces the song with the opening phrase of Kern and Hammerstein's pseudo-spiritual "Mis'ry's Comin' Round," deleted during the Washington tryouts and retained in the show only as background music.

Record Side 3

BLACKBIRDS OF 1928 5/9/28, Liberty Theatre; 518 performances. Music, Jimmy McHugh; lyrics, Dorothy Fields; orchestrations, Will Vodery, Ken MacComber, Arthur Goodman; producer-director, Lew Leslie; musical director, Allie Ross. ★ Adelaide Hall, Bill Robinson, Aida Ward, Tim Moore, Mantan Moreland, Elisabeth Welch, Hall Johnson Choir.
*Doin' the New Low Down—**Bill Robinson***
Don Redman's Orchestra. Brunswick 6520, mx B-12180-A; recorded 12/29/32.

Along with such exemplary book musicals as Sissle and Blake's *Shuffle Along* (1921) and *The Chocolate Dandies* (1924), the all-black revue was a popular Broadway

Bill "Bojangles" Robinson

Harlem's famed Cotton Club he borrowed songwriters Jimmy McHugh and Dorothy Fields to write the score, which included the suggestive doggerel of "Diga Diga Doo" and the standard "I Can't Give You Anything But Love" (introduced by Bert Lahr and Patsy Kelly earlier in the season in *Harry Delmar's Revels*).

Blackbirds was first produced as a floor show at the posh Manhattan nightclub Les Ambassadeurs, and its warm reception there persuaded Leslie to attempt a Broadway production. During the tryout in Atlantic City, he decided that a star specialty was badly needed to liven up its second act. The void was filled by vaudevillian Bill "Bojangles" Robinson, who made a belated but welcome Broadway debut performing a single number, "Doin' the New Low Down," which he sang while tap dancing up and down a small section of steps placed stage center. Robinson recorded the piece first in 1929 with the small jazz band Irving Mills's Hotsy-Totsy Gang. The recording included in this collection comes from Jack Kapp's 1932 Brunswick album of songs from the show. It preserves both Robinson's appealingly modest vocal and the unmatchable sound of his tap dancing.

Blackbirds of 1928, like *Shuffle Along*, became a real hit when its producer instituted a series of mid-week midnight performances that became the rage of New York café society. The subsequent editions of *Blackbirds*, staged in 1930, '33, and '39, provided momentary vehicles for the talents of Ethel Waters, Flournoy Miller, and Lena Horne but never came close to the original's style or financial prosperity.

phenomenon of the twenties. Unlike the book musicals, most black revues were written and produced by whites. Among the many presented in the era were *Africana* (1927), *Hot Chocolates* (1929), and four editions of *Blackbirds*, and of all these, *Blackbirds of 1928* holds the record for being the most artistically and commercially successful endeavor of its kind. Producer Lew Leslie originated the idea for these Afro-American extravaganzas in the early 1920s in London and Paris. The first Broadway edition was planned as a showcase for his discovery Florence Mills, who died suddenly during its planning stages and was replaced by the unknown Adelaide Hall. From the artistic staff of

WHOOPEE 12/4/28, New Amsterdam Theatre; 379 performances. Music, Walter Donaldson; lyrics, Gus Kahn; book & director, William Anthony McGuire; producer, Florenz Ziegfeld; choreographers, Seymour Felix & Tamara Geva; musical director, Gus Salzer. ★ Eddie Cantor, Ruth Etting, Ethel Shutta, Paul Gregory, Tamara Geva, Frances Upton, George Olsen Orchestra. *Makin' Whoopee*—**Eddie Cantor** Conductor, Nat Shilkret. Victor 21831, mx BVE-49001-2; recorded 12/18/28.

Eddie Cantor, of the pop-eyed double-take and the frantically clapping hands, achieved

Making 'Whoopee' at the New Amsterdam

A period caricature of Eddie Cantor, Frances Upton, and company.

one of the greatest hits of his career in this tuneful, lavishly mounted musical version of Owen Davis's 1923 comedy *The Nervous Wreck*. The production renewed Cantor's long association with Florenz Ziegfeld, for whom he had starred in the 1922 book musical *Kid Boots* and five editions of the *Follies,* and returned Ziegfeld to the more familiar terrain of musical comedy after his noble experiment with *Show Boat.* The reliable William Anthony McGuire converted Davis's eleven-character, three-set play into an opulently cast, multi-scened extravaganza, retaining the basic plot about a hypochondriac who goes west for a health cure and gets involved in a series of comic situations. McGuire's additions to the original included a Romeo and Juliet–derived subplot about a supposed Indian half-breed and his white sweetheart, an overbearing nurse who served as a foil for Cantor, and a torch-singing movie star who wandered in and out of the proceedings with only the slightest connection to the story. The show was mounted in characteristic Ziegfeldian splendor, with a parade of nearly nude showgirls on horseback and Joseph Urban's spectacular Grand Canyon setting as the high points.

Cantor made the most of his assigned

Donaldson-Kahn songs, which were more a string of extractable pop hits than a unified score. "Makin' Whoopee," with its title phrase borrowed from an expression coined by columnist Walter Winchell, was a naively suggestive ditty that became one of Cantor's great signature songs. He performed it early in the first act, along with a sextet of chorines in riding attire. Although he recorded the number many times during his career, he never surpassed his first try on Victor in 1928—even though the orchestration is nondescript and Nat Shilkret's conducting rather weak-willed. In addition to droll numbers for Cantor, the show also produced one of the great torch ballads, "Love Me or Leave Me," throbbingly sung by Ruth Etting as Leslie Daw, a melancholy movie actress with a penchant for the wrong men.

Whoopee was one of the biggest successes of the 1920s and might have run forever had Ziegfeld, a victim of the Wall Street crash, not been forced to sell the motion picture rights to Sam Goldwyn. Cantor's appearance in the 1930 film version launched him on a movie career that kept him away from the theater throughout the thirties. The musical had a Broadway revival in 1971 that originated at the Goodspeed Opera House. Though attractive in design and execution, it lacked a principal comedian who could compete with Cantor's memory and closed after a brief run.

GIRL CRAZY 10/14/30, Alvin Theatre; 272 performances. Music, George Gershwin; lyrics, Ira Gershwin; book, Guy Bolton & John McGowan; orchestrations, Robert Russell Bennett; producers, Alex A. Aarons & Vinton Freedley; director, Alexander Leftwich; choreographer, George Hale; musical director, Earl Busby. ★ Willie Howard, Ginger Rogers, Allen Kearns, William Kent, Ethel Merman, Eunice Healey, Lew Parker.
I Got Rhythm—**Ethel Merman** Decca 24453, mx 74230; recorded 12/12/47.

In many ways *Girl Crazy* marked the end of a theatrical era. It was the last commercially profitable show produced by the team of Aarons and Freedley, their final hit in collaboration with the Gershwins, and the Gershwins' penultimate success within a conventional musical comedy format. Bolton and McGowan's solidly crafted libretto, which vaguely recalled the milieu of *Whoopee,* was a predictable but often hilarious combination of the worlds of Broadway, burlesque, and the wild west. Its hero, Danny Churchill, a New York playboy perpetually tempted by the seductions of nightlife and gold-digging debutantes, is sent by his father to the isolated outpost of Custerville, Arizona. True to his inclinations, Danny transforms a broken-down dude ranch into a popular saloon and falls in love with the town's lovely postmistress, Molly Gray. The romantic leads, appealingly played by Allen Kearns and Ginger Rogers, were assigned some of the Gershwins' most entrancing ballads, including "Embraceable You" and "But Not for Me." As was the case with so many musicals of the period, *Girl Crazy* was created as a star vehicle. Bert Lahr was slated to play the comic lead, a manic Manhattan taxi driver named Gieber Goldfarb, who communicates with Indians in perfect Yiddish. When Lahr was unable to free himself from another contract, he

Ethel Merman and the girls in the "I Got Rhythm" number.

26

was succeeded by vaudevillian Willie Howard, who made a rare appearance without his brother, Joseph. As memorable as Howard, Rogers, and Kearns proved in their roles, the reviews saluted the Broadway debut of twenty-one-year-old Ethel Merman. In the minor role of Kate Fothergill, the salty wife of a saloonkeeper, she made Broadway history with her rendition of the Gershwins' "I Got Rhythm," a raucous paean to life's simple pleasures. Critics and audiences alike were dazzled by her commanding stage presence and a voice that Ira Gershwin claimed "could reach not only standees but ticket takers in the lobby." The role established her enduring Broadway persona, the brassy dame with a heart of gold and a larynx of anodized aluminum. Considering the hoopla that surrounded her performance, it is surprising that Merman did not record "I Got Rhythm" until over a decade later when she was under contract to Decca. With an uncredited orchestration similar to Robert Russell Bennett's original, she delivers the song with such full-throated élan and crystal clear diction that it is difficult to imagine any other singer attempting it.

OF THEE I SING 12/26/31, Music Box Theatre; 441 performances. Music, George Gershwin; lyrics, Ira Gershwin; book, George S. Kaufman & Morrie Ryskind; orchestrations, Robert Russell Bennett; producer, Sam H. Harris; director, Kaufman; choreographers, George Hale & William Daly; musical director, Charles Previn.
★ William Gaxton, Lois Moran, Victor Moore, Grace Brinkley, June O'Dea, George Murphy.
Of Thee I Sing, Baby—**Jack Carson, Betty Oakes, Jack Whiting, and Company** Conductor, Maurice Levine. Capitol S-350, mx S-350-Y1; recorded 5/11/52.

As *Show Boat* in the previous decade had brought a new maturity to the American operetta, 1931's *Of Thee I Sing* ushered in a refreshingly adult, if offbeat, approach to the native musical comedy. Its synthesis of vernacular musical traditions and comic opera/operetta techniques earned it the distinction of being the first Broadway musical to win a Pulitzer Prize for Drama.

George and Ira Gershwin and George S. Kaufman had first attempted to wed musical comedy and political satire in *Strike Up the Band,* a 1927 show about international relations that eventually made it to Broadway in 1930 with script revisions by Morrie Ryskind. For their next collaboration the Gershwins, Kaufman, and Ryskind concocted a follow-up of sorts, to be called *Tweedle-Dee,* but they soon discovered that their plot about Republicans and Democrats in competition over writing a new national anthem was a one-joke affair. Their second attempt, equipped with a title borrowed from a phrase in "My Country, 'Tis of Thee," was a far more skillful, non-partisan send-up of American institutions and establishments. The plot, which was really a series of pointed sketches linked by song and dance, centers on the campaign and presidency of dapper John P. Wintergreen. Although his political platform, "Love," meets with national approval, Wintergreen is threatened with impeachment when he rejects Diana Devereaux, winner of the beauty contest held to select his First Lady, and chooses instead his demure, corn muffin–baking secretary, Mary Turner. All ends happily as Mary gives birth to twins and Diana becomes the charge of the wistfully anonymous Vice President Alexander Throttlebottom.

The Gershwins' score was a real departure from their series of syncopated ditties for twenties musicals. In their interwoven succession of individual songs, recitatives, and complex extended musical scenes, they explored a new style of composition for the American musical theater that earned them the sobriquet "a jazz Gilbert and Sullivan." One of the most effective moments in the score occurs midway in act 1 at the campaign rally set at Madison Square Garden. Promoting his theme of "Love," Wintergreen proposes to Mary Turner in front of a suggested crowd of thousands by serenading her with his ironic campaign song, "Of Thee I Sing, Baby." As the voters and party workers join in, the number becomes a soaring chorale.

Perhaps because none of its cast members was familiar to record buyers or, more importantly, because the score was not as effective removed from its dramatic context, there are no extant commercial recordings of the first production. The version of the title song included here comes from the cast album of the financially unsuccessful 1952 revival starring Jack Carson and Paul Hartman in the roles created by William Gaxton and Victor Moore. A splendidly theatrical recording, it retains the dialogue leading into the song and boasts the brightest fidelity the pre-stereo LP could offer. The new orchestration, faithful to Russell Bennett's original, is by Broadway veteran Don Walker. *Of Thee I Sing* received a brand new concert production in 1987 starring Larry Kert, Jack Gilford, and Maureen McGovern, which was subsequently recorded by CBS.

In 1933 Messrs. Gershwin, Gershwin, Kaufman, and Ryskind returned to *Of Thee I Sing*'s characters with far less popular results in a sequel called *Let 'Em Eat Cake*. Its bitter vision of fascism in America was more scabrous than satiric, though Gershwin regarded his score for the work as "the composer's claim to legitimacy."

THE BAND WAGON 6/3/31, New Amsterdam Theatre; 260 performances. Music, Arthur Schwartz; lyrics, Howard Dietz; sketches, Dietz & George S. Kaufman; orchestrations, Robert Russell Bennett; producer, Max Gordon; director, Hassard Short; choreographer, Albertina Rasch; musical director, Al Goodman. ★ Fred & Adele Astaire, Frank Morgan, Helen Broderick, Tilly Losch, Philip Loeb, John Barker.
Hoops—**Fred and Adele Astaire** Leo Reisman and His Orchestra. Victor 22386, mx BS-7092-1; recorded 10/19/31.

Described by co-author Howard Dietz as "an experimental production, combining the sophistication and intelligence of the intimate revue with the opulence of a Ziegfeld extravaganza," *The Band Wagon* is recognized as the finest of 1930s revues. Impresario Max Gordon planned the show as a follow-up to his hit of the previous season, *Three's a Crowd,* but he had a difficult time persuading Dietz and Schwartz to undertake the task of devising another revue. Before accepting, Dietz demanded that he and George S. Kaufman alone be permitted to write its sketches, that the Astaires be signed as its stars, and that its Broadway residence be the legendary Ziegfeld house, the New Amsterdam Theatre. When Gordon accepted his conditions, Dietz began to develop the revue around the production concept of a double revolving stage, an idea he and designer Albert Johnson had worked out. The moving stage floor was used throughout the show, not just as a novelty but as an integral part of the performance. It was employed to particularly stunning effect in the first act finale, "I Love Louisa," in which the principals, dressed in lederhosen and dirndls, were spun around on a set resembling a Bavarian carousel.

Dietz and Kaufman's sketches were praised for their consistent wit and hilarity. The skit that most critics singled out was "The Pride of the Claghornes," in which an aristocratic family of the ante-bellum South is scandalized when the daughter, Breeze, confesses that she is still a virgin. A tone of clever sophistication also pervades the

"All day long, we play *avec ze hoops!*": Fred and Adele in *The Band Wagon*.

Dietz-Schwartz songs, most notably in the opening, when the company assembles onstage in theater seats and ironically echos the audience's sentiments by singing "It Better Be Good." Of the show's ballads, the stand-out was the brooding and angular "Dancing in the Dark," performed as a ballet solo by Tilly Losch on a set with slanted mirror floors and constantly shifting colored lights. Fred and Adele Astaire had one final opportunity to perform their celebrated "run-around" dance in the comic number "Hoops," in which they cavorted as two *enfants terribles* on the loose in Paris's Parc Monceau.

During the Broadway run, the Astaires collaborated with Leo Reisman's orchestra on 78s of the show's score (including the lively "Hoops" heard here), as well as in a more complete rendering on an experimental $33\frac{1}{3}$-rpm recording. Although the latter was not released at the time, it gives *The Band Wagon* the distinction of being the first Broadway show recorded on a long-playing record.

GAY DIVORCE 11/29/32, Ethel Barrymore Theatre; 248 performances. Music & lyrics, Cole Porter; book, Dwight Taylor, adapted by Kenneth Webb & Samuel Hoffenstein; orchestrations, Hans Spialek & Robert Russell Bennett; producers, Dwight Deere Wiman & Tom Weatherly; director, Howard Lindsay; choreographers, Carl Randall & Barbara Newberry; musical director, Gene Salzer. ★ Fred Astaire, Claire Luce, Luella Gear, G. P. Huntley, Jr., Erik Rhodes, Eric Blore. *Night and Day—***Fred Astaire** Victor 24193, mx BS-73977-1; recorded 11/22/32.

Cole Porter and Fred Astaire in their prime as theatrical artists were the principal distinctions of *Gay Divorce*. Dwight Taylor's libretto, originally called *An Almost Perfect Lady* and based on the unproduced comedy *An Adorable Adventure* by his stepfather, J. Hartley Manners, seems at best a curious amalgam of French bedroom farce, genteel British drawing-room comedy, and 1920s Broadway libretto à la Bolton and Wodehouse. The slightly frayed threads of the plot are woven on the somewhat overused framework of mistaken identity. Heroine Mimi Glossop travels to the French Riviera seeking a divorce and allows herself to be caught with a hired co-respondent named Tonetti, recommended by her acid-tongued, much-married aunt Hortense. Novelist Guy Holden adores her from afar and impersonates the co-respondent in order to capture her attention and win her love.

Cole Porter consented to write the score only on the condition that Fred Astaire be signed to play the hero. Astaire, in search of his first solo starring vehicle after his sister Adele's retirement from the stage, accepted the role after hearing Porter play the songs. His immediate favorite was the rhetorical "After You, Who?", but the song that turned the show into a hit was "Night and Day," which the composer had written specifically for Astaire's limited vocal range. Porter credited his insistent lyric to a remark made to him by Mrs. Vincent Astor about the "drip, drip, drip" of a leaky faucet, and his exotic melody to a Muslim call to worship that he had heard in Morocco. Astaire sang the number to leading lady Claire Luce and then proceeded to dance with her all over the

Roland Bottomley, Eric Rhodes, Claire Luce, and Fred Astaire in a farcical scene from *Gay Divorce.*

white and silver furniture that decorated Jo
Mielziner's exquisite resort hotel setting.

Following respectable productions of *Gay
Divorce* on Broadway and in London,
Astaire retired from the stage and devoted
the rest of his career to motion pictures.
The 1934 film version of the show, which
scrapped all of Porter's score except "Night
and Day," was retitled by film censors *The
Gay Divorcée*. Presumably they believed
that while a divorcée could conceivably be
gay (in the sense of "mirthful"), a divorce
most assuredly could not.

AS THOUSANDS CHEER 9/30/33, Music Box
Theatre; 400 performances. Music & lyrics, Irv-
ing Berlin; sketches, Moss Hart; orchestrations,
Frank Tours, Adolph Deutsch, Helmy Kresa;
producer, Sam H. Harris; director, Hassard
Short; choreographer, Charles Weidman; musical
director, Frank Tours. ★ Marilyn Miller, Clifton
Webb, Helen Broderick, Ethel Waters, Leslie
Adams, Leticia Ide, José Limon.
Easter Parade—**Clifton Webb** Leo Reisman
and His Orchestra. Victor 24418, mx BS-78071-2;
recorded 10/3/33.

Clifton Webb in "Easter Parade" finery.

The jewel-box elegance of *The Band Wagon*
found a worthy successor in *As Thousands
Cheer*. Combining the narrative structure of
a book musical with the format of a revue,
the show unfolded a satiric report on world
events, with its songs and sketches
masquerading as headlines in a daily
newspaper. Its "sections" ranged from the
front page and international news to the
comics and advice to the lovelorn. Author
Moss Hart also found the opportunity to
caricature a number of contemporary
celebrities, including Joan Crawford,
Douglas Fairbanks, Jr., John D. Rockefeller,
Herbert Hoover, Aimee Semple McPherson,
Josephine Baker, and Mahatma Gandhi.
Hart's wittiest skit cast all the principals as
hotel employees who fall under the influence
of former guest Noel Coward and neglect
their cleaning duties to spout *bons mots* and
affect continental accents.

Irving Berlin's score ranks among his
finest efforts for the theater. For each of his
stars he created a specialty designed to
display his or her unique talents. Ethel
Waters scored a double hit with the tragic
lament "Supper Time" and the frenetic
weather report "Heat Wave"; dancer
Marilyn Miller (in her final Broadway

appearance) cavorted daintily in "The
Funnies," with the ensemble costumed as
famous comic strip characters; and debonair
Clifton Webb (as Prince Mdivani wooing
Barbara Hutton) revealed new skills as a
balladeer in the lovely "How's Chances?"
Webb and Miller, along with comedienne
Helen Broderick, appeared in the first act
finale, a charming evocation of a turn-of-
the-century rotogravure section created in
glowing sepia tones by scenic designer
Albert Johnson and costumier Irene
Sharaff. For its musical number Berlin
unearthed a song he had written in 1917
called "Smile and Show Your Dimple."
With a new lyric, the piece became "Easter
Parade," one of the first of his many
tributes to holiday seasons. Webb's 1933
Victor recording, although a solo rendition
rather than an ensemble chorale, retains the
nostalgic charm of its original stage
incarnation. Leo Reisman's accompaniment, with its tolling tubular bells and
delicate violins, is remarkably appropriate,

especially since the recording was created more for dancing than for listening.

As Thousands Cheer was one of the most critically acclaimed and financially profitable of thirties revues. A 1935 London production, retitled *Stop Press,* retained the best of Berlin's score and added numbers by Dietz and Schwartz from *The Band Wagon* and several of their other revues.

ROBERTA 11/18/33, New Amsterdam Theatre; 295 performances. Music, Jerome Kern; lyrics & book, Otto Harbach; orchestrations, Robert Russell Bennett; producer, Max Gordon; directors, Kern & Hassard Short (uncredited); choreographers, José Limon & Robert Lonergan; musical director, Victor Baravalle. ★ Lyda Roberti, Bob Hope, Fay Templeton, Tamara, George Murphy, Sydney Greenstreet, Raymond Middleton, Fred MacMurray.
Smoke Gets in Your Eyes—**Tamara** Leo Reisman and His Orchestra. Brunswick 6715, mx B-14387; recorded 11/28/33.

Roberta was Jerome Kern's last successful musical for the Broadway theater. Although it was anticipated as a successor to his "continental" operettas *The Cat and the Fiddle* and *Music in the Air* and the landmark *Show Boat,* it turned out to be a conventional 1930s musical comedy with a succession of star specialties and a magnificent collection of songs. Like *Show Boat,* it was derived from a novel by a popular member of the Manhattan smart set; this time, the author was Alice Duer Miller, whose book *Gowns By Roberta* was a European romance involving an All-American halfback who inherits his aunt's modiste shop in Paris and falls in love with an employee who turns out to be a Russian princess. The work gave Kern a final opportunity to work with Otto Harbach. In adapting the novel as a libretto, Harbach added the characters of a comic hoofer and an onstage jazz band.

While Kern and Harbach were putting the finishing touches on the script and score, Kern went in search of a producer. Impresario Max Gordon, late of *The Band Wagon,* ended his longstanding feud with the composer when he was offered the project. In turn, he allowed Kern to make his first official bid as a stage director. The now legendary cast that Gordon assembled included venerable musical comedy star

Fay Templeton in her final stage role, exotic soprano Tamara, Polish bombshell Lyda Roberti, hoofer George Murphy, and a vaudeville comic named Bob Hope as the wisecracking confidant of leading man Raymond Middleton.

Entitled *Gowns by Roberta,* the musical braved its first audience at Philadelphia's Forrest Theatre on 21 October 1933. The reviews were mixed, with high praise for Kern's lovely score but severe criticism for the dawdling narrative and heavy-handed staging. Anxious to protect his investment, Gordon insisted that Kern relinquish his post as director to Hassard Short, who had guided *The Band Wagon* to a Broadway triumph. Short insisted on new sets and new costumes (particularly for a fashion show in the second act), bringing the budget up to the unheard-of figure of $115,000. The revisions strengthened the libretto, but the New York reviews were discouraging. The

Princess Stephanie (Tamara), wearing the peasant garb of her homeland, sings "Smoke Gets in Your Eyes" to her fellow expatriates.

outlook for the show was dismal, in spite of its vogue among Manhattan's carriage trade. What led the show to eventual success was the widespread popularity of "Smoke Gets in Your Eyes," which the *New York Herald-Tribune* reported "has swept the dance floors, radio studios, and glee clubs of the country." Kern had originally written the melody as a jaunty dance number for *Show Boat,* then later reworked it as a march for a series of original radio musicals that never reached the air. It was Harbach who persuaded him to slow the tempo and convert the tune into a pensive ballad, to which Harbach added a lyric based on a mythical Russian proverb. Onstage, Tamara, as the expatriate White Russian princess, performed the song, accompanying herself on the guitar, but in this recording she is backed by Leo Reisman's Orchestra, whose dance-band approach does nothing to alter the rubato phrasing of her stage interpretation.

Record Side 4
Cassette Side
Compact Disc II

ANYTHING GOES 11/21/34, Alvin Theatre; 420 performances. Music & lyrics, Cole Porter; book, Guy Bolton & P. G. Wodehouse, revised by Howard Lindsay & Russel Crouse; orchestrations, Robert Russell Bennett, Hans Spialek; producer, Vinton Freedley; director, Lindsay; choreographer, Robert Alton; musical director, Earl Busby. ★ William Gaxton, Ethel Merman, Victor Moore, Bettina Hall, Helen Raymond, Vera Dunn, Leslie Barrie, Vivian Vance.
I Get a Kick Out of You—**Ethel Merman**
Conductor, Johnny Green. Brunswick 7342, mx B-16397-A; recorded 12/4/34.

Anything Goes is one of the glittering Art Deco landmarks of 1930s Broadway musical comedy, with its farcical, depression-be-damned plot, its array of brassy cartoon characters, and its elegant parade of smart and melodic anthems. Its history began in 1934 when producer Vinton Freedley conceived the idea for a sophisticated musical to be called *Hard to Get,* about the comic aftermath of a luxury liner ship-wreck. He engaged champion librettists Guy Bolton and P. G. Wodehouse to flesh out his brief scenario, and when the Gershwins proved unavailable because of

Porgy and Bess, he hired Cole Porter to write the music and lyrics. For his stars, Freedley teamed the comedy duo of William Gaxton and Victor Moore with his *Girl Crazy* discovery Ethel Merman in a role first offered to troubled torch singer Libby Holman.

On 8 September 1934, just two weeks before rehearsals were scheduled to begin, the tragic sinking of the pleasure cruiser U.S.S. Morro Castle off the New Jersey coast rendered the premise of the script virtually unuseable. With Bolton and Wodehouse involved in other projects in Europe, Freedley persuaded the show's director, Howard Lindsay, to join forces with Theatre Guild press agent Russel Crouse in constructing a new libretto that would accommodate Porter's completed score and Donald Oenslager's nautical set designs. Their hastily assembled revision is among the wittiest musical comedy scripts of the decade, using its cast of intermingling high- and low-born characters on a transatlantic cruise as a microcosm of the changing social order emerging from the depression. These characters include Reno Sweeney, an evangelist turned cabaret entertainer; Wall Street refugee Billy Crocker; his sweetheart, Hope Harcourt, who is unhappily aboard with her titled English fiancé and her social-climbing mother; and Moonface Martin, the FBI's Public Enemy No. 13, disguised as the Reverend Dr. Moon.

Among its many other accomplishments, *Anything Goes* confirmed Ethel Merman's status as one of Broadway's great treasures. Appearing as a tough-talking, soft-hearted dame who was one part Aimee Semple McPherson, one part Texas Guinan, and one part Merman, she had the lion's share of the score, including the chief ballad, "I Get a Kick Out of You," sung to William Gaxton in a prologue to the first act. The song, which had grown out of Porter's background music for the 1933 British musical *Nymph Errant,* was banned from the airwaves for years because of its reference to cocaine. The show has enjoyed two major New York revivals to date: a 1962 off-Broadway edition with Eileen Rodgers and Hal Linden and a 1987 Lincoln Center production starring Patti Lupone.

J. Rosamond Johnson, Todd Duncan, and Anne Brown in a lighthearted scene from the 1942 Broadway revival of *Porgy and Bess*.

PORGY AND BESS 10/10/35, Alvin Theatre; 124 performances. Music & orchestrations, George Gershwin; libretto, DuBose Heyward & Ira Gershwin; producer, The Theatre Guild; director, Rouben Mamoulian; musical director, Alexander Smallens. ★ Todd Duncan, Anne Brown, Warren Coleman, Avon Long, Harriett Jackson, Edward Matthews, Georgette Harvey, Helen Dowdy, Ruby Elzy, J. Rosamond Johnson. *Bess, You Is My Woman Now*—**Todd Duncan and Anne Brown** Conductor, Alexander Smallens. Decca 29069, mx 67742; recorded 5/15/40.

Broadway's first bona fide American folk opera was George Gershwin's last and most breathtakingly adventurous effort for the musical theater. Gershwin had first expressed interest in writing an operatic version of DuBose Heyward's novel *Porgy* shortly after its publication in 1925. He was intrigued with the challenges offered by the tragic tale of life among the poor Gullah blacks of Charleston, South Carolina, but his plans were postponed when the Theatre Guild produced a dramatic adaptation by Heyward and his wife, Dorothy, during the 1927/28 season.

Interest in a musical adaptation of *Porgy* resurfaced in the early thirties when the Guild attempted to secure the rights for a version to be adapted by Jerome Kern and Oscar Hammerstein II to star Al Jolson. Heyward rejected their plan and persuaded them to sponsor Gershwin's more ambitious approach, which would expand on the musico-dramatic horizons explored earlier in *Of Thee I Sing*.

Gershwin wrote much of the score on Folly Island, not far from the tenements of Charleston's Cabbage Row district which Heyward had renamed Catfish Row in his narrative. Heyward and Ira Gershwin collaborated on a libretto that transformed the doomed affair between Porgy, a middle-aged cripple, and Bess, a drug-addicted prostitute, into the basis for an exalted theatrical experience, and George's music provided a glorious vehicle for their words. Unlike his other musical theater works which interspersed music and spoken dialogue, *Porgy and Bess* was sung throughout. Along with regular musical comedy turns like "It Ain't Necessarily So" and "There's a Boat That's Leavin' Soon for New York" (both written for the slinky dope peddler Sportin' Life), he turned out stirring ensembles ("Gone, Gone, Gone"), solos ("I Got Plenty o' Nuttin'," "I Loves You Porgy," and "Summertime") and duets ("Bess, You Is My Woman Now") all linked, as in traditional opera, by passages of recitative.

The Broadway premiere was deemed such a momentous occasion that newspapers sent both drama and music critics to cover it. Opinion was sharply divided, with the work being praised by theater reviewers but taken to task by the music reporters, who seemed to resent an American grand opera that had emerged more from the native idioms of jazz and musical comedy than from traditional European forms.

A commercial failure in its first New York engagement, *Porgy and Bess* succeeded in a 1942 Broadway revival sponsored by Cheryl Crawford which retained original 1935 cast members Todd Duncan and Anne Brown and replaced the passages of recitative with spoken dialogue. That version toured extensively in the early 1950s under the auspices of the U. S. State Department, with Leontyne Price and William Warfield in the leads. A full-scale 1976 revival of the opera in its original form by the Houston Grand Opera led eventually to the work's incorporation into the repertoire at the Metropolitan Opera in 1985. Although considered something of a sophisticated curiosity at the time of its premiere, *Porgy and Bess* became recognized as a model for a more mature approach to writing, both musically and dramatically, for the commercial musical theater. Its influence can be observed in works as diverse as Weill, Rice, and Hughes's *Street Scene* (1947) and Bernstein, Sondheim, and Laurents's *West Side Story* (1957).

BABES IN ARMS 4/14/37, Shubert Theatre; 289 performances. Music, Richard Rodgers; lyrics, Lorenz Hart; book, Rodgers & Hart; orchestrations, Hans Spialek; producer, Dwight Deere Wiman; director, Robert Sinclair; choreographer, George Balanchine; musical director, Gene Salzer. ★ Mitzi Green, Ray Heatherton, Duke McHale, Wynn Murray, Harold & Fayard Nicholas, Rolly Pickert, Grace MacDonald, Ray MacDonald, Alfred Drake, Robert Rounseville. *Johnny One-Note*—**Wynn Murray** Ruby Newman and His Orchestra. Victor 25546, mx 06194-1; recorded 3/12/37.

According to Richard Rodgers, *Babes in Arms* "was one of those shows that worked right from the start." Reunited with Dwight Deere Wiman, who had produced their 1936 musical *On Your Toes,* Rodgers and Hart provided not only a bountiful score but also the charming libretto, a breezy comedy about the children of vaudevillians in Seaport, Long Island. Because of the effects of the depression, the teenagers are threatened with being sent to a work farm while their parents are on tour with Federal Theatre projects. To support themselves, the kids put on a musical revue bankrolled by former child star Baby Rose, who at sixteen is anxious for a comeback. When she withdraws from the show and takes its financing with her, the young people nearly give up hope of staying together, but the accidental landing of a French aviator in their midst inspires them to convert a fallow field into a landing strip and promote their hometown as an aviation center.

Much of the show's success lay in the believable youthfulness of its cast. The romantic leads were played by Ray Heatherton, later known as TV's "merry mailman," and ex-movie moppet Mitzi Green. Also in the cast were such future stars as Alfred Drake, Robert Rounseville, and, in the chorus, Dan Dailey. Perhaps the most notable Broadway debut made by a member of the original company was that of Wynn Murray, an eighteen-year-old blonde butterball with no previous professional experience as a performer. Her Mermanesque delivery of "Johnny One-Note" remains one of the era's bright moments in the musical theater. The song was staged as part of the youngsters' show-in-a-barn and prefaced a satiric ballet inspired by Verdi's *Aida,* with the children

Babes-in-arms Mitzi Green, Rolly Pickert, Alfred Drake, Ray Heatherton, and Wynn Murray rescue aviator Aljan DeLouville from his wrecked plane.

costumed in improvised Egyptian costumes made of dishcloths, mops, and coat hooks. In addition to "Johnny One-Note," Rodgers and Hart's score contained at least three songs that became standards: "Where or When," "My Funny Valentine," and "The Lady Is a Tramp," all introduced by Mitzi Green.

PINS AND NEEDLES 11/27/37, Labor Stage; 1,108 performances. Music & lyrics, Harold J. Rome; sketches, Charles Friedman, Arthur Arent, Marc Blitzstein; producer, Labor Stage, Inc.; director, Friedman; choreographers, Benjamin Zemach & Gluck Sandor. ★ The ILGWU Players (including Millie Weitz, Ruth Rubenstein, Al Levy, Nettie Harary, Al Eben).
Chain Store Daisy—**Ruth Rubenstein** Pianists, Harold Rome and Baldwin Bergersen. Decca 23061-A, mx 6325-A; recorded 2/38.

The Great Depression brought a new awareness of social issues to the theater. A lighthearted example of this trend is *Pins and Needles,* the revue that grew out of a desire among members of the International Ladies Garment Workers Union to develop theatrical activities that would give voice to the struggle between labor and management. Originally they sought a serious

drama, but Louis Schaffer, head of the union's committee for theatrical endeavors, thought a contemporary revue with satirical songs, dances, and sketches would highlight their concerns in a more accessible way. To prove his point, he commissioned Harold Rome to write some topical songs and perform them for the committee. The audition convinced the ILGWU members, and they embarked on a spare-time rehearsal schedule that lasted over a year.

The show premiered at the home of the early Kern-Bolton-Wodehouse musical comedies, the Princess Theatre, which the ILGWU company renamed the Labor Stage. At first, performances were scheduled only on weekends so that cast members could maintain their daily jobs, but when the show's merits became known among theatergoers, the company happily adopted a regular policy of eight performances a week.

Among the virtues of *Pins and Needles* were its surprisingly versatile cast, made up of dressmakers and other assorted garment workers, and Harold Rome's exceptional score, which blended its left-of-center philosophies with humor and warmth. The

Ruth Rubenstein (left) and other *Pins and Needles* cast members with ILGWU president David Dubinsky (seated left) and FDR.

opening number, "Sing Me a Song with Social Significance" set the sunny, satirical tone of the revue with its insistence that a love song "must be packed with social fact." Among the various character pieces, "Chain Store Daisy," the plaint of a Vassar graduate reduced to a job in Macy's lingerie department, was cited as a comic highpoint. During the Broadway run, the song's original interpreter, Ruth Rubenstein, recorded the number with pit pianists Rome and Bergersen. Her understated delivery makes the self-deprecating pathos of its lyric all the more winning.

In order to maintain its topicality, the revue was altered and new material added throughout its 2½-year run, particularly in the number "Four Little Angels of Peace," which changed its satiric targets as the leaders of international power shifted.

THE CRADLE WILL ROCK 6/16/37, Venice Theatre; 14 performances. Music, lyrics, & book, Marc Blitzstein; producer, the Mercury Theatre (Orson Welles); director, Welles. ★ Howard Da Silva, Will Geer, John Adair, Hiram Sherman, Olive Stanton, Peggy Coudray, Blanche Collins, Bert Weston, John Hoysradt, Edward Fuller.

***The Cradle Will Rock*—Howard Da Silva**
Pianist, Marc Blitzstein. Musicraft 1080-A, mx GM331A; recorded 1937.

The Cradle Will Rock was a musical equivalent to such 1930s agitation-propaganda dramas as Clifford Odets's stirring *Waiting for Lefty* and other socio-political works produced by the Group Theatre. In its relentlessly militant indictment of American capitalism and its fervent plea for the unionization of downtrodden workers, it was unlike anything the musical theater had previously witnessed.

Composer-lyricist-librettist Marc Blitzstein patterned his "play in music" after the avant-garde, politically oriented musical theater traditions developed by Bertolt Brecht and Kurt Weill in 1920s Berlin. With a plot that came directly out of the newspaper headlines, his bitter morality play (or "immorality play," as critic Irving Kolodin called it) tells of the mythical Steeltown, U.S.A., ruled by despotic factory owner Mister Mister, the equally manipulative Mrs. Mister, and their dimwitted children, Junior and Sister Mister. Eventually the oppressed

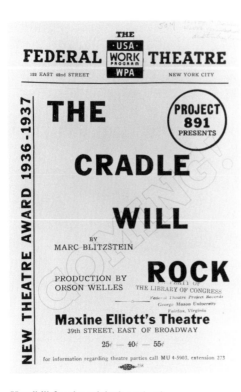

Handbill for the original production.

community is liberated by heroic Larry Foreman, a fiery labor organizer. As their names suggest, the characters are stereotypical abstractions rather than three-dimensional dramatic figures. Blitzstein's score is equally uncompromising, with its atonal harmonies and staccato rhythms. Its lyrics seem to have been lifted from left-wing political pamphlets, particularly in the explosive title song, a rallying cry aimed at blue-collar America.

Because of its controversial viewpoint and compositional style, the musical had trouble finding a producer. Chiefly through the influence of staff members John Houseman and Orson Welles, it was adopted by the one-year-old Federal Theatre project of FDR's Works Progress Administration. That the show seemed a questionable choice for the beleaguered government agency was confirmed on the morning before opening night, when military officers were dispatched to shut down the production, turn away ticket buyers, impound the elaborate expressionistic sets, and padlock the theater. Welles and Houseman sprang into action and, in a grand gesture commensurate with the political fervor of the era, led a parade of actors and patrons up Broadway to the out-of-the-way Venice Theatre. The version of *The Cradle Will Rock* that premiered that evening was very different from the one planned. Blitzstein sat alone onstage at an old upright piano and provided the only musical acccompaniment. Since Actors' Equity had forbidden its members to perform the work on any stage other than that announced by the WPA, the cast performed from various locations in the audience, being pulled into the dramatic action by lighting designer Abe Feder's single probing spotlight.

Following its brief run at the Venice Theatre, the no-frills production resurfaced first in December 1937, as a Sunday night attraction at Welles's experimental Mercury Theatre, and then in early January 1938, when it was transferred to Broadway's Windsor Theatre for a run of 108 performances. It has had numerous revivals since its premiere, most notably a 1947 Leonard Bernstein–supervised version, a 1964 off-Broadway edition, and a 1984 touring production by the Acting Company guided by original director Houseman.

One of the most significant theatrical works of the 1930s, *The Cradle Will Rock* was also the first Broadway musical to have an original cast album. Musicraft, a small company dedicated to non-traditional material, recorded the score in 1938 on seven ten-inch 78s with Blitzstein providing the piano accompaniment and narration. The original edition is among the rarest of American theater recordings.

KNICKERBOCKER HOLIDAY 10/19/38, Ethel Barrymore Theatre; 168 performances. Music & orchestrations, Kurt Weill; lyrics & book, Maxwell Anderson; producer, The Playwrights Company; director, Joshua Logan; choreographers, Carl Randall & Edwin Denby; musical director, Maurice Abravanel. ★ Walter Huston, Ray Middleton, Jeanne Madden, Richard Kollmar, Mark Smith.
September Song—**Walter Huston** Conductor, Maurice Abravanel. Brunswick 8272, mx B-23732; recorded 11/24/38.

A musical version of Washington Irving's satiric *Diedrich Knickerbocker's History of New York* (1809) marked the first collaboration of German expatriate composer Kurt Weill and Pulitzer Prize–winning American dramatist Maxwell Anderson. In keeping with the era's penchant for a more socially and politically aware lyric stage, the authors reinterpreted Irving's portrait of the seventeenth-century Dutch colony of Nieuw Amsterdam as an imaginative, though occasionally preachy, indictment of fascism. Their central theme, democracy versus totalitarianism, is personified in the conflict between hero Brom Broeck, a freedom-loving vendor, and the dictatorial Governor Pieter Stuyvesant. Not only do the two characters differ philosophically, they also compete for the attentions of Tina Tienhoven, the daughter of the corrupt chief councilor. Surrounding them are a group of bumbling Dutch burgomasters who speak in broad comic dialects akin to those of Weber and Fields a generation earlier. Washington Irving himself turns up as an omniscient figure who introduces the story and brings about the unexpected happy ending.

In the early drafts of the script, Stuyvesant was a secondary character and the villain of the piece. Anderson, an ardent opponent of the New Deal, intended his portrait of the historical figure as a venomous satire on FDR. Director Joshua Logan persuaded him to soften his political barbs against the current administration and to turn the character into a sympathetic leading role. Redesigned by Anderson and Logan as a star turn for Walter Huston, Stuyvesant became a wily but charming old codger, equally adept at dancing on his peg leg and crooning a tender ballad.

It was Huston who sparked the idea for the score's most famous number. Before he agreed to accept the part, he requested a song that would reveal a sentimental dimension of the character. After hearing him sing on a national radio broadcast, Weill and Anderson wrote the classic "September Song" over the course of one evening. Huston's performance of this touchingly melancholy piece ranks among the most cherished moments in the

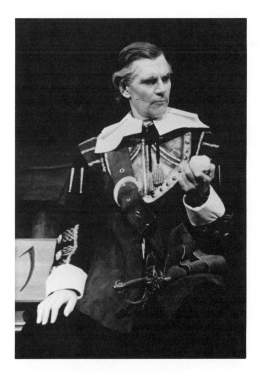

Walter Huston as Pieter Stuyvesant.

American musical theater. His first recording of the song (included here), ably supported by Weill's orchestration and the sensitive musical direction of Maurice Abravanel, captures much of the magic of his stage interpretation.

Because of its commercial failure and its artistic shortcomings, *Knickerbocker Holiday* has been given few major revivals. In May 1971 it received a handsome new production on the West Coast starring Burt Lancaster in a belated (and lamentable) musical stage debut. Plans for a Broadway transfer were dashed by the indifferent reviews and insufficient financing.

LEAVE IT TO ME! 11/9/38, Imperial Theatre; 291 performances. Music & lyrics, Cole Porter; book, Bella & Samuel Spewack; orchestrations, Don Walker; producer, Vinton Freedley; director, Samuel Spewack; choreographer, Robert Alton; musical director, Max Meth. ★ William Gaxton, Victor Moore, Sophie Tucker, Tamara, Mary Martin.
My Heart Belongs to Daddy—**Mary Martin** Decca 23149-A, mx 67129; recorded 1/25/40.

I Am an American was the original title of the libretto that became *Leave It to Me!*, adapted by Sam and Bella Spewack from their comedy *Clear All Wires,* based on their own madcap adventures as foreign news correspondents in the 1920s. Following a tradition established by *Of Thee I Sing,* the story was a political satire, but the topic that had inspired the Gershwins, Ryskind, and Kaufman to construct their one-of-a-kind comic opera was treated by the Spewacks and Cole Porter in the language of pure musical comedy. The plot concerns Alonzo P. "Stinky" Goodhue, a Topeka bathtub salesman who is appointed ambassador to the U.S.S.R. as a result of his wife's contributions to FDR's re-election campaign. To engineer his return to the states, he employs brash newspaperman Buckley Joyce Thomas, whose wily strategies backfire and turn Goodhue into a reluctant hero. Only when the bumbling ambassador proposes a plan for international peace does he bring about his recall to America. A highlight of the show was its first act finale with actor Walter Armin as a comic Josef Stalin dancing to "The Internationale."

Leave It to Me! gave Cole Porter his first real hit since *Anything Goes* (1934) and reunited him with its producer, Vinton Freedley, and two of its stars, William Gaxton and Victor Moore. After an absence of twenty-seven years, Sophie Tucker returned to the medium of the book musical to play Moore's politically ambitious wife, a role first planned for Mae West and then Charlotte Greenwood. Tamara, the leading lady of 1933's *Roberta,* portrayed Colette Arnaud, Gaxton's romantic interest. The show's surprise star was an unknown twenty-four-year-old Texan, Mary Martin, a last minute substitute for the originally cast June Knight. As Gaxton's sexy secretary Dolly Winslow, Martin parlayed a small role into a large triumph on the strength of her only solo number, the *faux-naif* "My Heart Belongs to Daddy." The song occurs midway in the second act, as Dolly continues her journey home to America by an out-of-the-way route through Siberia. Surrounded by fur-clad chorus boys (including Gene Kelly) and seated atop a steamer trunk, Martin performed the song with eyes cast heavenward and double entendres aimed considerably lower. As she offered her dubious pledge of allegiance to her paternal protector, she coyly stripped down to a pink chiffon chemise. Martin has recorded the number several times during her career, but her finest performance was the one included in a 1940 Decca album of Cole Porter songs. This rendition retains the original risqué lyrics and approximates the orchestration used in the theater.

DUBARRY WAS A LADY 12/6/39, 46th Street Theatre; 408 performances. Music & lyrics, Cole Porter; book, Herbert Fields & B. G. DeSylva; orchestrations, Hans Spialek; producer, DeSylva; director, Edgar MacGregor; choreographer, Robert Alton; musical director, Gene Salzer. ★ Bert Lahr, Ethel Merman, Betty Grable, Benny Baker, Ronald Graham, Charles Walters.
Friendship—**Bert Lahr and Ethel Merman** Conductor, Al Goodman. NBC Colgate Comedy Hour broadcast; recorded 2/28/54.

DuBarry Was a Lady was the fifth longest-running musical of the 1930s and the decade's last full-length musical comedy. Like several works of the era, it was born in Hollywood. Herbert Fields, while under contract to Paramount, had come up with a

Dolly Winslow (Mary Martin) pledges her heart to Daddy while flirting with a pack of Russian wolves (Gene Kelly is fourth from left).

racy scenario about the fabled French courtesan Madame DuBarry for the studio's star Mae West. When she rejected the script, he took the idea to B.G. "Buddy" DeSylva, a former songwriter and film executive who was eager to set up shop as a Broadway producer. DeSylva liked Fields's premise but asked him to combine it with his own idea for a show about a comic washroom attendant in an elegant New York club. The result was a raucous, extended burlesque sketch about Louis Blore, an employee at the Club Petite who pines with unrequited love for the club's headliner, May Daley. He mistakenly downs a Mickey Finn, then dreams that he is Louis XV and the flashy singer is his elusive mistress.

Bert Lahr, maintaining his position as one of Broadway's most endearing clowns, was an endless delight as the pathetically funny Louis. As the unwilling object of his affection, that bright brass trumpet known as Ethel Merman proved in fine fettle as both vocalist and comedienne. It was Merman's agreement to appear in the show that persuaded Cole Porter to write the score. Although admittedly not his finest effort, it did offer a number of appealing endeavors, including the suggestive "But in the Morning, No," the tender "Do I Love You?," and the mock-hillbilly "Friendship." The last, a hymn to platonic interdependence, was a show-stopping duet for Merman and Lahr. During their performance, each would try to convulse the other with spontaneous, improvised stage business. Although they never recorded the song commercially, they did perform it fourteen years after the original

"Just the perfect blendship": Ethel Merman and Bert Lahr in the dream sequence from *DuBarry Was a Lady.*

Broadway run, as an interpolated piece in a television adaptation of *Anything Goes.* In spite of the characterless, uncredited orchestrations, this soundtrack recording preserves all the ribald humor of Porter's lyric and the inspired trouping of two stars still very much at the top of their form. Merman's bravura Broadway bombast is tempered and complemented by Lahr's timid and insinuating approach to the material. The recording is a rare memento of an all-but-forgotten show.

Record Side 5

CABIN IN THE SKY 10/25/40, Martin Beck Theatre; 156 performances. Music, Vernon Duke; lyrics, John Latouche; book, Lynn Root; orchestrations, Domenico Savino, Charles Cooke, & Nathan Van Cleve; producers, Albert Lewis & Vinton Freedley; director, Albert Lewis; choreographer, George Balanchine; musical director, Max Meth. ★ Ethel Waters, Dooley Wilson,

Todd Duncan, Rex Ingram, Katherine Dunham, J. Rosamond Johnson.
***Taking a Chance on Love*—Ethel Waters**
Conductor, Max Meth. Liberty Music Shops L-310, mx 20931-1; recorded 11/7/40.

Cabin in the Sky began as a songless libretto entitled *Little Joe* by Lynn Root, a Hollywood screenwriter with his eye on Broadway. His story was a delicate fantasy about Little Joe Jackson's struggle with good and evil and his eventual salvation through the gentle strength of his wife, Petunia. The script passed through a number of theatrical hands before reaching Vernon Duke, who was looking for the right property for his first Broadway book musical. Despite his unfamiliarity with its poetic themes of black folklore, Duke committed himself enthusiastically to the project and went in search of a lyricist. He was turned down by Ira Gershwin, who was occupied with *Lady in the Dark,* and E. Y.

Harburg (ironically, Harburg and Harold Arlen later wrote several new songs for the show's film version), but he finally found a willing collaborator in John Latouche, also embarking on his first try at a book musical. At the recommendation of Louis "Doc" Bender (a celebrated dentist, theatrical agent, and cohort of Lorenz Hart), Albert Lewis and Vinton Freedley agreed to sponsor the show on Broadway, along with such illustrious silent partners as fellow producers Martin Beck, Gilbert Miller, and Sam Harris.

When Duke and Latouche had completed more than half the score, they approached Ethel Waters to star. At first she refused on the grounds that the role of Petunia was eclipsed by that of Little Joe, but after some extensive campaigning by the songwriters, she agreed to sign. Other principals in the illustrious cast were Dooley Wilson as the male lead, Todd Duncan and Rex Ingram as the opposing forces of good and evil, and dancer

Katherine Dunham as a sinuous agent of the Devil.

When rehearsals began, the press made much of the fact that a fable about American blacks was being created by three Russians: composer Duke, choreographer Balanchine, and set designer Aronson. Budgetary restrictions prevented the customary out-of-town tryouts; instead, the producers adopted the now-common practice of running a series of preview performances before the official Broadway opening. The previews revealed a need for a song in the first act to establish the heroine's forgiving nature and provide an introductory showcase for Waters's considerable talents. Duke and Latouche first wrote an offbeat lullaby, which proved unsatisfactory. Three days before the opening, Duke dug out an old song, "Fooling Around with Love," written earlier with lyricist Ted Fetter for an unproduced show. With Fetter's blessing, Latouche altered the title and lyric, and on

Ethel Waters and Dooley Wilson in *Cabin in the Sky*.

opening night, "Taking a Chance on Love" stopped the show and required eight encores.

Although its run was modest even by 1940s standards, *Cabin in the Sky* endures as Duke's theatrical masterwork. It also provided Ethel Waters with one of the finest moments of her long career. She first recorded "Taking a Chance on Love" during the Broadway run on the Liberty Music Shops label, a small company in Manhattan whose products were forerunners of the original cast recording. Her rendition is fresh, vital, and enchantingly in character, foreshadowing her later career as one of America's finest dramatic actresses.

PAL JOEY 12/25/40, Ethel Barrymore Theatre; 374 performances. Music, Richard Rodgers; lyrics, Lorenz Hart; book, John O'Hara & George Abbott (uncredited); orchestrations, Hans Spialek; producer-director, Abbott; choreographer, Robert Alton; musical director, Harry Levant. ★ Vivienne Segal, Gene Kelly, Leila Ernst, June Havoc, Jack Durant, Jean Casto.
Bewitched, Bothered, and Bewildered—
Vivienne Segal Conductor, Lehman Engel. Columbia OL-4364, mx XLP-3711; recorded 9/20/50.

Pal Joey, with its unsavory principal characters, frank dialogue, and sardonic score, shattered many a myth about the boundaries of commercial musical comedy. The show originated in John O'Hara's *New Yorker* short stories in letter form, about an unscrupulous but charming Chicago nightclub entertainer. At the suggestion of screenwriter George Oppenheimer, O'Hara adapted the stories as a libretto and found two enthusiastic collaborators in Rodgers and Hart, for whom the script's adult tone offered a welcome change from traditional musical formulas. George Abbott joined the team as producer, director, and uncredited co-author.

The libretto centers on Joey Evans's mercenary relationship with worldly society matron Vera Simpson, who eventually drops him when she learns of his plans to blackmail her. Around them are a collection of equally venal opportunists, including such Runyonesque characters as underhanded chorine Gladys Bumps and underworld thug Ludlow Lowell. The only sympathetic character is an excessively naive chorus girl, Linda English, who briefly becomes involved with Joey before seeing his true colors. The cynical tone of

Robert Alton's dream ballet, "Joey Looks into the Future," serves as *Pal Joey*'s first-act finale. Gene Kelly and Vivienne Segal are center.

O'Hara's script is matched by Hart's often risqué lyrics, which are tempered somewhat by Rodgers's characteristically lovely flow of melodies.

At Rodgers's insistence, singer-dancer-actor Gene Kelly was given the title role. The composer thought Kelly's Irish charm would make the self-serving Joey palatable to audiences. O'Hara favored Marlene Dietrich for Vera, but Rodgers and Hart convinced him that their friend Vivienne Segal was the ideal choice. The part of the scheming Gladys was expanded during rehearsals because of June Havoc's delightful interpretation of the character.

Contrary to popular belief, *Pal Joey* was a commercial success during its initial Broadway run, but its critical reception was mixed. The *New York Herald-Tribune*'s Richard Watts, Jr., pronounced it "an outstanding triumph" while Abel Green of *Variety* dismissed it as "quite an unpleasant evening." Its most emphatic detractor was Brooks Atkinson of the *New York Times,* who made the now-famous observation. "Although it is expertly done, can you draw sweet water from a foul well?"

In 1950 Goddard Lieberson of Columbia Records revived interest in the work by recording its score with Vivienne Segal back as the predatory heroine and *Kiss Me, Kate*'s Harold Lang in Kelly's role. Segal made the most of her chance to immortalize Vera's sweet-and-sour persona, particularly in the splendidly candid "Bewitched, Bothered, and Bewildered." The success of the recording led to a Broadway revival starring Segal and Lang which ran for 542 performances during the 1952 season.

LADY IN THE DARK 1/23/41, Alvin Theatre; 467 performances. Music & orchestrations, Kurt Weill; lyrics, Ira Gershwin; book, Moss Hart; producer, Sam H. Harris; directors, Hart & Hassard Short; musical director, Maurice Abravanel. ★ Gertrude Lawrence, Bert Lytell, Macdonald Carey, Victor Mature, Danny Kaye, Donald Randolph.
Tschaikowsky—**Danny Kaye** Columbia 36025, mx CO 29836; recorded 2/28/41.
Jenny—**Gertrude Lawrence** Conductor, Leonard Joy. Victor 27330, mx BS-060683-1; recorded 2/23/41.

Moss Hart was one of many 1930s show business cognoscenti to undergo

Gertrude Lawrence in *Lady in the Dark*.

psychoanalysis with the celebrated Freudian disciple Dr. Gregory Zillboorg. Hart eventually turned the experience into a play called *I Am Listening,* a sophisticated drama with occasional musical interludes, written expressly for actress Katherine Cornell. As the play began to evolve into a full-scale musical, however, Cornell dismissed any notion of singing onstage and abandoned the project. Shortly thereafter, Hart found himself on a bill with Gertrude Lawrence at a British War Relief benefit and was immediately convinced of her unique suitability as his star. He lined up Kurt Weill and Ira Gershwin for the score, then went in pursuit of the mercurial Miss Lawrence, who led him on a merry chase for nearly four months before agreeing to return to the American musical theater after a ten-year absence. In the supporting cast were soon-to-be Hollywood stars Victor Mature and Macdonald Carey and nightclub comedian Danny Kaye, making his first appearance in a Broadway book musical.

Although its treatment of psychiatry seems somewhat naive by today's standards, Hart's libretto remains an extraordinarily literate story about fashion magazine editor Liza Elliott's journey to self-knowledge with the help of an understanding Freudian analyst. Aside from the ballad "My Ship," which wafts in and out of the play as a leitmotif, all the musical numbers are contained in four stylized dream sequences deemed "little one-act operas" by Weill. In the original production these vignettes, chronicling manifestations of the heroine's troubled psyche, were depicted by designer Albert Johnson in bold, surrealistic hues and images that contrasted dramatically with the play's naturalistic scenes. In addition, Hart and co-director Hassard Short made extensive use of four revolving stages (twice as many as in *The Band Wagon* nine years earlier) to give a cinematic fluidity to the transitions between fantasy and reality.

The most pivotal sequence is the "Circus Dream," near the beginning of act 2: plagued by an inability to decide on the cover art for the Easter issue of her magazine, Liza imagines that her dilemma explodes into a gaudy *mise-en-scène* replete with a circus ring as a courtroom, acrobats as jurors, her suitors as performers cum attorneys, and her foppish staff photographer (Kaye) as a ringleader-judge. The scene contains two of the show's most memorable numbers. The first, Danny Kaye's tongue-twisting non sequitur "Tschaikowsky," was to catapult him to Broadway stardom. In rehearsals, his rapid-fire delivery of Ira Gershwin's rhythmic progression of the names of fifty-three Russian composers eclipsed the effect of the contemplative "Zodiac Song" assigned to Lawrence. Dismayed at the prospect of losing their star, Hart, Weill, and Gershwin devised "Jenny," a song about the sorrows that befell a woman "who would make up her mind." Lawrence turned the song into a personal triumph with uncharacteristic bumps and grinds that, according to one

observer, "out-Minskyed Minsky" in their good-natured ribaldry. Early in the run, a friendly competition developed between Lawrence and Kaye as each attempted to upstage the other during their back-to-back show-stopping numbers.

Kaye's 1941 recording of "Tschaikowsky" retains the Gilbert and Sullivan–inspired choral patter that opens the scene. It is paired in this collection for the first time with Lawrence's vivacious rendition of "Jenny" recorded the same year. The two recordings recreate important moments both in their stars' careers and in the evolution of the musical theater as a conscious art form.

Cassette Side D

THIS IS THE ARMY 7/4/42, Broadway Theatre; 113 performances. Music & lyrics, Irving Berlin; producer, Uncle Sam; directors, Ezra Stone & Joshua Logan; choreographers, Robert Sidney & Nelson Barclift; musical director, Milton Rosenstock. ★ 300 U.S. servicemen & Irving Berlin.

***Oh, How I Hate to Get Up in the Morning*—Irving Berlin with Supporting Cast and Soldier Chorus** Conductor, Milton Rosenstock. Decca 18777-A, mx 71228-A; recorded 7/28/42.

This Is the Army, Irving Berlin's contribution to the war effort, was a sequel of sorts to his World War I military revue, *Yip Yip Yaphank.* Both were written while Berlin was sequestered at Camp Upton, Long Island, both had casts composed entirely of inductees, and both featured Berlin singing the classic lament of military life, "Oh, How I Hate to Get Up in the Morning," dressed in the standard-issue puttees, jacket, and round-brimmed hat of 1918. His Decca recording of the song sparkles with the theatricality of an onstage performance, including the comic scene that introduces the piece.

For his cast, Berlin selected would-be singers, dancers, and comedians stationed at various military installations around the country. Among the notables to emerge from the company were Burl Ives, Gary Merrill, Jules (Julie) Oshins, and Ezra Stone (who also co-directed). The show played for twelve sold-out weeks on Broadway before embarking on a tour of theaters and military bases all over the world. Its final perform-

Irving Berlin in a vintage moment from *This Is the Army*.

ance was in Hawaii on 22 October 1945. Berlin donated the ten million dollars of ticket sales and song-sheet profits to the Army Emergency Relief, an unselfish gesture that brought him the Medal of Freedom, the highest civilian honor bestowed by the U.S. government.

Along with Berlin's cameo appearance, *This Is the Army* had a number of other memorable moments. Among the highlights was its opening, "a military minstrel show" with the entire company arranged on a proscenium-high bank of risers, performing "This Is the Army, Mister Jones," "I'm Getting Tired So I Can Sleep," and "I Left My Heart at the Stage Door Canteen." The show also included tributes to black soldiers in the jazzy "What the Well-dressed Man in Harlem Will Wear," the Army Air Corps in the ballad "With My Head in the Clouds," and sailors in the rousing act 1 finale, "How About a Cheer for the Navy?" The best of the (uncredited) sketches was a second act spoof of the famous Stage Door Canteen, in which the cast lampooned such stars as Jane Cowl, Lynne Fontanne, Alfred Lunt, and Charles Boyer.

ONE TOUCH OF VENUS 10/7/43, Imperial Theatre; 567 performances. Music & orchestrations, Kurt Weill; lyrics, Ogden Nash; book, S. J. Perelman & Ogden Nash; producers, Cheryl Crawford & John Wildberg; director, Elia Kazan; choreographer, Agnes de Mille; musical director, Maurice Abravanel. ★ Mary Martin, Kenny Baker, John Boles, Paula Laurence, Teddy Hart, Sono Osato, Allyn Ann McLerie.
Speak Low—**Mary Martin and Kenny Baker** Conductor, Maurice Abravanel. Decca 23296-A, mx 71493; recorded 11/7/43.

The juxtaposition of the ethereal and the mundane has been a recurring narrative device in the American musical theater since 1884, when matinee idol Henry E. Dixie cavorted in tights as the title character in *Adonis*. One of the most artful twentieth-century exemplars is *One Touch of Venus*, a sophisticated contemporary variation on the Pygmalion-Galatea myth. Its plot is derived from the obscure 1891 novella *The Tinted Venus* by British author F. Anstey, in which a meek little barber brings a marble statue to life by placing his fiancee's ring on its finger. In the autumn of 1941, costume designer Irene Sharaff suggested the story to Kurt Weill as possible musical comedy material. Weill was amused by the satiric humor inherent in the relationship between a noble, glamorous deity and the mortal nebbish upon whom she bestows her affections. Envisioning his adaptation as an "original kind of *opera comique* on the Offenbach line," he found an immediate ally in Cheryl Crawford, who agreed to produce the work. When his *Lady in the Dark* collaborator Ira Gershwin turned the project down, Weill had the inspired notion of hiring Ogden Nash, the celebrated writer of light verse, to pen his first set of musical comedy lyrics. Playwright Arthur Kober was Crawford's first choice as librettist; when he declined, the assignment went to Bella Spewack. Her script, entitled *One Man's Venus* (one of her rare efforts without her husband, Sam), depicted a cool, dignified goddess that Crawford and Weill agreed could only be played by Marlene Dietrich. The film star equivocated for months but eventually signed a contract to appear as Venus. Shortly thereafter, Crawford and Weill grew dissatisfied with the script and replaced Spewack with humorist S. J. Perelman, who

The goddess and the barber: Mary Martin and Kenny Baker, *One Touch of Venus*.

later recalled that he and Nash wrote the book "at the Harvard Club, interspersed with long lunches and martinis." Their revisions transformed the heroine into an earthier, more animated goddess whose uninhibited nature is at odds with the modern world's repressions. With everything set to proceed, Dietrich announced that the Perelman-Nash script was "too sexy and profane" and walked out on the project. Frantically, the creative team pursued Gertrude Lawrence, Leonora Corbett, and Vera Zorina before giving the role to Mary Martin, who had been absent from Broadway since 1938's *Leave It to Me!*.

Martin scored a great personal success as Venus, helped in no small way by a twenty-thousand-dollar wardrobe designed by *haute couturier* Mainbocher. Although Weill had planned the piece as a sort of modern-day comic opera in the nineteenth-century French tradition, it proved to be his most conventional, albeit lighthearted, work. The songs, which drew heavily on elements of current popular music, recalled the sophisticated rhythms of Cole Porter, particularly in the beguine "Speak Low,"

the show's hit song performed early in the second act by Venus and her reluctant lover, Rodney Hatch. The score also contains two of Weill's more ambitious orchestral compositions, the ballets "Forty Minutes for Lunch" and "Venus in Ozone Heights." The latter, which depicts Venus's unsuccessful attempts at urban domesticity and subsequent return to her celestial home, concluded the show in its world premiere in Philadelphia, but audiences were unsatisfied by the unresolved romance between the mortal and the goddess. Perelman and Nash supplied a happy ending by adding a new final scene in which the timid barber encounters a young woman who "might be Venus's country cousin."

OKLAHOMA! 3/31/43, St. James Theatre; 2,212 performances. Music, Richard Rodgers; lyrics & book, Oscar Hammerstein II; orchestrations, Robert Russell Bennett; producer, The Theatre Guild; director, Rouben Mamoulian; choreographer, Agnes de Mille; musical director, Jacob Schwartzdorf (Jay S. Blackton). ★ Alfred Drake, Joan Roberts, Betty Garde, Howard Da Silva, Joseph Buloff, Celeste Holm, Lee Dixon, Joan McCracken, Bambi Linn.
Oklahoma—**Alfred Drake and Company** Conductor, Jay S. Blackton. Decca 23283-B, mx 71474; recorded 10/20/43.

Easily the most influential musical of its generation, *Oklahoma!* fostered a new sensibility for operetta, ushering in a theatrical trend toward period Americana and a greater emphasis on dance as an integral narrative element. The now-legendary tales of its troubled journey to Broadway make its artistic and commercial triumphs seem all the more extraordinary.

The motive for the show's creation was more a financial than an artistic one. The Theatre Guild, a producing organization that had fallen on hard times, hoped to alleviate its impecunious state by sponsoring a musical version of Lynn Rigg's 1931 folk drama, *Green Grow the Lilacs*. Richard Rodgers and Lorenz Hart were first approached to do the score, but unbeknownst to the Guild, the team's twenty-five-year partnership was at an end because of the mercurial Hart's personal problems. Rodgers formed a new alliance with Oscar Hammerstein II, who, by coincidence, had tried unsuccessfully to interest his occasional partner Jerome Kern in the project.

The eloquent simplicity of *Green Grow the Lilacs* determined the style of its musical adaptation: no extraneous production numbers, no specialty acts, and no anachronistic costumes designed chiefly to display feminine pulchritude. Rodgers and Hammerstein's first dual effort for the show was its opening number, "Oh, What a Beautiful Morning." Set to one of Rodgers's characteristically lovely waltzes, the lyric was inspired by the act 1 stage directions in Riggs's original script, which described images of silent cattle and fields of tall corn bathed in a golden haze. Hammerstein's libretto makes much of a slender plot about cowboy Curly McLain's courtship of farmer's daughter Laurey Williams, set against the drama of Oklahoma's impending statehood. Their romance is threatened by Laurey's innocent flirtation with Jud Fry, her sinister farmhand. A subordinate narrative involving the triangular relationship of cowpoke Will Parker, farmer's daughter Ado Annie Carnes, and Persian peddler Ali Hakim restates the themes of the main plot in comic terms. Agnes de Mille, on the strength of her choreography for Aaron Copland's ballet *Rodeo,* was hired to create the dances. Her ballets for the show, particularly the act 1 finale "Laurey Makes Up Her Mind," were striking contributions to a work rich with innovation.

No musical had a tougher battle in raising funds to support its production. Rodgers and Hammerstein were reduced to what was known as "the cocktail party circuit"—giving private auditions of the show to potential backers. Although members of the Theatre Guild suggested casting Shirley Temple and Groucho Marx in an effort to increase box office potential, Rodgers and Hammerstein held out for performers who fit the parts. Of the original cast, Alfred Drake and Celeste Holm went on to stardom as a result of their performances. During the final days of backers' auditions, Theatre Guild member Theresa Helburn suggested to Hammerstein that the show needed "a song about the earth" that would build on the sentiment "all the sounds of the earth are like music" in "Oh,

Oklahoma!'s finale, featuring (from left) Marc Platt, George Church, Katherine Sergava, Lee Dixon, Celeste Holm, Alfred Drake, Joan Roberts, Joseph Buloff, Betty Garde, and other members of the original cast.

What a Beautiful Morning." Her idle observation resulted in the famous ensemble number that prompted a change of the show's title from *Away We Go!* to *Oklahoma!*.

In addition to its other innovations, *Oklahoma!* became the first full-scale Broadway production to preserve all its songs on records. Produced by Jack Kapp, the *Oklahoma!* album was the pioneer that established American original cast recordings as a commercially viable enterprise.

Record Side 6

CAROUSEL 4/19/45, Majestic Theatre; 890 performances. Music, Richard Rodgers; lyrics & book, Oscar Hammerstein II; orchestrations, Don Walker; producer, The Theatre Guild; director, Rouben Mamoulian; choreographer, Agnes de Mille; musical director, Joseph Littau. ★ John Raitt, Jan Clayton, Jean Darling, Eric Mattson, Christine Johnson, Murvyn Vye, Russell Collins, Bambi Linn.
Soliloquy—**John Raitt** Conductor, Joseph Littau. Decca DA 29175-A/B, mx 72883/4; recorded 5/21/45.

Shortly after *Oklahoma!* opened to tumultuous acclaim, Theatre Guild co-directors Theresa Helburn and Lawrence Langner approached Rodgers and Hammerstein with the idea that Hungarian playwright Ferenc Molnar's tragic fantasy *Liliom* might offer the basis for another unconventional musical play. At first the team refused: the somber tale of a ne'er-do-well and his faithful mistress seemed too dour for musicalization and the Hungarian setting impossible to work with. At the producers' insistence, however, they agreed to reconsider. Helburn suggested moving the story to Louisiana so as to keep a European flavor in an American setting, but it was not until Richard Rodgers made a counter-suggestion, late nineteenth-century New England, that the project began to take on a life of its own. The resulting musical is perhaps the most intriguing and ambitious of the Rodgers and Hammerstein collaborations.

Hammerstein's transformation of *Liliom* into *Carousel* is artful and ingenious. Molnar's original becomes the story of demure but strong-willed Julie Jordan and her enduring, selfless love for roughhewn carnival barker Billy Bigelow. When he learns he is to become a father, Billy tries to raise money by robbing the town's wealthy mill owner, Mr. Bascombe, but is thwarted in his attempt and commits suicide. After arriving in heaven, where one minute is equal to fifteen years on earth, Billy is given a chance to help his coltish, now-teenage daughter by returning to earth for one day in the company of "The Starkeeper" (a replacement for Hammerstein's earlier notion of characters named Mr. and Mrs. God). In *Liliom* the anti-hero's efforts prove futile, but Hammerstein injected hope into the melancholy narrative: in Billy's reappearance on earth he convinces Julie of his eternal love for her and their child.

Rodgers always ranked the score of *Carousel* as his favorite among his own works; indeed, it is the finest achievement of his long career in writing for the musical theater. The first half-hour of the show is told almost entirely through music, including the haunting "Carousel Waltz," which accompanied Agnes de Mille's superb ballet-pantomime depicting Billy's and Julie's first meeting, and the "Park Bench Scene" containing the show's principal ballad, "If I Loved You." Billy Bigelow's "Soliloquy," the first piece the authors composed for the score, is one of the most remarkable accomplishments in their canon. In a seven-minute sequence of operatic proportions, the character contemplates his impending fatherhood and considers the pros and cons of having a son or a daughter. John Raitt's performance of the song-aria in the original production helped propel him to stardom.

BLOOMER GIRL 10/5/44, Shubert Theatre; 654 performances. Music, Harold Arlen; lyrics, E. Y. Harburg; book, Sig Herzig & Fred Saidy; orchestrations, Robert Russell Bennett; producers, John C. Wilson & Nat Goldstone; directors, Harburg & William Schorr; choreographer, Agnes de Mille; musical director, Leon Leonardi. ★ Celeste Holm, David Brooks, Dooley Wilson, Joan McCracken, Mabel Taliaferro, Richard Huey, Matt Briggs, Margaret Douglass, Blaine Cordner.
The Eagle and Me—**Dooley Wilson and Chorus** Conductor, Leon Leonardi. Decca DA 23337-A, mx 72547; recorded 10/44.

A costume sketch by designer Miles White adorns the *Bloomer Girl* song sheet.

Rodgers and Hammerstein's popularization of stylized Americana in *Oklahoma!* immediately inspired a number of similar shows. The first was *Bloomer Girl,* which combined historical nostalgia with the flag-waving patriotism of the wartime musical. Its creation began when theatrical agent Nat Goldstone received a review copy of an unproduced comedy by Lilith and Dan James set during the Civil War and dealing with such still-timely issues as feminism and racial equality. Goldstone convinced his client Harold Arlen that the script would provide the perfect vehicle for the composer's return to the musical theater after a long tenure as a Hollywood songwriter. Arlen called for the services of his friend and frequent collaborator E. Y. Harburg, who found the original script funny but facile and insisted that screenwriters Sig Herzig and Fred Saidy be brought in to rework the play and develop

its inherent concern for "the indivisibility of human freedom."

While Arlen, Harburg, Herzig, and Saidy honed the libretto and songs at their various residences in Beverly Hills, Goldstone, in New York, secured the services of the esteemed John C. Wilson as co-producer. Wisely, Wilson touted the show to potential backers as another *Oklahoma!,* an idea strengthened by his reassembly of several members of that show's artistic team, including actresses Celeste Holm and Joan McCracken, orchestrator Robert Russell Bennett, scenic designer Lemuel Ayers, costumer Miles White, and choreographer Agnes de Mille.

De Mille brought about the only major crisis that confronted the show during its development. Her impassioned "Civil War Ballet," a depiction of war's effect on women, had the creative team divided: Harburg and Wilson loathed it, insisting that it injected a jarring tone of tragedy into an otherwise light-hearted view of America's past, while Arlen shared de Mille's belief that the ballet brought a sense of contemporary relevance to the work. Arlen was overjoyed when the dance stopped the show during the world premiere in Philadelphia. *Bloomer Girl* received a largely favorable response in New York and was a popular attraction with wartime audiences for over two seasons. During the second year of its run, Nanette Fabray succeeded Celeste Holm as the lead.

The libretto contrasts the heroine's rebellion against the double standards of nineteenth-century America with the plight of southern blacks and their bondage in slavery. Herzig and Saidy's book occasionally missed its ideological mark, but the Arlen and Harburg songs promoted the musical's intended message, most notably in the simple, eloquent "The Eagle and Me," sung by Dooley Wilson as Pompey, an escaped slave. Set to a jaunty melody, Harburg's lyric celebrates his own philosophical views on the principles of human freedom, man's eternal dream "since the world was an onion."

ST. LOUIS WOMAN 3/30/46, Martin Beck
Theatre; 113 performances. Music, Harold Arlen;
lyrics, Johnny Mercer; book, Arna Bontemps &
Countee Cullen; producer, Edward Gross; direc-
tor, Rouben Mamoulian; choreographer, Charles
Walters; musical director, Leon Leonardi.
★ Harold and Fayard Nicholas, Ruby Hill, Rex
Ingram, June Hawkins, Pearl Bailey, Robert
Pope.
Come Rain or Come Shine—**Ruby Hill
and Harold Nicholas** Conductor, Leon Leon-
ardi. Capitol 10055, mx A-4738; recorded ca.
4/46.

In 1935 *Porgy and Bess* had introduced
Broadway audiences to a more serious
musical theater about, and performed by,
blacks. *St. Louis Woman,* in both theme
and tone, may be regarded as its immediate
successor. Like the earlier work, its plot
was derived from a novel; in this instance,
Arna Bontemps's *God Sends Sunday,* a
moralistic fable of gamblers, jockeys, and
sporting ladies in turn-of-the-century
Missouri. With a masterful pseudo-jazz and
blues score by Harold Arlen and Johnny
Mercer added to Bontemps' and poet
Countee Cullen's dramatization of the
narrative, producer Edward Gross planned
the endeavor as a unique variation on the
vogue for period Americana so prevalent
since *Oklahoma!*.

Ruby Hill and Harold Nicholas

MGM Pictures was the show's chief
investor. The studio brass, particularly
producer Arthur Freed, hoped that MGM
contractee Lena Horne would consent to
appear as the wayward heroine, Della
Green. When Horne rejected the part, it
went to Ruby Hill, a young West Coast
singer and actress recommended by veteran
Broadway vocal coach Al Seigel (who was
instrumental in Ethel Merman's early
career). Also prominent in the cast were
dancer Harold Nicholas as the horse-riding
hero, Li'l Augie; Harold's brother, Fayard,
as fellow jockey Barney; Rex Ingram as the
villain, Biglow Brown; and Pearl Bailey in
her musical theater debut as the comic
Butterfly.

Trouble plagued the show almost from
the start. Co-librettist Cullen died shortly
before rehearsals began. Bontemps, a fine
novelist but an inexperienced playwright,
proved unable to harmonize the tonal
inconsistencies of the script, which resulted
in a comic first act, a tragic second act, and

a third act of pure melodrama with an
abrupt happy ending. Out of town, MGM
dance director Charles Walters replaced
choreographer Antony Tudor, and Rouben
Mamoulian succeeded director Lemuel
Ayers, who also designed the lavish scenic
decor. Mixed reviews greeted the Broadway
opening, and insufficient financing killed the
possibility of building an audience on the
strength of the show's considerable merits.
In 1959 Arlen revised the work as a "blues
opera" called *Free and Easy,* which toured
Europe to acclaim but was closed
prematurely by its feuding producers before
coming to Broadway.

St. Louis Woman was the first of the
great American cult musicals. It has kept its
legendary status beyond its brief Broadway
run primarily through its original cast
album, recorded and distributed by Johnny
Mercer's company, Capitol Records.
Divorced from its ambitious but flawed
libretto, the score is one of the masterworks
of the musical stage. Arlen and Mercer
composed its most enduring number,
"Come Rain or Come Shine," during one

evening in October 1945. The song occurs in the otherwise tragic second act and functions as Li'l Augie's and Della's pledge of mutual devotion, a situation that comes as a happy surprise to both. Although justly famous as a standard for jazz and pop singers, the song takes on an appealing freshness when heard in its original context as a duet.

ON THE TOWN 12/28/44, Adelphi Theatre; 463 performances. Music, Leonard Bernstein; lyrics & book, Betty Comden & Adolph Green; orchestrations, Bernstein, Hershy Kay, Don Walker & Ted Royal; producers, Oliver Smith & Paul Feigay; director, George Abbott; choreographer, Jerome Robbins; musical director, Max Goberman. ★ Sono Osato, Nancy Walker, Betty Comden, Adolph Green, John Battles, Cris Alexander, Alice Pearce.
New York, New York—**Adolph Green, Cris Alexander, and John Reardon** Conductor, Leonard Bernstein. Columbia OL-5540, mx XLP 50597; recorded 5/31/60.

When the Leonard Bernstein–Jerome Robbins ballet *Fancy Free* premiered on April 18, 1944, it was hailed as a breakthrough in American dance. Among those captivated by its striking choreography and jazz-oriented score were set designer Oliver Smith and his associate Paul Feigay, who offered the creators a chance to convert the work into a musical comedy. For their lyricists-librettists, Bernstein and Robbins turned to their friends Betty Comden and Adolph Green, who also wrote featured parts for themselves in the show. In their

first Broadway libretto, Comden and Green used the basic premise of Robbins's ballet scenario about three sailors on twenty-four hours' shore leave. To this they added three female principals as the sailors' opposites, and a raft of eccentric but lovable supporting characters which constituted the first of their many portraits of Manhattan as essentially a small town with a big heart. Not one note of the *Fancy Free* score was used; instead, Bernstein composed a new collection of ballads, ballets, and ensemble numbers to convey the rhythms of wartime Manhattan. Similarly, Robbins created a series of dances that enriched the breezy narrative and acted as contemporary urban counterparts to Agnes de Mille's pseudo-folk dances for *Oklahoma!*.

Veteran director George Abbott was signed to guide the team of Broadway neophytes. On the strength of his reputation in the theater, MGM Studios backed the production in exchange for the film rights. Abbott assembled a cast of promising young talent including, besides Comden and Green, dancer Sono Osato, who had been principal danseuse of *One Touch of Venus,* and comediennes Nancy Walker and Alice Pearce. John Battles took over the romantic lead shortly before rehearsals began, when original choice Kirk Douglas proved unable to sing the role's demanding songs.

The most astute account of the musical's merits was offered by critic Louis Kronenberger: "It has its faults, to be sure, but even they are engaging, for they are

Cris Alexander, Adolph Green, and John Battles salute the wonders of New York in *On the Town.*

faults of people trying to do something different, of people trying to take a chance." Its extensive use of dance as an integral part of the plot and its satirical but basically sentimental story, songs, and characters make *On the Town* a major innovational work of its era. It contains one of the musical theater's most effective opening scenes. Set in the Brooklyn Navy Yard at dawn, the sleepy lament of a dockworker is interrupted by the three sailors who celebrate the beginning of their twenty-four-hour passes by naively extolling the splendors of the big city in the syncopated anthem "New York, New York." Although no cast album was produced during the run of the first Broadway production, *On the Town*'s score was committed to disc in 1960 as part of Goddard Lieberson's musical theater series for Columbia. Featured on the recording are original cast members Nancy Walker, Cris Alexander, and Comden and Green. Former Metropolitan Opera baritone John Reardon, soon to appear in the Comden and Green musical *Do Re Mi,* sings the role originally assigned to John Battles.

ANNIE GET YOUR GUN 5/16/46, Imperial Theatre; 1,147 performances. Music & lyrics, Irving Berlin; book, Herbert & Dorothy Fields; orchestrations, Philip J. Lang, Robert Russell Bennett & Ted Royal; producers, Richard Rodgers & Oscar Hammerstein II; director, Joshua Logan; choreographer, Helen Tamiris; musical director, Lew Stone. ★ Ethel Merman, Ray Middleton, Marty May, Kenny Bowers, Betty Anne Nyman, William O'Neal, Lea Penman.
***There's No Business Like Show Business*—Ethel Merman, Bruce Yarnell, Jerry Orbach, and Rufus Smith** Conductor, Franz Allers. RCA Victor LOC-1124, mx TPRM-4254; recorded 6/5/66.

Had fate taken a different turn, Irving Berlin's *Annie Get Your Gun* might have been Jerome Kern's *Annie Oakley*. Rodgers and Hammerstein, in their only joint effort at producing a musical written by other authors, planned the score as a reunion between Kern and his frequent Hollywood songwriting partner, Dorothy Fields, who had originally conceived the notion of starring Ethel Merman as America's beloved "Little Sure Shot." Fields was also slated to collaborate with her brother, Herbert, on the libretto. Kern's sudden

Ethel Merman as Annie Oakley, in an oil painting by Rosemarie Sloat.

death of a cerebral hemorrhage in November 1945 left the show temporarily without a composer. When Irving Berlin consented to write the whole score, Fields agreed to step down as lyricist and devote all her energies to the script.

Although at first unsure that his Tin Pan Alley style of songwriting was right for the show, Berlin quickly found inspiration in the Fieldses' libretto. With their blessing, he transformed portions of their dialogue into songs that delineated character and propelled the action of the story. He celebrated the heroine's lackadaisical but appealing philosophy of life in "Doin' What Comes Natur'lly and "I Got the Sun in the Morning," traced her romantic awkwardness in "You Can't Get a Man with a Gun," and portrayed her first brush with love in "They Say It's Wonderful." Stalwart hero Frank Butler was given dimension in "I'm a Bad, Bad Man," a mock-operetta gambol with the ladies of the chorus, and in the solo "The Girl That I Marry." The good-natured rivalry between Annie and Frank became the competition duet "Anything You Can Do (I Can Do Better)." Ironically, Berlin very nearly dropped "There's No Business Like Show Business" from the score because he mistakenly thought Rodgers and Hammerstein disliked it. The number acts as Annie's initiation into the entertainment world by Wild West Show members Buffalo Bill, Frank Butler, and Charley Davenport. When Decca recorded its cast album in 1946, the song was included only as part of the finale medley sung by the chorus. Twenty years later RCA Victor corrected the omission by including the song as it was originally staged, as part of its cast recording of Richard Rodgers's Music Theatre of Lincoln Center production. Back in the role written for her was Ethel Merman, in glorious voice and surrounded by a fine supporting cast.

In addition to its importance in Merman's career, the role of Annie has acted as a springboard for a number of musical comedy actresses, including Mary Martin in the first national touring company, Dolores Gray in the 1947 London production (which ran longer than the Broadway original), and Debbie Reynolds in a spectacular 1977 West Coast production supervised by Gower Champion.

FINIAN'S RAINBOW 1/10/47, 46th Street Theatre; 725 performances. Music, Burton Lane; lyrics, E. Y. Harburg; book, Harburg & Fred Saidy; orchestrations, Robert Russell Bennett & Don Walker; producers, Lee Sabinson & William Katzell; director, Bretaigne Windust; choreographer, Michael Kidd; musical director, Milton Rosenstock. ★ Ella Logan, Albert Sharpe, Donald Richards, David Wayne, Anita Alvarez, Robert Pitkin.
How Are Things in Glocca Morra?—**Ella Logan** Conductor, Milton Rosenstock. Columbia MM-686, mx CO 37552; recorded 4/3/47.

Satire and fantasy are delightfully blended in *Finian's Rainbow,* E. Y. Harburg's

masterwork for the musical theater. His wise and witty script, written with his *Bloomer Girl* collaborator Fred Saidy, was a combination of ideas he had conceived for two separate non-musical dramas to address issues of racial inequality and the American economic system. Its story concerns Finian, an eccentric old Irishman who has stolen a crock of gold from Og, a feisty leprechaun. Finian arrives with his daughter, Sharon, in Rainbow Valley, Missitucky, to bury the gold, believing that the reason Americans plant their gold in the ground at Fort Knox is that American soil causes it to grow like any other crop. His idea brings optimism to Rainbow Valley's oppressed black and white sharecroppers, including a romantic, free-thinking populist, Woody Mahoney, with whom Sharon falls in love. Complications appear in the guise of Senator Billboard Rawkins, a southern bigot who tries to trick Finian and his friends out of their potential wealth. Three wishes, made over Og's buried pot of gold, turn the racist

Ex-Glocca Morrans Sharon (Ella Logan) and Finian (Albert Sharpe) arrive in Missitucky, U.S.A.

Senator black, turn him white again, and restore the power of speech to Woody's mute sister, Susan. The wishes deplete the gold of its magic, but leave the populace a happier, if poorer, community.

Harburg had planned for Burton Lane to collaborate on the score with Earl Robinson, an ardent exponent of politically oriented Broadway theater and co-author (with John Latouche) of the famous "Ballad for Americans." Lane felt uneasy about the differences in their compositional styles and eventually persuaded Harburg to let him write the music alone. Together, Lane and Harburg produced some of the loveliest and most intelligent songs ever composed for the theater. The show's hit was the wistful, nostalgic "How Are Things in Glocca Morra?", which star Ella Logan, as Sharon, sang in her appealing (though some thought inappropriate) Scottish burr. The narrative elements of socio-economic satire were given voice in "Necessity," an ironic blues lament for black sharecroppers, and the production number "When the Idle Poor Become the Idle Rich," a humorous piece enhanced immeasurably by Michael Kidd's antic choreography. The requisite romantic numbers were given refreshingly unconventional treatment in "If This Isn't Love" and "Old Devil Moon." Harburg's characteristic gift for whimsicality reached its peak in Og's "Something Sort of Grandish," which rhymed "outlandish" with "hand-in-handish" and "sugar candish."

Finian's Rainbow grew out of the same social fervor begun in the thirties by *The Cradle Will Rock* and *Pins and Needles* and sparked a trend for fantasy in the musical theater that continued in a number of later works, most notably the gentler *Brigadoon,* which premiered during the same season.

Record Side 7
Compact Disc III

BRIGADOON 3/13/47, Ziegfeld Theatre; 581 performances. Music, Frederick Loewe; lyrics & book, Alan Jay Lerner; orchestrations, Ted Royal; producer, Cheryl Crawford; director, Robert Lewis; choreographer, Agnes de Mille; musical director, Franz Allers. ★ David Brooks, Marion Bell, Pamela Britton, Lee Sullivan, George Keane, James Mitchell.
***Almost Like Being in Love*—David Brooks and Marion Bell** Conductor, Franz Allers. RCA Victor 52-0069-B, mx D7-VB-683; recorded 3/23/47.

Brigadoon might well have wafted from the pen of the Scottish master of whimsy, James M. Barrie, had he been writing for the American musical theater in the 1940s. Alan Jay Lerner, an avowed admirer of Barrie's plays, credited his inspiration for the script to an offhand remark made by his collaborator Frederick Loewe about faith moving mountains. Lerner converted the idle observation into a tale of faith transporting an entire eighteenth-century village, Brigadoon, which protects itself from the evils of the world by emerging from the highland mist for only one day in every century. Intentionally or not, Lerner's libretto resembles the German story *Germelshausen* by Wilhelm Friederich Gerstacker, a debt first recognized by critic George Jean Nathan.

Showman Billy Rose was the first to option the musical for production, but he eventually relinquished the property to Cheryl Crawford, producer of *One Touch of Venus* four seasons earlier. The biggest stars associated with the show were those on its production team. Oliver Smith's evocative sets, with their shaded hills, glens, thatched cottages, and cathedral ruins, complemented the vibrant and dramatic ballets of Agnes de Mille, by then the dean of Broadway choreographers. The cast was made up of comparative newcomers. David Brooks, fresh from a long run as the southern hero of *Bloomer Girl,* assumed the leading role of Tommy Albright, a jaded twentieth-century New Yorker who happens upon the enchanted Scottish village and falls in love with one of its citizens. Soprano Marion Bell (later to be, briefly, Mrs. Alan Jay Lerner) left the

David Brooks and Marian Bell in *Brigadoon.*

West Coast world of operetta and film to make her only appearance in a Broadway musical, as Tommy's beloved. For the traditional comic subplot, Hollywood's Pamela Britton scored in the role of Meg Brockie, a man-hungry street vendor (who bore more than a passing resemblance to *Oklahoma!*'s Ado Annie), and George Keane won good notices as Jeff Douglas, a sardonic American who is nonplussed by the ethereal quaintness of the hamlet. *Brigadoon* was the first of Lerner and Loewe's three great Broadway hits (the others being *My Fair Lady* and *Camelot*). The score is a graceful fusion of Scottish folk rhythms and sophisticated Broadway sounds, from the atmospheric production number "Down on MacConnachy Square" to the romantic leads' hit ballad "Almost Like Being in Love," which recalls Rodgers and Hammerstein's "If I Loved You" from *Carousel* in its indirect expression of affection. Thirteen of *Brigadoon*'s numbers

are preserved in the original cast recording, the first of its kind to be issued by RCA Victor.

Cassette Side E

STREET SCENE 1/9/47, Adelphi Theatre; 148 performances. Music & orchestrations, Kurt Weill; book, Elmer Rice; lyrics, Rice & Langston Hughes; producers, The Playwrights Company & Dwight Deere Wiman; director, Charles Friedman; choreographer, Anna Sokolow; musical director, Maurice Abravanel. ★ Polyna Stoska, Anne Jefferys, Brian Sullivan, Norman Cordon, Hope Emerson, Sheila Bond, Danny Daniels. *Lonely House*—**Brian Sullivan** Conductor, Maurice Abravanel. Columbia 72041-D, mx XCO 37408; recorded 2/23/47.

An adaptation of Elmer Rice's 1929 Pulitzer Prize-winning play, *Street Scene,* gave Kurt Weill the chance to fulfill a long-harbored dream: the creation of "a special brand of musical theater which would completely integrate drama and music, spoken word and movement." Called "a dramatic musical" by its authors, the work is an opera in the Broadway idiom, a link between the traditions established by *Porgy and Bess* and the innovations of *West Side Story.* Weill's combination of spoken passages and extended musical scenes owes a stylistic debt to the *Singspiel,* a form of musical theater indigenous to his native Germany.

Like its source, the opera is a tragic slice of life about twenty-four hours in the lives of Manhattan tenement dwellers. Central to the plot are the characters Rose Maurrant and Sam Kaplan, two star-crossed dreamers oppressed by their environment who find fleeting happiness in each other's company. Rose's mother, Anna, also seeks escape from her dismal surroundings in a love affair with a neighbor but meets her death at the hands of her jealous husband. The secondary characters are a colorful sampling of urban types, ranging in tone from a comic Italian violin teacher to a pathetic German-American family threatened with dispossession. The stark, unsentimental narrative unfolds before the single setting of a street of faded brownstones, as atmospheric a locale as *Porgy and Bess*'s Catfish Row.

Weill's score combines operatic arias,

Ray Bolger cavorts as the hero of *Where's Charley?*

ensembles, and recitatives with musical play set pieces à la Rodgers and Hammerstein, pseudo-blues, and even a wild jitterbug called "Moon-faced, Starry-eyed." "Lonely House," the lament of the young Jewish protagonist Sam Kaplan, is both poignant and powerful. The melody, half Broadway ballad, half operatic soliloquy, reflects the score's vivid eclecticism. Langston Hughes's sensitive lyric conveys the isolation of the big city and underscores the tragic nature of the story.

Critically acclaimed for its experimentation with both serious and commercial music theater forms, *Street Scene* was a financial failure in its brief Broadway run. Unlike *Carousel* and other comparable works with tragic elements, it offered little hope or optimism in its sociological treatment of the urban economically oppressed. Its achievements live on in productions by major opera companies and in its sterling 1947 original cast recording.

WHERE'S CHARLEY? 10/11/48, St. James Theatre; 792 performances. Music & lyrics, Frank Loesser; book, George Abbott; orchestrations, Ted Royal, Hans Spialek, & Philip J. Lang; producers, Cy Feuer & Ernest Martin, in association with Gwen Rickard (Bolger); director, Abbott; choreographer, George Balanchine; musical director, Max Goberman. ★ Ray Bolger, Allyn Ann McLerie, Byron Palmer, Doretta Morrow, Paul England.
Once in Love with Amy—**Ray Bolger**
Decca DU-40065, mx 74761; recorded 2/15/49.

This musical version of *Charley's Aunt,* Brandon Thomas's classic Edwardian farce, reconfirmed Ray Bolger's status as one of the musical theater's most versatile stars and gave him the best role of his career. As Charley Wykeham, a turn-of-the-century Oxford student who is forced by circumstance to impersonate his aunt from Brazil ("where the nuts come from"), he made the most of his opportunities to sing, dance, and clown in both school blazers and the get-up of a manic Whistler's Mother.

Aside from seasoned veterans like Bolger, director-librettist George Abbott, and choreographer George Balanchine, *Where's Charley?* introduced an array of new talent, including cast members Allyn Ann McLerie and Doretta Morrow and novice producers Cy Feuer and Ernest Martin, all of whom would make their mark on the Broadway theater. The most auspicious debut was scored by thirty-eight-year-old Frank Loesser essaying his first set of songs for a book musical. His score is full of promising surprises: a witty, tongue-in-cheek tribute to "The New Ashmolean Marching Society and Students' Conservatory Band"; the love song "My Darling, My Darling," which made the Hit Parade; and the refreshingly theatrical "Make a Miracle," a contrapuntal duet for the hero and his sweetheart in which they ponder the wonders to come in the twentieth century. The show's most famous number is the bumptious "Once in Love with Amy," Bolger's soft-shoe show-stopper which occurred early in the second act. Nightly, Bolger would invite the entire audience to join in with him on the refrain, creating an ambiance akin to that of a revival meeting. On Bolger's vintage recording of the number, done late in the show's Broadway run, the audience is simulated by using members of the chorus. An ASCAP strike in effect at the time of the Broadway opening was instrumental in preventing a complete original cast album.

Where's Charley? is so strongly associated with Ray Bolger that it has seldom been attempted by other performers, in spite of its many virtues. In 1958 British comedian Norman Wisdom triumphed in the first West End production, and in 1974 Raul Julia appeared in a scaled-down off-Broadway revival.

KISS ME, KATE 12/30/48, New Century Theatre; 1,077 performances. Music & lyrics, Cole Porter; book, Bella & Sam Spewack; orchestrations, Robert Russell Bennett; producers, Arnold Saint Subber & Lemuel Ayers; director, John C. Wilson; choreographer, Hanya Holm; musical director, Pembroke Davenport. ★ Alfred Drake, Patricia Morison, Lisa Kirk, Harold Lang, Harry Clark, Jack Diamond, Annabelle Hill, Lorenzo Fuller.

Where Is the Life That Late I Led?— **Alfred Drake** Conductor, Pembroke Davenport. Columbia 55045, mx XCO 40361; recorded 1/14/49.

None of the Broadway crowd predicted much of a future for *Kiss Me, Kate* when it was first announced. Its producers were neophytes, its composer was considered passé, and its stars were not of sufficient magnitude to ensure success at the box office. That the show went on to establish itself as a masterpiece is a testament to the unswerving faith of its creators.

The idea for a musical version of *The Taming of the Shrew* originated in 1935 with Arnold Saint Subber. While working as a stagehand in a Theatre Guild revival of Shakespeare's comedy, he was amused and intrigued by the similarities between the offstage behavior of stars Alfred Lunt and Lynn Fontanne and their brawling onstage roles. Twelve years later, Saint Subber found a willing production partner in set designer Lemuel Ayers, and together they persuaded Bella and Sam Spewack to convert the idea into a full-length script. The Spewacks contrived a witty story about a troupe of actors involved in a Baltimore tryout of a musical *Shrew*. At the center of the story is egomaniacal producer-director-actor Fred Graham (a caricature of Orson Welles) and his equally volatile star and ex-wife, Lilli Vanessi. In spite of flirtations elsewhere, they are reunited, much the same as are their onstage counterparts Petruchio and Katherina, at the conclusion. A secondary plot deals with Graham's dalliance with Lois Lane, a former night club chorine who is really in love with Bill Calhoun, a fellow thespian whose gambling debts involve him with a pair of comic gangsters. The original cast was headed by Alfred Drake and former MGM contractee Patricia Morison, who became a star in a role that had been turned down by everyone from Mary Martin to Lily Pons.

Despite the brilliance of the Spewacks' script, the show's real triumph is Cole Porter's score, an endlessly inventive mating of the Bard and Broadway. His skill at turning out hit tunes is evident in the ballads "Why Can't You Behave?" and "So in Love," but he achieved a new maturity in plot-oriented material that seemed to grow organically out of the dramatic scenes and characters. In the boisterous soliloquy "Where Is the Life That Late I Led?," its title a direct quote

Alfred Drake as Fred Graham as Petruchio.

from Shakespeare's text, he conveys the braggadocio and swagger of Petruchio with the skill of a seasoned dramatist. Performed on the cast recording with great zest and style by Alfred Drake, for whom Porter and the Spewacks designed the role, the piece stands as one of the musical theater's great solo numbers, with its mock–Italian opera flourishes and clever lyric.

GENTLEMEN PREFER BLONDES 12/8/49, Ziegfeld Theatre; 740 performances. Music, Jule Styne; lyrics, Leo Robin; book, Anita Loos & Joseph Fields; orchestrations, Don Walker; producers, Herman Levin & Oliver Smith; director, John C. Wilson; choreographer, Agnes de Mille; musical director, Milton Rosenstock. ★ Carol Channing, Yvonne Adair, Jack MacCauley, Eric Brotherson, Alice Pearce, Rex Evans, George S. Irving, Reta Shaw.

Diamonds Are a Girl's Best Friend— **Carol Channing** Conductor, Milton Rosenstock. Columbia ML 4290, mx XLP 2076; recorded 12/19/49.

The 1949 musical version of *Gentlemen Prefer Blondes* represents the triumph of three legendary ladies: diminutive author Anita Loos; her foxy-dumb heroine, Lorelei Lee; and Lorelei's most famous impersonator, the incomparable Carol Channing.

Loos's celebrated satire of the quintessential jazz age demimondaine first appeared in the 1925 issues of *Harper's Bazaar*. A year later Florenz Ziegfeld asked the author to transform it into a musical comedy, but she had already signed an agreement with producer Edgar Selwyn for its adaptation as a straight play, which became the hit of the 1926 season. In 1948 the idea of a musical conversion resurfaced at the instigation of co-producers Oliver Smith and Herman Levin and director John C. Wilson. Their combined efforts persuaded Loos to supervise an adaptation by the usually reliable Joseph Fields. Fields's treatment of her story, which interpolated a gangster plot and changed the leading character's name to Mabel, did not suit Loos, and she insisted on writing much of the libretto herself. Her script, faithful to its previous incarnations, returned the focus to the Parisian exploits of blonde gold digger Lorelei Lee and her pragmatic friend, brunette Dorothy Shaw. On the recommendation of Mike Todd, Loos approved the hiring of Jule Styne and Leo Robin as composer and lyricist.

The creative team hoped to find a full-fledged star to play Lorelei. Dolores Gray and Gertrude Neisen were among those considered, and the part was eventually offered to Nanette Fabray, who turned it down to appear in the 1948 Lerner-Weill musical, *Love Life*. At a performance of Charles Gaynor's revue *Lend an Ear*, Jule

Styne was impressed by a tall blonde who appeared as an addle-brained flapper in the sketch "The Gladiola Girl." Anita Loos accompanied him on a subsequent visit to the show and agreed that they had found their Lorelei in newcomer Carol Channing. In a triumph of casting against type, Channing revealed a prodigious gift for satire, suggesting not so much a coyly manipulative kept woman as an Amazon in ingenue's clothing. She was greatly abetted by the Styne-Robin score, which gave her the tongue-in-cheek "A Little Girl from Little Rock" and her signature piece, "Diamonds Are a Girl's Best Friend," with its title paraphrased from Lorelei's observation in the novel, "Kissing your hand may make you feel very good, but a diamond and safire [sic] bracelet lasts forever."

Channing returned to the role in 1973 in a revised version of the show called *Lorelei*

Carol Channing as Lorelei Lee.

and bearing the subtitle "Gentlemen Still Prefer Blondes." Although her hybrid vehicle was inferior in nearly every way to the original, it offered new audiences, on Broadway and on tour, an opportunity to witness a classic performance by one of the theater's great comediennes.

SOUTH PACIFIC 4/7/49, Majestic Theatre; 1,925 performances. Music, Richard Rodgers; lyrics, Oscar Hammerstein II; book, Hammerstein & Joshua Logan; orchestrations, Robert Russell Bennett; producers, Rodgers, Hammerstein, Logan, Leland Hayward; director, Logan; musical director, Salvatore Dell'Isola. ★ Mary Martin, Ezio Pinza, William Tabbert, Juanita Hall, Myron McCormick, Betta St. John.
A Wonderful Guy—**Mary Martin**
Some Enchanted Evening—**Ezio Pinza**
Conductor, Salvatore Dell'Isola; Columbia ML 4180, mx XLP 1116; recorded 4/18 & 19/49.

The Rodgers-Hammerstein-Logan adaptation of James Michener's *Tales of the South Pacific* resulted in one of the most colossally successful musicals ever created. Its advance ticket sales totalled a Broadway record of over $400,000, and after the premiere, the struggle to get seats became a hot topic at cocktail parties. The show reaped virtually all the major theatrical awards for the season: eight Tonys, nine Donaldsons, the Drama Critics' Circle Award, and the Pulitzer. It also yielded the earliest LP original cast album to become a million seller.

Joshua Logan was the first to see the musical theater possibilities in Michener's collection of stories about life in the Pacific during World War II. He was especially taken with "Fo' Dolla'," a melancholy tale about a doomed romance between young Marine lieutenant Joe Cable and Liat, an ethereally beautiful Tonkinese girl. Logan immediately approached his agent, Leland Hayward, about securing the stage rights to the work and began trying to interest Rodgers and Hammerstein in the property. Eventually, all four agreed to act as producers.

Although Hammerstein was intrigued by the exoticism of "Fo' Dolla'," he felt that its downbeat fragility and all-too-apparent similarity to Puccini's *Madama Butterfly* necessitated relegating it to the subsidiary position and selecting another of Michener's

Nellie Forbush (Mary Martin) and her fellow nurses celebrate "the world-famous feeling."

stories as the main plot. This he found in "Our Heroine," about an adult romance between Army nurse Nellie Forbush and Emile de Becque, a rich, middle-aged French planter with a shadowy past. To link the two plots, he borrowed the comic character of wheeler-dealer Luther Billis from "The Boar's Tooth," another tale in the collection.

Before the script and score were completed, Rodgers and Hammerstein began casting. Juanita Hall, a veteran performer who had appeared in the original company of *Show Boat*, was picked for the role of the wily Tonkinese peddler Bloody Mary, while dancer Betta St. John, an alumna of the Broadway company of *Carousel*, stepped out of the chorus line to portray the delicate Liat. For Lt. Cable the authors hoped to hire their Curly from the London cast of *Oklahoma!*, but when Howard Keel elected instead to star in the MGM film version of *Annie Get Your Gun*, they chose newcomer William Tabbert. Logan's old

Princeton roommate Myron McCormick played the resourceful Billis. For the first time in their collaboration, Rodgers and Hammerstein decided to fill the leading roles with bona fide stars instead of such talented young hopefuls as had headlined *Oklahoma!* and *Carousel*. Ezio Pinza, in search of the right property for his Broadway debut, was the first cast member to be signed. Mary Martin, whose unaffected exuberance and southern charm made her a natural for Nellie Forbush, accepted the part after Rodgers assured her she would not be given duets that would place her musical comedy voice in competition with Pinza's operatic basso.

It is an accepted fact that Rodgers and Hammerstein's score for *South Pacific* is one of the great achievements of their seventeen years of collaboration. More than half its songs have become standards, and every piece seems uniquely suited for its character and situation. Not since the booming ensembles of *Rose-Marie*'s

Mary Martin and Ezio Pinza

entity, Joshua Logan and scenic artist Jo Mielziner changed settings in full view of the audience, creating a stage effect similar to the cinematic dissolve, which allowed one scene to dovetail immediately into another.

Record Side 8

GUYS AND DOLLS 11/24/50, 46th Street Theatre; 1,200 performances. Music & lyrics, Frank Loesser; producers, Cy Feuer & Ernest Martin; orchestrations, George Bassman, Ted Royal; director, George S. Kaufman; choreographer, Michael Kidd; musical director, Irving Actman. ★ Robert Alda, Vivian Blaine, Sam Levene, Isabel Bigley, Stubby Kaye, Pat Rooney, Sr., Johnny Silver, Douglas Deane, B. S. Pully. *Runyonland Music/ Fugue for Tinhorns/ Follow the Fold*—**Stubby Kaye, Johnny Silver, Douglas Deane, Isabel Bigley, and Company** Conductor, Irving Actman. Decca DL 8036, mx 80219; recorded 12/3/50.

A "musical fable of Broadway" based on characters and incidents extracted from stories by Damon Runyon yielded one of the great American musical comedies. Producers Feuer and Martin first saw inherent musical possibilities in Runyon's short story "The Idyll of Miss Sarah Brown," which focused on the unlikely romance between professional gambler Sky Masterson and Salvation Army worker Brown, and planned the work as a serious musical drama in the grand tradition of *South Pacific*. Frank Loesser, fresh from winning laurels as composer of Feuer and Martin's *Where's Charley?*, agreed to supply the score, but eleven authors, including screenwriters Robert Carson and Jo Swerling, tried and failed to come up with a suitable libretto. Finally the producers decided their story was a comedy, not a drama, and called in Abe Burrows, a radio writer with no theatrical experience, to create a new libretto around Loesser's collection of songs.

Burrows's libretto, a comic masterpiece, creates a brassy but strangely poetic underworld of hoods, chorines, and hangers-on whose sun and stars are made of the brightest Broadway neon. To the romance first planned by Feuer and Martin he added a comic subplot about the on-again, off-again love affair between gambler

mounties had a male chorus been used for such effects as in the ribald "There Is Nothin' Like a Dame." Joe Cable's moral dilemma is chillingly stated in "You've Got to Be Carefully Taught," a bitter, ironic indictment of racial intolerance. The songs designed for the leads have their own special appeal. "A Wonderful Guy" is a joyous statement of love that is perfectly suited to the straightforward, uncomplicated Nellie. Martin's delightful, full-speed-ahead performance on the cast album is a vivid memento of what was arguably her best role in the theater. "Some Enchanted Evening," de Becque's first-act solo, creates an intoxicating aroma of sophisticated romance worthy of a passionate Frenchman. Pinza's rendition is definitive, from his simon-pure bass notes in the main melody to the thrilling falsetto of its coda.

Aside from its textual and casting virtues, the original production of *South Pacific* heralded a greater fluidity in direction and set design for the American musical theater. Previously, most shows would cover scene changes by lowering the house curtain and striking up an orchestral reprise to muffle the noise of shifting wings and drops. In order to keep the narrative a continuous

The guys and dolls of *Guys and Dolls*: Isabel Bigley and Robert Alda (left), Vivian Blaine and Sam Levene (right), backed by the Hot Box Girls.

Nathan Detroit and his platinum blonde sweetheart, Miss Adelaide. The supporting characters were borrowed from other Runyon stories: Harry the Horse, Angie the Ox, Nicely-Nicely Johnson, and others. The most remarkable aspect of the libretto is the peculiarly appropriate patois Burrows adopted for his raffish characters, a mixture of the king's English and pure Broadwayese.

Loesser's witty, wise, and warm music and lyrics constitute his finest effort for the musical theater. His ballads for Sky and Sarah are romantic and melodically adventurous, especially their first duet ''I'll Know.'' Likewise, ''Adelaide's Lament,'' an account of a psychosomatic head-cold triggered by the ups and downs of her romance, and the title tune are comic gems, all the more effective because their jokes are rooted in character and situation. The tone of the show is established by Loesser's comic opera opening. After a brief, frantic chase ballet, Nicely-Nicely Johnson, Benny Southstreet, and Rusty Charlie introduce the principal narrative theme, gambling, in

''Fugue for Tinhorns.'' (Loesser's first draft of the song, ''Three-Cornered Tune,'' was planned as a trio for Sky, Sarah, and Nathan). The entrance of the Save-a-Soul Mission Band led by Sarah Brown conveys the second theme of the plot, setting up the dramatic conflict to follow.

Of the original cast, Vivian Blaine, Robert Alda, and Stubby Kaye went on to long careers in both musical and nonmusical theater. The show received an all-black Broadway revival in 1976 headed by Robert Guillaume as Nathan Detroit.

THE KING AND I 3/29/51, St. James Theatre; 1,246 performances. Music, Richard Rodgers; lyrics & book, Oscar Hammerstein II; producers, Rodgers & Hammerstein; orchestrations, Robert Russell Bennett; director, John Van Druten; choreographer, Jerome Robbins; musical director, Frederich Dvonch. ★ Gertrude Lawrence, Yul Brynner, Dorothy Sarnoff, Doretta Morrow, Larry Douglas, John Juliano, Johnny Stewart. ***Shall We Dance?*—Gertrude Lawrence and Yul Brynner** Conductor, Frederick Dvonch. Decca DL 9008, mx MG 2211; recorded 4/16/51.

The history of *The King and I* begins with Gertrude Lawrence, who came up with the idea of musicalizing Margaret Landon's 1944 novel, *Anna and the King of Siam*, as a vehicle for her own talents. She first approached Cole Porter, who rejected her offer outright. A copy of the novel was then dispatched to Rodgers and Hammerstein, who also had their doubts about attempting such a project. They had never authored a work with one specific actor in mind; furthermore, the kissless relationship between two middle-aged principals hardly seemed suited to the type of musical romance for which they were famous. But both men were intrigued by the drama inherent in the clash of nineteenth-century eastern and western cultures, as embodied in the barbaric Siamese monarch and the prim but strong-willed Victorian governess. Putting their misgivings aside, they accepted Lawrence's proposal.

Noel Coward, Rex Harrison, and Alfred Drake all turned down the role of the king, fearing that it would be overshadowed by the part designed for Lawrence. Mary Martin, then appearing in *South Pacific*, urged Rodgers and Hammerstein to consider her leading man from the 1946

musical play *Lute Song*. A single audition brought Yul Brynner the role that launched his career in musical theater.

Instead of attempting an accurate reproduction of nineteenth-century Siamese music in the score, Rodgers suggested the exotic locale through a frequent use of musical colorations based vaguely on the oriental pentatonic scale. By his own description, it was as if the regionalist American artist Grant Wood had painted his impressions of Bangkok. Likewise, Hammerstein, instead of using pidgin English for the members of the royal household, often conveyed their dialogue by a series of oriental musical sounds emanating from the orchestra pit. Like *South Pacific*, the show was short on dance elements, but it found room for two choreographic triumphs staged by Jerome Robbins. The first was the ballet "The Small House of Uncle Thomas," an imaginative retelling of the Civil War classic *Uncle Tom's Cabin* as understood by Tuptim, the King's unhappy Burmese concubine. The other was the "Shall We Dance?" number, put into the show during its Boston tryout. In it, Anna recalls the formal dances of her youth in England and

Yul Brynner and Gertrude Lawrence

proceeds to teach the King how to polka. One of the most memorable scenes in theatrical history was the sight of Gertrude Lawrence making graceful arcs with the billowing hoopskirt of her pale lavender ball gown and glowing with what Hammerstein called "her magic light." Lawrence's onstage energy and personification of healthy high spirits belied the fact that she was suffering from cancer and would die in the eighteenth month of the show's three-year Broadway run. As preserved on the Decca original cast album, "Shall We Dance?" presents Lawrence at the climax of her career and Brynner on the brink of stardom. In 1977 Brynner starred in a fabulously successful Broadway revival of the show, ending its marathon road tour four years later, only several months before his death from cancer.

A TREE GROWS IN BROOKLYN 4/19/51, Alvin Theatre; 270 performances. Music, Arthur Schwartz; lyrics, Dorothy Fields; book, Betty Smith & George Abbott; orchestrations, Don Walker; producers, Robert Fryer & Abbott; director, Abbott; choreographer, Herbert Ross; musical director, Max Goberman. ★ Shirley Booth, Johnny Johnston, Marcia Van Dyke, Nathaniel Frey, Albert Linville, Nomi Mitty. *He Had Refinement*—**Shirley Booth** Conductor, Max Goberman. Columbia ML 4405, mx XLP 6986; recorded 4/22 & 23/51.

Brooks Atkinson summed up the overall critical reaction to *A Tree Grows in Brooklyn* when he called it "one of those happy inspirations that the theatre dotes on." Yet the piece was one of the curious commercial failures of its era and is thus denied the status of a classic which, in retrospect, it so richly deserves. Before its transformation into a lavish period musical, Betty Smith's episodic urban idyll of Irish immigrants in Brooklyn's Williamsburg district had been a best-selling novel and a superior motion picture. In their libretto, Smith and director-producer Abbott preserved the integrity of the source and revealed a keen ear for dialogue and period slang. The story has two parallel plots, one tragic, one comic. The principal narrative concerns the ill-fated romance between Katie Rommely Nolan and her husband, Johnny, a charming but weak dreamer who succumbs to alcoholism. (Johnny's self-destruction was strikingly portrayed in a

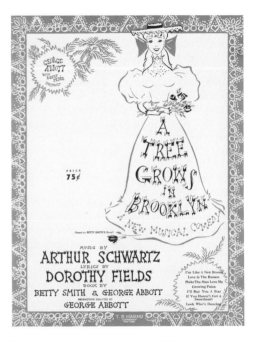

Song sheet cover bearing the original poster art.

nightmarish second act "Hallowe'en Ballet" designed by Herbert Ross.) To soften the relentless despair of the Nolans' saga, Smith and Abbott built up the part of Cissy, Katie's endearingly amoral sister, into a starring role. Cissy's exploits take the form of a series of uproarious but static sketches built around her infatuation with the memory of her first "husband," a bigamist named Harry Swanswine. If the musical had a flaw, it was that the two plots added up to less than their individual strengths, causing the show to waver in tone between the romantic drama of a *Carousel* and the madcap comedy of a *Where's Charley?*

Whatever the minor shortcomings of the libretto, the show was blessed with a superlative score that represented Arthur Schwartz and Dorothy Fields at the peak of their formidable powers as theatrical songwriters. There was period atmosphere galore in the ensemble numbers "Payday" and "If You Haven't Got a Sweetheart."

The melancholy love story was unfolded in "Make the Man Love Me" and "I'll Buy You a Star." For the raucous Cissy, Fields wrote one of the finest comic lyrics of her long career, "He Had Refinement," in which the character catalogues all the dubious attributes of her long-lost first love. Shirley Booth turned the song, and the role, into a personal triumph, overriding her vocal limitations and capitalizing on her twin talents as dramatic actress and comedienne.

In the mid-1960s *A Tree Grows in Brooklyn* rose from its undeserved obscurity when Sammy Davis, Jr., and Pearl Bailey were announced to star in an all-black version of the show. Alas, it never progressed beyond the planning stages, and the musical still awaits a new production to affirm its considerable merits for another generation.

Cassette Side F

WONDERFUL TOWN 2/25/53, Winter Garden Theatre; 559 performances. Music, Leonard Bernstein; lyrics, Betty Comden & Adolph Green; book, Joseph Fields & Jerome Chodorov; orchestrations, Don Walker; producer, Robert Fryer; director, George Abbott; choreographers, Donald Saddler, Jerome Robbins (uncredited); musical director, Lehman Engel. ★ Rosalind Russell, Edith Adams, George Gaynes, Henry Lascoe, Dort Clark, Jordan Bentley, Cris Alexander.
Ohio—**Rosalind Russell and Edith Adams** Conductor, Lehman Engel. Decca DL-9010, mx 84091; recorded 3/8/53.

The idea of adapting the 1940 comedy *My Sister Eileen* into a musical engaged a number of Broadway's leading craftsmen. In 1948 its original producer Max Gordon attempted to interest Burton Lane, Herbert and Dorothy Fields, and George S. Kaufman in concocting an adaptation. Two years later Leland Hayward, fresh from his producing chores with *South Pacific*, announced a version to be written by the Fieldses and scored by either Cole Porter or Irving Berlin. Concurrently, still another musicalization of the play was proposed as a vehicle for Ella Logan. But because of seemingly insurmountable problems in clearing the rights from its owner, Columbia Pictures, none of these projects went beyond the preliminary planning stages.

In June 1952 producer Robert Fryer went after the property and succeeded where others had failed. For the libretto, he hired Jerome Chodorov and Joseph Fields, who had adapted the original comedy from a series of semi-autobiographical *New Yorker* short stories by Ruth McKenney. When Frank Loesser proved unavailable, Fryer handed the responsibility for the songs to light-classics composer Leroy Anderson and lyricist-sketchwriter Arnold B. Horwitt. In an inspired bit of casting, Fryer signed as his leading lady the glamorous comedienne Rosalind Russell, who had enlivened the film version of the play.

In November 1952 Fryer was faced with an unsatisfactory score and the possibility of losing his star to other prospects. At the insistence of Russell and director George Abbott, Anderson and Horwitt were replaced by Leonard Bernstein, Betty Comden, and Adolph Green. In less than five weeks, they completed new music and

"Oh, why-o, why-o did we leave Ohio?": Rosalind Russell and Edie Adams in *Wonderful Town*.

lyrics. Known in the creative stages as *My Beautiful Sister*, *A Likely Story*, and *The Sherwood Sisters*, the show finally took on the title of *Wonderful Town*, clearly reminiscent of *On the Town*, the previous Bernstein-Comden-Green salute to Manhattan. Once the musical entered rehearsals, it underwent few alterations. Out of town, Russell received the humorously self-deprecating "One Hundred Easy Ways" to replace "The Story of My Life," and Jerome Robbins came in to rework the opening number, "Christopher Street." Following its Broadway opening, *Wonderful Town* was proclaimed the best musical of the year and swept the season's Tony Awards.

Its plot hinges on the exploits of Ruth and Eileen Sherwood, two sisters from the Midwest in pursuit of careers and romance in 1930s Manhattan. Eileen, a delectable blend of beauty and naiveté, longs to be an actress, while her older sister, Ruth (whose dilapidated typewriter no longer strikes the letter *W* since she completed a paper on Walt Whitman) is determined to become a magazine writer. The songwriters took full advantage of the story's 1930s setting in such witty pastiches as "Conga" and "Swing." The sisters' urban misadventures. which acquaint them with everyone from a group of singing policemen to the dance-crazed sailors of the Brazilian navy, lead eventually to happiness and success. Early in act 1, the girls find they have been hoodwinked into renting a basement apartment in Greenwich Village just inches above the blasting for the new subway system. In the nostalgic Brahmsian lullaby "Ohio," they remind themselves of the hometown comforts they have abandoned.

THE GOLDEN APPLE 3/11/54, Phoenix Theatre; 173 performances. Music, Jerome Moross; lyrics & book, John Latouche; orchestrations, Moross & Hershy Kay; producers, T. Edward Hambleton & Norris Houghton for the Phoenix Theatre Co.; director, Norman Lloyd; choreographer, Hanya Holm; musical director, Hugh Ross. ★ Kaye Ballard, Priscilla Gillette, Stephen Douglass, Jack Whiting, Bibi Osterwald, Jonathan Lucas, Portia Nelson.
Lazy Afternoon—**Kaye Ballard** Conductor, Hugh Ross. RCA Victor LOC 1014, mx E4VP-8168; recorded 4/12/54.

By the mid-1950s, Manhattan's loosely defined off-Broadway district was fast becoming a haven for small, experimental works that were judged too special, too avant-garde for the typical mainstream commercial theater audience. Of the musicals to emerge from that era and environment, the seminal work is *The Golden Apple,* an imaginative retelling of Homer's *Iliad* and *Odyssey* set in turn-of-the-century America. Authors John Latouche and Jerome Moross planned the show as a traditional scene-song-and-blackout musical comedy to be presented on Broadway by veteran producer Cheryl Crawford, but when the work was completed, it had evolved into a highly unconventional opera drawn from the American idioms of folk songs and dances, operetta, vaudeville, and Tin Pan Alley ditties. Crawford, along with several other big-name producers, rejected the work for the very reasons that made it so breathtakingly unique, fearing that such an uncompromising and erudite musical would never sell.

To the rescue came T. Edward Hambleton and Norris Houghton, founders of the Phoenix Theatre on Manhattan's Lower East Side. Seeking something different in musicals, they took a chance on the show and produced it for a mere $60,000 as the final play in their spring season. The modest production was hailed by reviewers as a breakthrough in musical theater tradition. *New York Daily Mirror* critic Robert Coleman judged it "the most original and imaginative work of its kind to blaze across the theatrical horizon in many a moon." Lured by the critical response and packed houses at the tiny Phoenix Theatre, producers Roger Stevens and Alfred De Liagre, Jr., adopted the show and moved it uptown to the considerably larger Alvin Theatre on Broadway, where it continued for a brief, disappointing run before succumbing to the summer doldrums.

Moross's score, in its amalgam of classical, pop, and folk genres, anticipates such later sung-throughout works as Andrew Lloyd Webber's *Evita*. Latouche's libretto transposes the classic Greek myths to the fictional hamlet of Angel's Roost, Washington. Ulysses and his men become U.S. soldiers returning from the Spanish-

Jonathan Lucas, Kaye Ballard, Priscilla Gillette, and Stephen Douglass, *The Golden Apple*.

American war; Helen of Troy, a bored, libidinous hausfrau; Paris, a wily traveling salesman who communicates solely through Hanya Holm's choreography; and the three goddesses, small-town gossips. The second act conveys the narrative elements of the *Odyssey* in a clever pastiche of vaudeville numbers, ranging from a typical soft-shoe to an intentionally campy Hawaiian number. Although most of the score did not lend itself to non-contextual excerpt, the sinuous "Lazy Afternoon," which brings about Helen's seduction of Paris, propelled Kay Ballard to stardom through both the original cast album and her 45-rpm recording of the song. Over the years, the piece has become a favorite among jazz and pop singers.

FANNY 11/4/54, Majestic Theatre; 888 performances. Music & lyrics, Harold Rome; book, S. N. Behrman & Joshua Logan; orchestrations, Philip J. Lang; producers, David Merrick & Logan; director, Logan; choreographer, Helen Tamiris; musical director, Lehman Engel. ★ Ezio Pinza, Walter Slezak, Florence Henderson, William Tabbert, Gerald Price, Nejla Ates, Edna Preston.

Welcome Home—**Ezio Pinza** Conductor, Lehman Engel. RCA Victor LOC 1015, mx E4VP-8511; recorded 11/21/54.

A musical adaptation of Marcel Pagnol's trilogy of plays *Marius, Fanny,* and *Cesar* established the career of one of the musical theater's most prolific producers, former St. Louis attorney David Merrick. Launching the kind of promotional hoopla that would become his trademark, Merrick parlayed the show into a runaway box office success—not that *Fanny* needed any of his Barnumesque gimmicks, for it was a remarkably mature and touching work that surely would have succeeded on its own.

Set "not so long ago" in the French port of Marseilles, the bittersweet story focuses on the complex relationships among Cesar, a Rabelaisian barkeeper; his restless son, Marius, who longs for a life at sea; Cesar's friend Panisse, a rich, middle-aged sailmaker; and Fanny, a winsome street vendor who loves Marius. When Marius joins the navy and unwittingly abandons the pregnant Fanny, she marries Panisse, who has always longed for a son to carry on the family business. Marius is shocked to learn the truth upon his return to the village. Years later, the couple is reunited by old Panisse, who, on his deathbed, dictates a letter to Cesar instructing Marius to marry Fanny and care for their child.

In adapting Pagnol's trilogy, authors Behrman and Logan regrettably sacrificed some of its intimacy for pure 1950s stage spectacle, including overblown scenic effects and a couple of ambitious but extraneous ballets by choreographer Helen Tamiris. Logan was involved with the work almost from its inception and served as not only co-librettist but also director and co-producer. At first he planned the musical as a reunion vehicle for his *South Pacific* cohorts Mary Martin, Richard Rodgers, and Oscar Hammerstein II, but Martin declined in order to fulfill a long-cherished desire to portray *Peter Pan,* and Rodgers and Hammerstein left when Merrick refused to give up even partial credit as producer. Undaunted, Logan raised

Ezio Pinza as Cesar in *Fanny.*

the secondary role of Cesar to star status and recruited Ezio Pinza, who, along with juvenile lead William Tabbert, was also a *South Pacific* alumnus. Harold Rome was hired to supply the music and lyrics, which are unquestionably the best of his career. The score is something of a precursor of Frank Loesser's more ambitious *The Most Happy Fella,* with "pop" songs, like the title ballad, intertwined with full-blown operatic arias and recitatives. Cesar's "Welcome Home," with its stately, reflective melody and introspective lyric, is a fine example of the intense emotionalism of the score. Pinza's rendition of the piece on the original cast recording is masterful and affecting, made all the more touching by the fact that the show marked his final Broadway appearance.

PETER PAN 10/20/54, Winter Garden Theatre; 152 performances. Music, Mark Charlap; lyrics, Carolyn Leigh; additional music, Jule Styne; additional lyrics, Betty Comden & Adolph Green; book, Jerome Robbins; orchestrations, Albert Sendrey; director-choreographer, Robbins; producers, Richard Halliday & Edwin Lester; musical director, Louis Adrian. ★ Mary Martin, Cyril Ritchard; Kathy Nolan, Margalo Gillmore, Joe E. Marks, Sondra Lee, Joseph Stafford, Robert Harrington.
I've Gotta Crow—**Mary Martin with Kathy Nolan** Conductor, Louis Adrian. RCA LOC-1019, mx E4VP-8479; recorded 11/4/54.

James M. Barrie's whimsical fairy tale about "the boy who would not grow up" has always featured a woman in the title role and music in its presentation. The original 1905 New York production, with Maude Adams as Peter, included songs and incidental music by John Crook; a 1924 revival starring Marilyn Miller boasted two songs by Jerome Kern; and a 1950 edition with Jean Arthur and Boris Karloff had interpolations by Leonard Bernstein. The play became a full-fledged Broadway musical in 1954 as a showcase for Mary Martin.

At first, director-choreographer Jerome Robbins planned to follow in his predecessors' footsteps and use only a handful of songs, to be composed by newcomers Carolyn Leigh and Mark Charlap. During the development process he added one more number, "The Old

Gavotte," by Nancy Hamilton and Morgan Lewis. Following the show's premiere on the West Coast as part of Edwin Lester's Los Angeles and San Francisco Light Opera series, the Hamilton-Lewis song was deleted, and the score was bolstered by contributions from Jule Styne, Betty Comden, and Adolph Green. The New York opening was greeted with praise for Robbins's adaptation, particularly in his extensive use of dance, and wild approval for Martin's performance, both on the ground and soaring high above on invisible wires. Also singled out for kudos were Cyril Ritchard, who played Captain Hook with the stylized panache of a Restoration rake, and platinum-haired pixie Sondra Lee, refreshingly offbeat as Indian princess Tiger Lily. The Broadway run was relatively brief because the show was sold for television broadcast on the NBC network, where it has reached millions of viewers. In 1979 Sandy Duncan starred in a welcome, 551-performance Broadway revival.

Peter Pan (Mary Martin) and Captain Hook (Cyril Ritchard) size each other up.

The 1954 production's hybrid score is surprisingly effective. Of the Styne-Comden-Green material, the standouts are the campy "Captain Hook's Waltz," the dreamy "Never-Never Land" (which recalls Victor Herbert's "Toyland"), and the bravura duet, "Mysterious Lady," in which Martin had a chance to show off her coloratura range and Ritchard punctuated his movements with hilariously ostentatious shouts of "misericordia!" The Leigh-Charlap songs hit just the right tone of innocence and braggadocio for Peter, most notably in "I've Gotta Crow." Used as Martin's introductory number, the song established Peter's character with a lilting melody and lyrics that asserted "If I'm pleased with myself, I have every good reason to be!"

Record Side 9

HOUSE OF FLOWERS 12/30/54, Alvin Theatre; 165 performances. Music, Harold Arlen; lyrics, Arlen & Truman Capote; book, Capote; orchestrations, Ted Royal; producer, Arnold Saint Subber; director, Peter Brook; choreographer, Herbert Ross; musical director, Jerry Arlen. ★ Pearl Bailey, Diahann Carroll, Juanita Hall, Dino DiLuca, Ray Walston, Rawn Spearman, Geoffrey Holder, Dolores Harper, Ada Moore, Enid Mosier, Carmen De Lavallade. **A *Sleepin' Bee*—Diahann Carroll with Ada Moore, Dolores Harper, and Enid Mosier** Conductor, Jerry Arlen. Columbia OL-4969, mx XLP 32982; recorded 1/9/55.

Broadway has not witnessed a more exotically beautiful or beguilingly different musical comedy than *House of Flowers*. Its source was Truman Capote's 1950 O. Henry Award–winning short story based on his colorful experiences as a tourist in the bars and bordellos of Haiti. The narrative is a gossamer fable about Ottilie (known professionally as Violet), a young resident of the brothel Maison des Fleurs, who falls in love with Royal, a naive country boy. While short on plot, the story was long on island atmosphere, a blend of sophistication, innocence, and native rituals. Capote set about transforming it into a straight play but soon found himself with a libretto for a musical. Producer Arnold Saint Subber thought the results fascinating and insisted that Capote team with Harold Arlen on the score.

Cover of the original cast album.

The collaboration began by mail between Arlen in Hollywood and New York and Capote on an extended tour of Europe, and continued through Arlen's long hospitalization for a bleeding ulcer. Capote's lyrical scenario was matched by Arlen's sensuous music, which made much of West Indian rhythms and instruments. When the adaptation was finished, Capote's narrative of the two young lovers had become secondary to a new story about bordello keeper Madame Fleur, primarily because Pearl Bailey had agreed to star in the role. Other featured cast members were former opera singer Rawn Spearman; *South Pacific*'s original Bloody Mary, Juanita Hall; comedian Ray Walston; dancer Geoffrey Holder; and nineteen-year-old Diahann Carroll, making her first appearance in a Broadway musical as the ingenue Violet/Ottilie. The show's production team consisted of theatrical royalty, including Shakespearean and operatic director Peter Brook, choreographer George Balanchine, and designer Oliver Messel.

The Philadelphia tryout exploded in a series of contretemps between Pearl Bailey and the production staff, resulting in the departure of Brook and Balanchine and their replacement by Herbert Ross. The battles took their toll on the company without correcting what were seen as the production's shortcomings. Press reaction to the Broadway premiere was mixed, ranging from the *World-Telegram Sun* drama critic's endorsement of the musical as "first-rate" to *Variety's* dismissal of it as a "dull thud." Subsequent raves from George Jean Nathan and Walter Kerr could not keep the show on the boards for more than five months. A 1968 off-Broadway revival was truer to Capote's short story, but its threadbare production all but eliminated the exotic, extravagant beauty that made the original production unique.

Like *St. Louis Woman* nearly ten years earlier, *House of Flowers* has earned a lasting reputation through its original cast album. Its unique charm is apparent from the opening strains of the steel drum–punctuated overture to the exuberant coda in the production number "The Turtle Song." The melody for the song-aria "A Sleepin' Bee" was originally composed by Arlen for the Judy Garland film *A Star Is Born*. Drawing on a voodoo myth described in Capote's story, the piece contrasts the innocence of Ottilie, bewitchingly sung by Diahann Carroll, with the knowing innuendo of the other Maison des Fleurs residents Pansy, Tulip, and Gladiola.

THE PAJAMA GAME 5/13/54, St. James Theatre; 1,063 performances. Music & lyrics, Richard Adler & Jerry Ross; book, George Abbott & Richard Bissell; orchestrations, Don Walker; producers, Frederick Brisson, Robert E. Griffith, & Harold Prince; directors, George Abbott & Jerome Robbins; choreographer, Bob Fosse; musical director, Harold Hastings. ★ John Raitt, Janis Paige, Eddie Foy, Jr., Carol Haney, Reta Shaw, Stanley Prager, Ralph Dunn. *Hey There*—**John Raitt** Conductor, Harold Hastings. Columbia OL-4840, mx XLP-31707; recorded 5/16/54.

The Pajama Game is something of a spiritual successor to *Pins and Needles,* since both focus on the American garment industry and share a sincere, if lighthearted, viewpoint on the issues of labor

John Raitt and his dictaphone in *The Pajama Game.*

and management. Like the novel *7½ Cents* on which it is based, the 1954 musical centers on a threatened strike in an Iowa pajama factory and its effects on the romances of two pairs of employees. True to musical comedy tradition of the era, one set of lovers is serious, one comic.

Producer Robert E. Griffith first learned of Richard Bissell's novel from a review in the *New York Times* and immediately suggested to his partner, Harold Prince, that they obtain the rights for a musical comedy adaptation. When the necessary permissions were secured, they offered the show to George Abbott, who found the narrative drab and ill-suited for a libretto but agreed to direct if it could be suitably adapted. Griffith and Prince offered the project to every major librettist, composer, and lyricist working in the theater at the time and were turned down by virtually everyone. Abbott eventually consented to collaborate with the novel's author on the adaptation. (Bissell's amusing roman à clef *Say, Darling*, a fictional production history of *The Pajama Game*, became "a comedy about a musical" in 1958 with songs by Comden, Green, and Styne.) At the

suggestion of Frank Loesser (then caught up in the on-again, off-again preparations for *The Most Happy Fella*), pop songwriters Richard Adler and Jerry Ross were hired to create their first score for a book musical. Dancer Joan McCracken, who had worked with Abbott in Rodgers and Hammerstein's *Me and Juliet*, suggested as choreographer Bob Fosse, her husband and a refugee from characterless dancing assignments in MGM musicals. In exchange for co-director credit, Jerome Robbins agreed to supervise the overall staging of the musical numbers. In the final stages of pre-production, Frederick Brisson joined Griffith and Prince as co-producer.

The cast was made up of familiar faces—but none that guaranteed box office success—and talented unknowns. At the helm were Janis Paige, a film actress who had never before appeared in a Broadway musical, and John Raitt, an experienced stage performer who had starred in a string of failures since his debut ten years earlier in *Carousel*. In supporting roles were Carol Haney, who had been Gene Kelly's assistant on several movies and had danced briefly with Bob Fosse in the film version of *Kiss Me, Kate*, and ex-vaudevillian Eddie Foy, Jr. The chorus included future choreographer Peter Gennaro and Shirley MacLaine, who became a star overnight when she substituted for an ailing Carol Haney early in the run.

The hit song of *The Pajama Game* was the ballad "Hey There." Alone in his office, the hero (John Raitt), the factory supervisor, tries to talk himself out of his attraction to the heroine, the beautiful but tough-talking head of the employees' grievance committee. In staging the number, Abbott and Robbins had Raitt record his soliloquy on a dictaphone and then play it back onstage as if it were his own psyche offering advice. The technique was similar to a current fad among recording artists like Patti Page and Kay Starr, who sang duets with themselves through the newly discovered wonders of multi-track audiotape.

"And, little man, little Lola wants you": Stephen Douglass receives a seductive pitch from Gwen Verdon in *Damn Yankees*.

DAMN YANKEES 5/5/55, 46th Street Theatre; 1,019 performances. Music & lyrics, Richard Adler & Jerry Ross; book, George Abbott & Douglass Wallop; orchestrations, Don Walker; producers, Frederick Brisson, Robert E. Griffith, & Harold Prince; director, George Abbott; choreographer, Bob Fosse; musical director, Harold Hastings. ★ Gwen Verdon, Stephen Douglass, Ray Walston, Russ Brown, Robert Shafer, Shannon Bolin, Jimmie Komack, Rae Allen, Nathaniel Frey, Jean Stapleton, Eddie Phillips.
***Whatever Lola Wants*—Gwen Verdon**
Conductor, Harold Hastings. RCA LOC-1021, mx F2PP-3749; recorded 5/8/55.

Just two weeks after *The Pajama Game*'s Broadway premiere, George Abbott received a call from William Morris agent Albert Taylor suggesting that a novel by his client Douglass Wallop, *The Year the Yankees Lost the Pennant*, was ideal source material for a new musical comedy. Abbott admired the novel's satirical blending of baseball with the Faust legend and consented to direct and collaborate with

Wallop on the adaptation. Besides its producers Brisson, Griffith, and Prince, the show reunited Abbott with a number of other *Pajama Game* alumni, including songwriters Adler and Ross, choreographer Fosse, and author Richard Bissell, who gave uncredited assistance on the libretto.

The cast assembled for *Damn Yankees* was another mix of seasoned professionals and talented new faces. Comic actor Ray Walston gave the most memorable stage performance of his career as a modern-day Mephistopheles named Mr. Applegate. Robert Shafer and Stephen Douglass, as middle-aged and youthful incarnations of the romantic hero, ably captured two aspects of the same personality. Jean Stapleton scored in a minor part not unlike her later persona in the television series *All in the Family*. Excellent though they all were, the show really belonged to Gwen Verdon, who won the leading role of Lola, a ravishingly beautiful witch, only after it was turned down by both Mitzi Gaynor and Zizi Jeanmaire. Of Verdon's performance, Boston critic Elliot Norton observed, "Not since Mary Martin's heart first belonged to Daddy has the Broadway stage produced such a gifted girl star."

A considerable amount of revision occurred during the musical's tryout tour, with Adler and Ross rewriting nearly one-third of their original score. The Broadway opening was nothing short of a home run, but on the following afternoon perfectionist Abbott assembled the cast for a rehearsal that eliminated one song, moved another to the second act, reworked the ending, and trimmed twenty minutes from the running time. Apart from occasional cast replacements, the show then remained unchanged for the rest of its 2½-year run.

Like *The Pajama Game*, *Damn Yankees* is a perfect specimen of pure 1950s commercial musical comedy, with its clever but untaxing story, ensemble playing, and succession of Hit Parade tunes. Its plot tells of insurance salesman Joe Boyd, who makes a pact containing an escape clause with the devil in order to lead his beloved Washington Senators to a World Series victory. Lola, the most enticing lost soul in Applegate's stable, is assigned to lure Joe to eternal destruction, but the plan backfires when Lola falls in love with her intended prey, helps him triumph as a baseball star, and then returns him to his faithful wife. The highlight of Adler and Ross's score is the humorous "Whatever Lola Wants," a burlesque tango brilliantly staged in the original production by Bob Fosse in the Senators' locker room. Dressed, according to the authors, as "a sort of latter-day Sadie Thompson," Lola purrs, cajoles, and performs a coy striptease to win over the ingenuous hero. Verdon's performance of the number established her as the finest dancing comedienne of her generation, as adept at a punch line as a tour jeté.

THE MOST HAPPY FELLA 5/3/56, Imperial Theatre; 676 performances. Music, lyrics, & book, Frank Loesser; orchestrations, Don Walker; producers, Kermit Bloomgarden & Lynn Loesser; director, Joseph Anthony; choreographer, Dania Krupska; musical director, Herbert Greene. ★ Robert Weede, Jo Sullivan, Art Lund, Susan Johnson, Shorty Long, Mona Paulee, Keith Kaldenberg.
Excerpt, Act 2 (Like a Woman Loves a Man/My Heart Is So Full of You)—Robert Weede and Jo Sullivan Conductor, Herbert Greene. Columbia 03L-240, mx XLP-38351; recorded 5/13, 14, 20/56.

After his *Guys and Dolls* had established itself as an out-and-out Broadway smash in 1950, Frank Loesser went looking for a new dramatic property completely unlike its brash urban milieu. His search was ended when he discovered Sidney Howard's 1927 Pulitzer Prize–winning play, *They Knew What They Wanted*, a rueful tale of a triangular relationship involving Tony, an aging Italian immigrant in California's Napa Valley; Amy, the young waitress from San Francisco who becomes his mail-order bride; and Joe, the handsome and hedonistic farmhand who comes between them. Loesser took its study of basically good people caught in uncomfortable circumstances, stripped away the political overtones, and revealed an adult love story that offered something completely different as source material for a musical.

For over four years Loesser, in his first outing as a librettist, slaved away at the adaptation, often abandoning it in frustration only to find himself too compelled by the material and its challenges to shelve it. He reshaped the basic theme and three-act structure of Howard's play, making both Tony and Amy (or Rosabella, as Tony calls her) more sympathetic figures. To add variety and lighten the melodramatic tone of the narrative, Loesser added a comic romance between Cleo, the brassy but good-hearted friend of the heroine, and Herman, a worker on Tony's farm—two characters who might well be distant cousins of *Oklahoma!*'s Ado Annie and Will Parker. Little of Loesser's script took the form of spoken dialogue; he had written a work of such ambitious proportions that it approached the texture and scope of grand opera. Like that of *The Golden Apple*, the score was an amalgam of recitative, arias, operetta duets, and raucous musical comedy numbers. In spite of, or perhaps because of, its eclecticism, the nearly forty musical numbers provided an uncommonly rich emotionality while remaining completely accessible to typical Broadway audiences. Most of the lighter numbers, including "Standing on the Corner" and the hoedown "Big D," went to either Cleo or Herman, energetically played by Susan Johnson and Shorty Long. The more obviously operatic numbers, such as the impassioned duet "My Heart Is So Full of You," were assigned to basso Robert Weede and soprano Jo Sullivan in the roles of Tony and Rosabella. Joe's indulgent rootlessness was voiced in the haunting "Joey, Joey, Joey," a combination of pop and arioso styles. However the work may be classified by critics and audiences, Loesser himself refused to identify it as either an opera or a musical play, preferring instead to call it "a musical with music."

MY FAIR LADY 3/15/56, Mark Hellinger Theatre; 2,717 performances. Music, Frederick Loewe; lyrics & book, Alan Jay Lerner; orchestration, Robert Russell Bennett, Philip J. Lang; producer, Herman Levin; director, Moss Hart; choreographer, Hanya Holm; musical director, Franz Allers. ★ Rex Harrison, Julie Andrews, Stanley Holloway, Robert Coote, Cathleen Nesbitt, John Michael King, Philippa Bevans, Christopher Hewett.
The Rain in Spain—**Rex Harrison, Julie Andrews, Robert Coote, and Servants (Rosemary Gaines, Glenn Kezer, Colleen O'Connor, Muriel Shaw, Reid Shelton, Gloria van Dorpe)** Conductor, Franz Allers. Columbia OL 5090, mx XLP 37804; recorded 3/25/56.

The idea of a musical based on George Bernard Shaw's *Pygmalion* began with Gabriel Pascal, the colorful Hungarian impresario responsible for the 1938 film version of the comedy. Although Shaw refused permission for musicalization during his lifetime, his executors granted Pascal a limited option on the material in 1952. A legion of seasoned professionals rejected the project outright: Rodgers and Hammerstein, Dietz and Schwartz, Noel Coward, E. Y. Harburg, and Cole Porter. After much searching Pascal secured the services of Lerner and Loewe, but their initial efforts proved unsatisfactory and led to a temporary rift in their partnership. At the time of Pascal's death in 1954, they had resumed the partnership and solved the problem of adapting an intimate romance into a lavish musical by simply including onstage those incidents that occur offstage in Shaw's play. Lerner's libretto hewed close to its source, recounting the rise of Eliza Doolittle from guttersnipe to grande dame under the tutelage of phonetics professor Henry Higgins. As in the Pascal film, Lerner's only major alteration of Shaw's plot was to imply at the conclusion that Eliza and Higgins belonged together. With the Cinderella overtones of its story, the show was something of a successor to *Irene* (1919) and *One Touch of Venus* (1943).

With Herman Levin as producer and CBS financing the $400,000 production in exchange for exclusive rights to the cast recording, *My Lady Liza* began casting in early 1955. No one but Rex Harrison was seriously considered to play the misogynistic Higgins. When Mary Martin rejected the role of Eliza after hearing five songs from the score, a number of leading ladies were tested before the nod was given to twenty-year-old Broadway newcomer Julie Andrews. Joining the supporting cast were such distinguished British actors as Stanley Holloway, Robert Coote, and Cathleen Nesbitt. Shortly before the tryout tour, the show's title was changed to *My Fair Lady*, from the coda lyric in the nursery song "London Bridge Is Falling Down." It suggests Eliza's miraculous shedding of her Lisson Grove cocoon and indicates a Cockney mispronunciation of "Mayfair lady," the very pinnacle of English gentility to which the heroine aspires. The original Broadway production ran for over seven years, won countless awards, and enhanced the theatrical reputations of all the leading players.

"The Rain in Spain" was written during the final weeks before rehearsals started, when the authors decided that Eliza's mastery of Higgins's speech lessons should be expressed in song. According to Lerner, once he and Loewe had decided on the tango rhythm, they completed a draft of the song in ten minutes. During the New Haven tryout they added a choral lament by Higgins's servants to preface the number.

Robert Coote, Julie Andrews, and Rex Harrison record "The Rain in Spain" for *My Fair Lady*'s original Broadway cast album.

Critic Wolcott Gibbs described the segment as "just about the most brilliantly successful scene that I recall seeing in a musical comedy."

Record Side 10
Cassette Side G
Compact Disc IV

CANDIDE 12/1/56, Martin Beck Theatre; 73 performances. Music, Leonard Bernstein; lyrics, Richard Wilbur; additional lyrics, John Latouche & Dorothy Parker; book, Lillian Hellman; orchestrations, Bernstein & Hershy Kay; producers, Ethel Linder Reiner & Lester Osterman, Jr.; director, Tyrone Guthrie; musical director, Samuel Krachmalnick. ★ Max Adrian, Robert Rounseville, Barbara Cook, Irra Petina, William Olvis, Boris Aplon, William Chapman, Conrad Bain.
Glitter and Be Gay—**Barbara Cook** Conductor, Samuel Krachmalnick. Columbia OS-2350, mx XSM-58052; recorded 12/9/56.

Barbara Cooke as Candide's beloved Cunegonde.

As early as 1950, Lillian Hellman contemplated a stage version of the eighteenth-century Voltaire classic, with incidental music by Leonard Bernstein, but previous artistic commitments temporarily prevented their collaboration. When she and Bernstein returned to the project nearly four years later, they changed their original conception of a play with music to a full-scale comic operetta. Hellman's libretto was remarkably faithful to its source, retaining its picaresque saga of Candide, his giddy fiancée, Cunégonde, and his teacher Dr. Pangloss, as they wander from their home in Westphalia, center of "the best of all possible worlds," to Lisbon, Paris, Venice, and Buenos Aires. After they endure such devastations as rape, insurrection, slavery, and the Spanish Inquisition, their gullible idealism gives way to a more earthbound and realistic outlook. Hellman also shaded the scenario with her own brand of subtle political commentary, alluding to Senator Joseph McCarthy's recent red-baiting reign of terror in the hero's various trials and persecutions.

James Agee was initially selected as lyricist. He was soon replaced by Dorothy Parker, who, in rapid succession, was supplanted first by John Latouche and, after Latouche's sudden death in 1956, finally by poet Richard Wilbur. In the interim, Hellman wrote the words for "El Dorado" and Bernstein (with help from his wife, Felicia Montealegre) devised the lyrics for "I Am Easily Assimilated." Bernstein's score was a complete triumph of style, or more precisely, styles, for it consisted of comic opera pastiches that ridiculed the genre's pomposity while revelling in its rich flow of melody. In addition to its splendid overture, which is a whole show in itself, the work's most famous number is Bernstein and Wilbur's mock–coloratura aria "Glitter and Be Gay." Thrillingly sung by Barbara Cook, the piece is Cunégonde's lament at her temporary status as a Parisian demi-mondaine who finds comfort in the fact that "If I'm not pure, at least my jewels are."

Although the original production had a wealth of attractions, director Tyrone Guthrie, at the helm of his first and only musical, failed to unify the elements of script, score, cast, and design. Treasured by a sophisticated few during its brief Broadway run, *Candide* maintained a following through its classic original cast recording. The album's popularity, coupled with a continuing fascination with the show among theater professionals and audiences, led to a highly successful new Broadway production in 1974, with rediscovered Bernstein melodies, a new script by Hugh Wheeler, additional new lyrics by Stephen Sondheim, and a raucous, sideshow-flavored staging by Harold Prince which preserved the manic spirit of Voltaire's original.

BELLS ARE RINGING 11/29/56, Shubert Theatre; 924 performances. Music, Jule Styne; lyrics & book, Betty Comden & Adolph Green; orchestrations, Robert Russell Bennett; producer, The Theatre Guild; director, Jerome Robbins; choreographers, Robbins & Bob Fosse; musical director, Milton Rosenstock. ★ Judy Holliday, Sydney Chaplin, Jean Stapleton, Eddie Lawrence, Dort Clark, Frank Aletter, George S. Irving, Peter Gennaro, Bernie West.

Just in Time—**Sydney Chaplin and Judy Holliday** Conductor, Milton Rosenstock. Columbia OS-2006, mx XSM 44385; recorded 12/4/56.

Following their profitable partnership on *Peter Pan*, Comden and Green vowed to collaborate again soon with Jule Styne and Jerome Robbins. The vehicle that brought about their reunion was inspired by an illustration on the back of the Manhattan phone directory showing an attractive young operator with various telephone cords sprouting from her head as if she were a benevolent Medusa. At the center of Comden and Green's story was the character of Ella Peterson, an endearingly neurotic answering-service employee who applies lipstick before taking a call and who falls in love with one of her clients, frustrated playwright Jeff Moss, known to her as "Plaza-oh Double-four Double-three." Surrounding the Little Miss Fix-It heroine are a group of urban eccentrics and a warmly charitable view of New York City

Sydney Chaplin and Judy Holliday

78

that recalled the team's previous shows *On the Town* (1944) and *Wonderful Town* (1953).

The musical was jerry-built for one of Comden and Green's oldest friends, the adorable comedienne Judy Holliday, who yearned to return to the stage after a long stint as a film star. John Raitt, Alfred Drake, and Lloyd Bridges were offered the male lead; eventually cast at Holliday's suggestion was all-but-unknown thirty-year-old Sydney Chaplin, a West Coast actor and scion of cinema royalty who had never before appeared in a Broadway musical. In the supporting cast was Jean Stapleton as Sue, the proprietress of Susanswerphone Telephone Service; Eddie Lawrence as Sandor, a bookie who uses Sue's company as a front for off-track betting operations; Dort Clark as a menacing police detective; and Bernie West as a dentist who composes popular songs on his air hose. Future stage and television star Hal Linden appeared in a small part as a nighclub emcee and understudied (and eventually succeeded) Chaplin as Judy Holliday's vis à vis.

Although Comden and Green labored over a year to complete the libretto, together with Jule Styne they composed the score in a week. Among the many delightful songs are the ballads "The Party's Over" and "Long Before I Knew You," the joyous polka "Hello, Hello There," and the heroine's larger-than-life, Jolson-styled "eleven o'clock" number "I'm Going Back (to the Bonjour Tristesse Brassiere Company)." The melody for the soft-shoe duet, "Just in Time," had long been in Styne's cocktail party canon of lyricless tunes. As staged by Robbins and Bob Fosse, the song finds Ella and Jeff proclaiming their mutual joy at discovering each other, amidst the vocal encouragement of others within Raoul Pene du Bois's stylized Central Park setting. Aside from its artistic merits, *Bells Are Ringing* bears the distinction of being the first American musical comedy recorded in stereo.

THE MUSIC MAN 12/19/57, Majestic Theatre; 1,375 performances. Music & lyrics, Meredith Willson; book, Willson & Franklin Lacey; orchestrations, Don Walker; producers, Kermit Bloomgarden, with Herbert Greene & Frank Productions; director, Morton DaCosta; choreographer, Onna White; musical director, Herbert Greene. ★ Robert Preston, Barbara Cook, David Burns, Pert Kelton, Iggie Wolfington, Helen Raymond, Eddie Hodges, the Buffalo Bills.
76 Trombones—**Robert Preston and Company** Conductor, Herbert Greene. Capitol SWAO-990, mx SWA01-990; recorded 12/22/57.

In a 1957 interview in the *New York Herald-Tribune*, Meredith Willson modestly observed that "the existence of *The Music Man* proves Somerset Maugham's contention that anybody with a good memory can write down a story." Willson's preoccupation with nostalgic recall began in 1951, when producers Cy Feuer and Ernest Martin, at Frank Loesser's insistence, asked him to write a show for them about his small-town Iowa boyhood. Remembering sunlit images of the parades, picnics, and front porches of his youth, Willson drafted a scenario he called *The Silver Triangle*, centering on a charming rascal of a traveling salesman named Harold Hill, whose con game of collecting money to organize a boys' band brings unexpected optimism and self-knowledge to the fictional community of River City, Iowa. Along the way, he falls in love with Marion Paroo, the town's prim but romantic librarian, who is as much an outcast in her own way as the fast-talking Hill. Early in the creative process, Willson discovered an ingenious way to hint at the similarities of these seemingly dissimilar characters: he provided each with a variation of the same melody, first as the heroine's ballad waltz "Goodnight, My Someone" and then as the trickster-hero's rousing, Sousaesque march "76 Trombones." After supervising countless revisions and suggesting the new title of *The Music Man,* Feuer and Martin finally bowed out as producers, citing what they considered insurmountable problems in the show's second act. Undaunted, Willson continued to draft new scenes and songs, taking on as collaborator Franklin Lacey, with whom he had worked on an outdoor pageant in California. Lacey's chief contribution was the deletion of an

Robert Preston and the River City kids

extraneous subplot about a River City
janitor and his dystrophic son and the
substitution of the character of Marion's
withdrawn little brother, Winthrop, as an
added link between her and Harold Hill's
dream of a boys' band. After amassing over
thirty drafts and forty songs, Willson
persuaded producer Kermit Bloomgarden to
present the work during the 1957/58
theatrical season. Frank Loesser pledged
his faith in the project by agreeing to serve
as associate producer and to publish the
score through his Frank Productions.

The role of Harold Hill was first offered
to Danny Kaye. When he turned it down,
dozens of others were considered, among
them Dan Dailey, Phil Harris, Ray Bolger,
Jackie Gleason, Milton Berle, Jason
Robards, Art Carney, Bert Parks, Lloyd
Bridges, Van Heflin, James Whitmore, and
Andy Griffith. At the urging of the show's
director, Morton DaCosta, the role went to
seasoned film and stage actor Robert

Preston, who had never before sung or
danced onstage. As his leading lady,
Barbara Cook gave yet another of the
glowing performances that made her
Broadway's finest soprano ingenue. Also in
the cast were the reliable character actors
Pert Kelton, Iggie Wolfington, and David
Burns, and the added attraction of the
Buffalo Bills, the first barbershop quartet to
appear as characters in a Broadway
musical. Taking all the major awards for the
1957/58 season, *The Music Man* reminded
audiences of another era. It recreated the
all-American spirit and innocence of a
George M. Cohan musical comedy.

Preston's biggest show-stopper occurred
in the fourth scene of act 1. As the "River
Citizians" are gathered in the high school
gymnasium for their Fourth of July
activities, which include stereopticon slides,
historical tableaux à la Del Sarte, and a
pompous mayor forever trying to deliver
the Gettysburg Address, Hill seizes the

occasion to promote his community band scheme and brings the assembled crowds to fever pitch with his galvanizing delivery of "76 Trombones."

WEST SIDE STORY 9/26/57, Winter Garden Theatre; 734 performances. Music, Leonard Bernstein; lyrics, Stephen Sondheim; book, Arthur Laurents; orchestrations, Bernstein, Sid Ramin, & Irwin Kostal; producers, Robert E. Griffith & Harold Prince, in association with Roger L. Stevens & Robert Whitehead; director-choreographer, Jerome Robbins; musical director, Max Goberman. ★ Carol Lawrence, Larry Kert, Chita Rivera, Mickey Calin, Ken LeRoy, Art Smith, Martin Charnin, Lee Becker, Reri Grist, Marilyn Cooper.
Tonight—**Carol Lawrence and Larry Kert** Conductor, Max Goberman. Columbia OS-2001, mx XSM-41521; recorded 9/29/57.

No musical of the 1950s took more chances than *West Side Story*. Its score was a fusion of pop and serious music styles alien to the typical Broadway audience, its narrative violent and tragic without any reference to the traditional wish-fulfillment mold, and its youthful cast of dancer-singer-actors relatively unknown. That such an uncompromising and original work became a commercial success was a testament to the growing sophistication of the musical theater and its patrons.

Jerome Robbins's original title was *East Side Story* for his modern retelling of *Romeo and Juliet*. The warring houses of Shakespeare's tragedy became feuding families of Catholics and Jews on Manhattan's Lower East Side during the Easter-Passover season. Leonard Bernstein and Arthur Laurents shared Robbins's enthusiasm for the idea, but artistic differences and previous commitments led to a temporary abandonment of the project. In 1954, nearly six years after their first planning sessions, Laurents and Bernstein found a more appropriate contemporary metaphor in a series of *Los Angeles Times* articles about teenage Anglo-Hispanic warfare. Robbins approved their changes and enthusiastically resumed work on the adaptation. When Bernstein relinquished his plan to write his own lyrics, twenty-five-year-old Stephen Sondheim joined the creative team, embarking on his first produced effort. Robbins later recalled his

Tony (Larry Kert) and Maria (Carol Lawrence) vow eternal love on Oliver Smith's evocative fire-escape set.

collaboration with Bernstein, Laurents, and Sondheim as "the most exciting I have ever had in the theater."

Prominent among the show's accomplishments was its extensive use of dance as an important dramatic element. Robbins propelled the story in a series of ballets: a frenetic community dance evolves into a poetic cha-cha when the lovers first meet; a wild street fandango extols the dubious pleasures of living in "America"; a brutal gang war becomes a series of violent pas de deux; and the dream ballet concept popularized in *Oklahoma!* receives a new interpretation in which the hero and heroine briefly imagine a world without urban strife and racial prejudice. If Robbins, Laurents, Bernstein, and Sondheim made the characters of Tony and Maria as one-dimensional as their Elizabethan counter-parts, they also devised a striking equivalent to Shakespeare's famous balcony scene as the two declare their love atop the fire escape of a West Side tenement. Originally, the scene contained the songs "Somewhere" and "One Hand, One Heart." When Sondheim's mentor Oscar Hammerstein II saw an early run-through of the show, he insisted that the scene required a soaring ballad. His advice resulted in the romantic "Tonight," in which the lovers transform their oppressive surroundings into a world "with suns and moons all over the place."

Ethel Merman records "Rose's Turn" as Stephen Sondheim looks on.

GYPSY 5/21/59, Broadway Theatre; 702 performances. Music, Jule Styne; lyrics, Stephen Sondheim; book, Arthur Laurents; orchestrations, Sid Ramin & Robert Ginzler; producers, David Merrick & Leland Hayward; director-choreographer, Jerome Robbins; musical direction, Milton Rosenstock. ★ Ethel Merman, Jack Klugman, Sandra Church, Lane Bradbury, Maria Karnilova, Paul Wallace, Jacqueline Mayro, Mort Marshall.

Rose's Turn—**Ethel Merman** Conductor, Milton Rosenstock. Columbia OS-2017, mx XSM-47188; recorded 5/24/59.

Gypsy originated in a splendid, though fictionalized, memoir by vaudevillian-turned-stripper Gypsy Rose Lee. It centered on neither Gypsy herself nor her sister, actress June Havoc, but on their indomitable mother, Rose, whom the author described as "courageous, resourceful, and . . . in a feminine way, ruthless."

In late 1956 David Merrick acquired the rights to the autobiography after reading only one chapter. Joining forces with Leland Hayward, he set about transforming the story into a star vehicle for Ethel Merman. Betty Comden and Adolph Green were the first to attempt the task of adapting the work but soon gave up because they were unable to find a workable approach to the story, particularly in portraying the larger-than-life character of Rose. Hayward then asked *West Side Story* librettist Arthur Laurents to take on the challenge. Laurents held little enthusiasm for the property at first, regarding it as just another backstage musical until he hit upon the theme of a woman who lives vicariously through the successes of her children without ever creating a success completely her own. For the score, both Irving Berlin and Cole Porter were approached, and both declined. Merrick and Hayward briefly gave the assignment to Stephen Sondheim, but because Merman had been burned by neophyte songwriters in her most recent Broadway outing, *Happy Hunting* (1956), she insisted on Jule Styne as composer. Eventually, the producers persuaded Sondheim to postpone his composing ambitions and provide the lyrics for Styne's melodies.

Originally, director-choreographer Jerome Robbins conceived the show as a great nostalgic panorama of American vaudeville, with a collection of variety acts sprinkled throughout the narrative. But as rehearsals progressed, he realized that the show Laurents had written was a tight drama focusing on two people: the monomaniacal Rose, who becomes a victim of her own dreams, and her mousey daughter, Louise, who turns into the glamorous Gypsy Rose Lee. A major casting problem was finding a performer capable of portraying Rose's sheepish lover, Herbie. A number of character actors were considered, including Lew Parker and Victor Jory. The role went to the now-famous Jack Klugman, who made his musical debut in the show.

When *Gypsy* went into rehearsal, it was apparent that Styne and Sondheim had synthesized the raucous Merman persona with the character of Rose, in such songs as "Some People" and the insistent, whistle-in-the-dark first-act finale "Everything's Coming Up Roses"; All ended in blackouts, however, and denied Merman the opportunity to stay on stage and acknowledge the applause. Determined to create something dramatically richer than the typical Merman show-stopper, Laurents, Styne, Sondheim, and Robbins envisioned a coda to be titled "Rose's Turn" that would be something of a brassy *Walpurgisnacht* for Rose as she is confronted with the lonely emotional limbo within which her blind ambition has trapped her. The number was planned as a ballet with Rose haunted by specters of the people who have abandoned her, but Styne and Sondheim turned it into a dramatic song-aria based on fragments of several songs in the score, including "Everything's Coming Up Roses," "Mr. Goldstone, I Love You," and a number called "Momma's Talking Soft" that was dropped during the out-of-town tryout. "Rose's Turn" gives the character a chance to vent her frustrations in a nightmarish, neon-lit frenzy of bumps, grinds, and psychodrama. The song revealed both Merman's previously untapped versatility as an actress and Jule Styne's ability to write a theater score consisting of more than a string of pop hits, a score that was light years beyond the charming but modest ambitions of *Gentlemen Prefer Blondes* (1949) and *Bells Are Ringing* (1956).

In 1973 Angela Lansbury triumphed in the first London production of the show, which came to Broadway the following season. In his review of the revival, critic Walter Kerr pronounced *Gypsy* a "still mysteriously perfect venture."

THE SOUND OF MUSIC 11/16/59, Lunt-Fontanne Theatre; 1,443 performances. Music, Richard Rodgers; lyrics, Oscar Hammerstein II; book, Howard Lindsay & Russel Crouse; orchestrations, Robert Russell Bennett; choral arrangements, Trude Rittman; producers, Leland Hayward, Richard Halliday, Rodgers, & Hammerstein; director, Vincent J. Donehue; choreographer, Joe Layton; musical director, Frederick Dvonch. ★ Mary Martin, Theodore Bikel, Patricia Neway, Kurt Kasznar, Marion Marlowe, John Randolph, Nan McFarland, Lauri Peters, Brian Davies, Marilyn Rogers, Muriel O'Malley. *Do Re Mi*—**Mary Martin, with Lauri Peters, Marilyn Rogers, William Snowden, Kathy Dunn, Joseph Stewart, Mary Susan Locke, and Evanna Lein** Columbia KOS-2020, mx XSM 48557; recorded 11/22/59.

Rodgers and Hammerstein's last musical was also ultimately their most successful, with long runs on Broadway, on tour, and in the West End, followed by a film version that became one of the top-grossing movies of all time. The work, based on a memoir by Maria von Trapp, received its first dramatic treatment in a mid-1950s German film. Asked by Paramount Pictures to screen it as a possible vehicle for Audrey Hepburn, director Vincent J. Donehue instead saw the narrative as a perfect stage showcase for his friend Mary Martin. As Martin later recalled in her autobiography, *My Heart Belongs*, "the idea was just irresistible . . . a semi-Cinderella story, but true."

Donehue and Richard Halliday, Martin's husband, embarked on an international search for the Baroness von Trapp and her surviving stepchildren in order to secure clearances for a stage adaptation. In the autumn of 1957, with all rights in hand, Halliday hired playwrights Howard Lindsay and Russel Crouse to write the script. Somewhat reminiscent of the plot of *The King and I*, their story is a gentle (some critics said overly sentimental) account of Maria Rainer, a lively, music-loving postulant at Salzburg's Nonnberg Abbey, who is sent to the home of stern navy captain Georg von Trapp as governess for his seven unruly children. In time she wins the hearts of both Herr von Trapp and his family. When the threat of Nazism becomes a reality, Maria leads them to safety in her beloved Alps. Lindsay and Crouse planned originally to use authentic German folk and religious songs throughout, with the interpolation of one or two new pieces to be composed by Rodgers and Hammerstein. Not wanting to compete with the old masters, Rodgers and Hammerstein agreed to supply a complete score if the production could be delayed a year to allow them to finish work on *Flower Drum Song*. The wait proved wise for all concerned, for it enabled the show to attract audience interest to the tune of a record advance ticket sale of over 3¼ million dollars, an accomplishment that overrode the mixed critical reception the show received at its Broadway premiere.

Rodgers and Hammerstein's score is a fitting climax to their unique approach to the operetta genre. There is charm to spare in "Do Re Mi," a sprightly production number which grows out of Maria's efforts to win over the von Trapp children; warmth and a love for nature in the title song and "Edelweiss," which bears the sad distinction of being Oscar Hammerstein's final completed lyric; and dramatic power in the "Preludium," a liturgical chorale which replaces the traditional overture, and the Mother Abbess's hymn "Climb Ev'ry Mountain," the team's follow-up to *Carousel*'s "You'll Never Walk Alone."

During the Broadway run, Mary Martin was succeeded by such future stars as Florence Henderson and Nancy Dussault. In 1981 pop singer Petula Clark headed a well-received London revival. Julie Andrews starred in the fabulously successful 1965 movie version.

"Do-re-me-fa-so-la-ti-do!": Maria (Mary Martin) teaches the Von Trapp children to sing.

Ben Marino (Howard Da Silva, center) and his political cronies in *Fiorello!*

Record Side 11

FIORELLO! 11/23/59, Broadhurst Theatre; 795 performances. Music, Jerry Bock; lyrics, Sheldon Harnick; book, Jerome Weidman & George Abbott; orchestrations, Irwin Kostal; producers, Robert Griffith & Harold Prince; director, Abbott; choreographer, Peter Gennaro; musical director, Harold Hastings. ★ Tom Bosley, Howard Da Silva, Patricia Wilson, Ellen Hanley, Mark Dawson, Nathaniel Frey, Eileen Rodgers, Pat Stanley, Bob Holiday.
Little Tin Box—**Howard Da Silva, with Stanley Simmonds, Julian Patrick, Del Horstman, Ron Husmann, and David London** Conductor, Harold Hastings. Capitol SWAO-1321, mx SWAO2-1321; recorded 11/29/59.

The third musical to receive a Pulitzer Prize for drama, *Fiorello!* was also the first musical since Rodgers and Hart's *I'd Rather Be Right* (1937) to depict a real figure from American politics at the center of its plot.

With amazingly few touches of fiction, Jerome Weidman and George Abbott's libretto recounts the rise of Fiorello La Guardia, "Little Flower," from idealistic young lawyer on "the side of the angels" to reforming mayor of New York City. The script is something of a pop history lesson, with vignettes about World War I, the need for labor unions, and Tammany Hall political scandals, interspersed with quaint references to La Guardia's penchant for chasing fire engines and swinging sledge hammers against mobsters' slot machines. Weidman and Abbott even found time to include a love story, or, more precisely, two love stories: Fiorello's brief first marriage to Thea Almerigatti and his rescue from a widower's life by his faithful secretary, Marie. The authors initially planned for one actress to portray both wives, but their expansion of

Marie's character made the idea unworkable.

Bock and Harnick's solidly crafted score was their first Broadway hit. The songs, written in the Rodgers and Hammerstein mold of romantic realism, with more than a touch of Frank Loesser in their rhythms, have an uncommon measure of both dramatic purpose and period flavor. The First World War is suggested in the Tin Pan Alley pastiche "'Til Tomorrow," and the twenties are ushered in on the strains of the Charleston-cum-campaign-song, "Gentleman Jimmy," in dubious homage to La Guardia's flamboyant predecessor James J. Walker. The political climate of the era is imaginatively conveyed in two songs assigned to the character of Ben Marino, the Republican ward leader who becomes Fiorello's ally. The first, a humorous equation of "Politics and Poker," proved a hit with tryout audiences and inspired Bock and Harnick to add a similar number, "Little Tin Box," to the second act shortly before the New York premiere. The song is an ironic retelling of the Seabury hearings on the corrupt Walker administration, set to the free and easy rhythms of the soft-shoe. Its satiric words and ingratiating melody are reminiscent, in feeling if not compositional style, of the comic songs in the Gershwins' *Of Thee I Sing.*

Fiorello! was first and foremost an ensemble show, with a cast largely made up of fine young singing actors rather than established musical stars. Long before his television fame on *Happy Days*, Tom Bosley earned his earliest acclaim as the crusading Fiorello. Ellen Hanley and Patricia Wilson had the best roles of their respective careers as the two women in his life, and Eileen Rodgers made the most of a cameo appearance as a madcap 1920s musical comedy queen. The most famous member of the original cast was Howard Da Silva. As the rabble-rousing Ben Marino, he conjured up memories of his first major role, in *The Cradle Will Rock* nearly a quarter of a century earlier.

THE FANTASTICKS 5/3/60, Sullivan Street Playhouse; still running as of 12/31/88. Music, Harvey Schmidt; book & lyrics, Tom Jones; orchestrations & musical director, Julian Stein; producers, Lore Noto, Sheldon Baron, & Dorothy Olim; director, Word Baker. ★ Jerry Orbach, Rita Gardner, Kenneth Nelson, Hugh Thomas, William Larsen, Thomas Bruce, George Curley. *Try to Remember*—**Jerry Orbach and Company** Conductor, Julian Stein. MGM SES-3872OC, mx 960-17G-647; recorded 5/60.

Tom Jones and Harvey Schmidt wrote two complete, and completely different, versions of *The Fantasticks* before discovering a satisfying and wildly successful approach in their third try. Freely adapted from Edmond Rostand's turn-of-the-century comedy *Les Romanesques*, the musical was first drafted in 1956 under the working title *Joy Comes to Deadhorse*. The authors transplanted the story to the American Southwest and recast its variation of *Romeo and Juliet* with an Anglo hero and a Mexican heroine, whose battling families live on adjacent ranches. Unwittingly, Jones and Schmidt had conceived a Texas version of *West Side Story* in the grand Rodgers and Hammerstein tradition of the epic musical, requiring elaborate sets, a large cast and chorus, and a full orchestra. Their ambitious, overblown concept all but paralyzed them creatively, and after four years of steady work they were ready to abandon the project.

A second chance at the material came when director and fellow Texan Word Baker asked them to scale down their original concept to an intimate one-act musical for the 1959 summer season of experimental theater at Barnard College. Inspired by the challenge, they kept the bare bones of Rostand's farce about two young lovers whose fathers bring them together by pretending to keep them apart, and reset it in the minimalist, presentational techniques of the Italian commedia dell'arte and the Japanese traditions of the Noh drama and Kabuki theater. As a result of the show's brief run at Barnard, producer Lore Noto agreed to remount it for off-Broadway presentation. Jones and Schmidt briefly considered pairing the musical with another one-act but decided to expand it into a full evening's entertainment. With the exception of former Broadway juvenile

New faces from off-Broadway: Jerry Orbach, Rita Gardner, and Kenneth Nelson in *The Fantasticks*.

popularity of the original cast album and various satellite recordings of its songs, propelled *The Fantasticks* to an open-ended New York engagement that has made it "the world's longest-running musical." Among its other attributes, the show built on the foundations established by *The Golden Apple* (1954) in promoting the off-Broadway theater as an alternative outlet for new trends in musicals.

"Try to Remember" functions as an atmospheric prologue to the story proper. It is performed by El Gallo, a dashing and mysterious one-man "Greek chorus," who introduces the musical's leitmotif, seasonal rebirth, and then assembles the rest of the cast onstage to join him in the song.

BYE BYE BIRDIE 4/16/60, Martin Beck Theatre; 607 performances. Music, Charles Strouse; lyrics, Lee Adams; book, Michael Stewart; orchestrations, Robert Ginzler; producers, Edward Padula & L. Slade Brown; director-choreographer, Gower Champion; musical director, Elliott Lawrence. ★ Chita Rivera, Dick Van Dyke, Kay Medford, Paul Lynde, Dick Gautier, Michael J. Pollard, Susan Watson, Marijane Maricle, Charles Nelson Reilly.
A Lot of Livin' to Do—**Dick Gautier, Susan Watson and Teenagers** Conductor, Elliott Lawrence. Columbia KOS-2025, mx XSM 49659; recorded 4/24/60.

The surprise hit of the 1959/60 season, *Bye Bye Birdie* was a lighthearted antidote to *West Side Story's* portrait of hostile American youth. The show evolved from stage manager Edward Padula's idea of a musical about the rock-and-roll craze sweeping the country's teenage population. At first he and the songwriting team of Charles Strouse and Lee Adams planned to do a musical version of the novel *Let's Go Steady* by Warren Miller and Raphael Millan but eventually decided to commission an entirely new plot. After working with a number of potential librettists (including Mike Nichols), they settled on Michael Stewart, a TV and off-Broadway sketch writer who went on to become one of the musical theater's leading librettists.

Stewart's breezy script cashed in on the popularity of rock-and-roll's chief proponent, Elvis Presley (with a nod to Conway Twitty). It focused on Conrad Birdie and the national havoc caused by his

Kenneth Nelson, the cast of eight (including co-author Jones, who appeared under the pseudonym Thomas Bruce) were unknowns. Ed Wittstein's set design was spare and consisted of a stool bearing a block of wood, to suggest the wall that separates the young lovers, and a circle suspended from the flies, to represent the moon in the first half and the sun throughout the second. The orchestra was made up of a piano, a harp, and percussion. The entire budget for the initial production was a meager $16,500. When the show opened in spring 1960 at the tiny 155-seat Sullivan Street Playhouse in Greenwich Village, it received mixed reviews and was threatened with an early closing, but favorable word-of-mouth among professionals and theatergoers, along with the induction into the peacetime army. When Conrad's songwriter-agent, Albert Peterson, sees his sole source of income about to disappear, his resourceful girlfriend and secretary, Rose Grant, hatches the scheme of having Conrad sing Albert's ditty "One Last Kiss" to an adoring fan on national television. The expected royalties will bankroll Albert's agency (and his long-delayed marriage to Rose) until Conrad is discharged. Much of the libretto's humor hinges on the effect that the primitive, egotistical Birdie has on the placid community of Sweet Apple, Ohio, the home of teenager Kim McAfee, who has been selected to appear with him on "The Ed Sullivan Show."

Like its creative team, most of *Bye Bye Birdie's* original cast was relatively unknown. Top-billed were Chita Rivera, fresh from the Broadway and London companies of *West Side Story*, and Dick Van Dyke, who parlayed his success in the role of Albert into a prosperous career in television situation comedy. The leads were first offered to Gower and Marge Champion, but Gower countered with an offer of his services as director-choreographer, thereby launching his career as one of the leading lights of 1960s musical theater. Among the high points of the original production were his staging of "The Telephone Hour," with a whole community of teenagers arranged in a series of stacked cubicles by designer Robert Randolph, and "Shriners' Ballet," a splendid showcase for Chita Rivera's dancing talents.

Strouse and Adams's score, their first major effort for Broadway, contains precious little pure rock-and-roll, although they captured the sounds of the era in Conrad's solos "Honestly Sincere" and "One Last Kiss." The show's hits were Albert's soft-shoe "Put On a Happy Face" and the ensemble number "A Lot of Livin' to Do." The latter, performed with appealing freshness by Susan Watson as Kim and Dick Gautier as Birdie, is a youthful "seize the day" sounded by an energetic but not alienated youth.

Kim (Susan Watson), Birdie (Dick Gautier), and the Sweet Apple teenagers let off steam to the beat of "A Lot of Livin' to Do."

Cassette Side H

DO RE MI 12/26/60, St. James Theatre; 400 performances. Music, Jule Styne; lyrics, Betty Comden & Adolph Green; book & director, Garson Kanin; orchestrations, Luther Henderson; producer, David Merrick; choreographers, Marc Breaux & DeeDee Wood; musical director, Lehman Engel. ★ Phil Silvers, Nancy Walker, John Reardon, Nancy Dussault, David Burns, George Mathews, George Givot.
Adventure—**Phil Silvers and Nancy Walker** Conductor, Lehman Engel. RCA Victor LSOD 2002, mx M5PY-1127; recorded 1/8/61.

Like *Bye Bye Birdie*, *Do Re Mi* had fun at the expense of the American pop music business. Based on Garson Kanin's satirical novel with the same title, the story was first dramatized by Frank Tashlin and Herbert Baker as the screenplay for the 1957 film *The Girl Can't Help It* starring Tom Ewell and Jayne Mansfield. Dissatisfied with the screen adaptation, Kanin redesigned the work in 1960 as a stage musical. At the center of the libretto is Hubie Cram, a likeable small-time operator who briefly wins fame and fortune when he invades the jukebox industry with the help of a trio of out-to-pasture mobsters. Although his dreams of glory are short-lived, he succeeds in promoting the career of waitress–turned–singing star Tilda Mullen, chiefly through the help of his sardonic, long-suffering wife, Kay.

The script was unexceptional, but the actors who performed it were letter-perfect. John Reardon and Nancy Dussault brought extraordinary charm and fine singing voices to their portrayals of the romantic leads. The starring roles of Hubie and Kay Cram were entrusted to the superb clowns Phil Silvers and Nancy Walker, who kept the show rolling merrily along, even when the dialogue they had been given was less than hilarious.

Along with its remarkable cast, *Do Re Mi* had the virtue of Styne, Comden, and

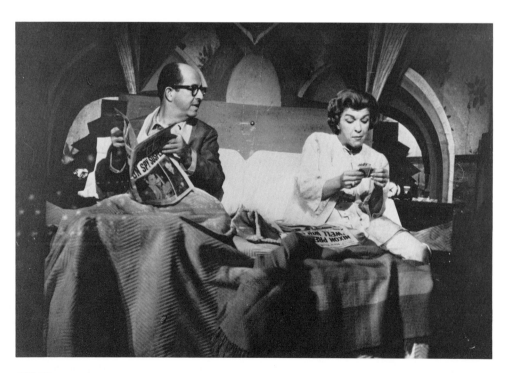

Phil Silvers and Nancy Walker in *Do Re Mi*.

Green's bright and rhythmic score, which contains some of their most felicitous collaborations. The sounds of rock-and-roll get the once-over in the parody "What's New at the Zoo?", while the wistful "Cry Like the Wind" anticipates the folk music revival of the early 1960s. The show's principal ballad, "Make Someone Happy," has become a popular standard through recordings by Perry Como and Tony Bennett. But the score's pièce de résistance is an achingly funny duet for Silvers and Walker called "Adventure." Occurring at the top of act 2, the number gives Kay Cram the chance to ponder what might have been, while Hubie tries unsuccessfully to sleep through her lively musings. Kanin, Marc Breaux, and DeeDee Wood staged the number with the Crams in bed and Walker continually rousing Silvers with operatic cackles, matador leaps, and melodramatic sighs worthy of a Duse or Bernhardt.

Met with generally favorable reviews, *Do Re Mi* did a tidy business at the box office until producer David Merrick moved it to a smaller, uptown theater. The shift proved fatal, and the production closed in the red at the end of the season. A subsequent, unsuccessful London production with an all-British cast served only to reconfirm the irreplaceability of Silvers and Walker.

CAMELOT 12/3/60, Majestic Theatre; 873 performances. Music, Frederick Loewe; lyrics & book, Alan Jay Lerner; orchestrations, Robert Russell Bennett & Philip J. Lang; producers, Loewe, Lerner, & Moss Hart; director, Hart; choreographer, Hanya Holm; musical director, Franz Allers. ★ Richard Burton, Julie Andrews, Robert Goulet, Roddy McDowall, Robert Coote, Bruce Yarnell, John Cullum.
*Camelot—***Richard Burton** Conductor, Franz Allers. Columbia KOS-2031, mx XSM-51698; recorded 12/11/60.

By 1958 *My Fair Lady* was safely established as an international hit, and its creators were eager to find a new property that would allow them a chance to capitalize on their huge success as a production team. They found it in T. H. White's *The Once and Future King*, a newly published historical novel based on the ancient Arthurian legends. Lerner and Hart decided to focus the libretto on the last portion of the narrative, which depicts the final glory of Camelot and its destruction as a result of the infidelity of King Arthur's wife, Queen Guenevere, and his bosom friend Sir Lancelot. Loewe, then recovering from a heart attack, had strong misgivings about the plot: he felt that no matter how cerebral its treatment, the theme of cuckoldry was more suited to the traditions of farce than those of the romantic musical. He eventually accepted the challenge, however, and obtained medical clearance from his doctor to embark on the creation of a new work. As soon as they secured the rights from the author, Lerner, Loewe, and Hart concerned themselves with casting. From the first New York and London productions of *My Fair Lady*, they recruited Julie Andrews to play the faithless queen and Robert Coote for the bumbling King Pellinore. After much pleading, Richard Burton agreed to appear as King Arthur for a year's run in what would be his only Broadway musical. In Lerner's autobiography, *On the Street Where I Live*, he recalled that "the writing of *Camelot* took 21 months and 21 thousand miles," the latter due to the fact that most of the script and score were written on the French Riviera because of Loewe's precarious health.

A series of disasters began to assail the production in July 1960, just two months before rehearsals were to start. Lerner, involved in a marital crisis, developed writer's block and suffered a temporary nervous breakdown. The death of costume designer Adrian and his replacement by Tony Duquette placed an additional strain on the show's development. The world premiere at Toronto's O'Keefe Centre, a newly-opened theater with surprising acoustical deficiencies, ran an ungainly four and one-half hours and received largely unfavorable reviews. During the overwhelming process of revisions, Lerner was suddenly hospitalized with a bleeding ulcer. On the day of his release, he watched in horror as Hart, stricken by a heart attack, was rushed into Lerner's just-vacated hospital room. Lerner took over as director at Hart's request, and the jinxed musical moved on to Boston en route to New York. Despite record advance ticket sales of $3,000,000, the mixed reaction from critics

King Arthur (Richard Burton) charms Guenevere (Julie Andrews) with his description of Camelot.

and audiences predicted a short life for *Camelot*. But by February 1961 Hart was sufficiently recovered to supervise a number of improvements that, along with appearances by Burton, Andrews, and Robert Goulet on "The Ed Sullivan Show," turned the musical into a commercial success. The ballad "If Ever I Would Leave You," sung by Goulet as the ardent Lancelot, became the pop hit in Lerner and Loewe's soaringly beautiful score, but the jaunty, regal "Camelot," first sung by Arthur in the opening scene to comfort a somewhat recalcitrant Guenevere, took on new meaning as it came to be identified with the Kennedy administration's lofty goals, gifted cast of characters, and eventual untimely demise.

CARNIVAL! 4/13/61, Imperial Theatre; 719 performances. Music & lyrics, Bob Merrill; book, Michael Stewart; orchestrations, Philip J. Lang; producer, David Merrick; director-choreographer, Gower Champion; musical director, Saul Schechtman. ★ Anna Maria Alberghetti, Jerry Orbach, Kaye Ballard, James Mitchell, Henry Lascoe, Pierre Olaf.
Mira—**Anna Maria Alberghetti** Conductor, Saul Schechtman. MGM SE-39460C, mx 61-ST-360-RE-1; recorded 4/17/61.

Few musicals possess the lyrical enchantment and pure imagination to be found in *Carnival!* Paul Gallico's short story about a waif who links up with a down-at-heels carnival troupe and falls in love with a dour puppeteer had first served as the basis for the 1953 MGM film *Lili* starring dancer-actress Leslie Caron. In turning Helen Deutsch's screenplay into a libretto, Michael Stewart preserved its wistful charm and added some welcome humor, particularly in the characters of the dashing magician, Marco the Magnificent, and his bibulous assistant and mistress, Rosalie, dazzlingly portrayed by James Mitchell and Kaye Ballard. Stewart's major alteration of the source was the conversion of the leading role of Lili into a star turn for a lyric soprano. Although Carol Lawrence was a strong contender for the part, David Merrick eventually cast Anna Maria Alberghetti, who enjoyed great success in her only Broadway appearance.

Bob Merrill's score remains something of a neglected treasure, with its calliope rhythms and innocent lyrics. Never before or since has his work been so consistently fresh and appropriate to character and plot. Especially lovely are the pieces composed for the wide-eyed heroine, most notably "Mira," in which she sings of her hometown "where everybody knew my name." In his review of the show's world premiere at the National Theatre, *Washington Post* critic Richard L. Coe praised Alberghetti's performance of the song, citing "as exactly audible a pianissimo as I have heard since Richard Tauber's day."

The greatest star of *Carnival!* was director-choreographer Gower Champion. Following in the traditions forged by Jerome Robbins, Champion's work was an unmistakable forward march for the "concept musical," a philosophy of staging in which all elements of the production contribute to a consistent point of view. His theatrical ingenuity was evident throughout, particularly in the show's opening. To the quaint wheezes of a concertina, the carnival performers straggle onto a bare stage, pulling wagons, practicing their routines, adjusting the lights, and setting up a tent, gradually metamorphosing into a shabby but enthusiastic circus parade. Champion's direction was instrumental in winning *Carnival!* the 1961 Drama Critics' Award for best musical of the season.

"I came on two buses and a train," sings Lili (Anna Maria Alberghetti) to a sympathetic Jacquot (Pierre Olaf).

92

HOW TO SUCCEED IN BUSINESS WITH-OUT REALLY TRYING 10/14/61, 46th Street Theatre; 1,417 performances. Music & lyrics, Frank Loesser; book, Abe Burrows, Jack Weinstein, & Willie Gilbert; orchestrations, Robert Ginzler; producers, Cy Feuer & Ernest Martin, with Frank Productions; directors, Abe Burrows & Bob Fosse; choreographer, Hugh Lambert; musical director, Elliott Lawrence. ★ Robert Morse, Rudy Vallee, Bonnie Scott; Claudette Sutherland, Charles Nelson Reilly, Ruth Kobart, Virginia Martin, Sammy Smith.
I Believe in You—**Robert Morse and Men** Conductor, Elliott Lawrence. RCA Victor LSO-1066, mx M2PY-5374; recorded 10/22/61.

Not since Harburg, Saidy, and Lane's *Finian's Rainbow* of two decades earlier had there been as successful a musical comedy satire as *How to Succeed in Business Without Really Trying*, a send-up of the Horatio Alger rags-to-riches myth set in the never-neverland of American big business. Based loosely on Sheperd Mead's tongue-in-cheek guide for climbing the corporate ladder, the work began as a songless comedy by Jack Weinstock and

Willie Gilbert. Producers Feuer and Martin bought the play and handed it over to their *Guys and Dolls* collaborators Abe Burrows and Frank Loesser for adaptation as a musical.

Burrows's sharp and funny script traces the meteoric rise of J. Pierrepont Finch from lowly window washer to chairman of the board of World Wide Wickets Company. Finch claws his way to the top through a strangely appealing mixture of boyish guile and underhanded conniving. Throughout his libretto, Burrows used an intentionally one-dimensional cast of characters to lampoon such corporate rituals as the coffee break, the office party, executive board meetings, TV ad campaigns, office wolves, and nubile secretaries. His broad, cartoon-strip style direction was complemented by quirky and comic musical staging by Bob Fosse and Hugh Lambert.

Frank Loesser's glib, brightly syncopated score was unfairly criticized for its supposed lack of hummable melodies.

J. Pierrepont Finch (Robert Morse) in the executive washroom, surrounded by his rivals.

Ultimately, what the critics were carping about was its deliberate departure from lyrical romanticism, for the songs were perfectly in tune with the show's characters and situations. Its single love song, "I Believe in You," originally written for the anti-hero's girlfriend Rosemary, was reassigned to Finch and staged in what became one of musical comedy's great *coups de théâtre*. Finch sings the song to his own reflection in the imaginary mirror of the executive washroom as he prepares for an important meeting. In ironic counterpoint, his colleagues and rivals sing their interior hopes for thwarting his success. (The sounds of their electric razors are amusingly simulated by kazoos in the orchestra.)

In addition to its skillful meshing of songs, story, and staging, *How to Succeed* was blessed with a splendid cast. Robert Morse's experience as a Broadway juvenile made him the perfect choice for the boyish Finch and earned him a Tony as the year's best actor in a musical. Rudy Vallee made a surprising comeback as the pompous company president, J. B. Biggely, who inadvertently helps Finch fulfill his ambitions. The supporting cast included some capital clowning by Charles Nelson Reilly as Biggely's prissy nephew, Bud Frump, and Virginia Martin as the absurdly sexy Hedy LaRue, the siren of the secretarial pool and Biggely's mistress.

How to Succeed in Business Without Really Trying was the fourth musical to win the coveted Pulitzer Prize for drama. The show was both a triumph and a climax in the careers of Burrows and Loesser. Although they continued to work in the musical theater throughout the decade, they never were able to duplicate *How to Succeed*'s commercial and artistic achievements.

Record Side 12

A FUNNY THING HAPPENED ON THE WAY TO THE FORUM 5/8/62, Alvin Theatre; 964 performances. Music & lyrics, Stephen Sondheim; book, Burt Shevelove & Larry Gelbart; orchestrations, Irwin Kostal; producer, Harold Prince; director, George Abbott; choreographer, Jack Cole; musical director, Harold Hastings. ★ Zero Mostel, Jack Gilford, David Burns, Raymond Walburn, John Carradine, Ruth Kobart, Brian Davies, Preshy Marker, Ronald Holgate. *Comedy Tonight*—**Zero Mostel and Company** Conductor, Harold Hastings. Capitol SWAO 1717, mx SWAO 1-1717; recorded 5/13/62.

When Burt Shevelove was an undergraduate at Yale, he used the comedies of Plautus as the basis for a campus musical. Years later he teamed with television writer Larry Gelbart (later of the "M*A*S*H" series) and returned to the material as a possible Broadway project. Their resulting "scenario for vaudevillians" had as its underlying theme the obvious parallels between the low humor of ancient Roman comedy and the pratfalls and leers of modern burlesque. Their plot drew upon a variety of stock characters and situations from Plautus's twenty-one surviving plays: the callow hero and his equally dim-witted beloved, the shrewish wife and her timid but lecherous husband, the doddering old man in search of his long-lost children, the braggart soldier who is more bombastic than brave. Shevelove and Gelbart linked the disparate, farcical plot threads through the character of Pseudolus, a clever and conniving slave who endures a series of trials in order to win his freedom.

The role was written for Phil Silvers, who chose instead to star in *Do Re Mi*. Briefly Milton Berle was to assume the part, but he withdrew when his contractual demand for final script approval was rejected. The role finally went to Zero Mostel, who was well-respected for his dramatic work but inexperienced in the ways of the commercial musical theater. The show also underwent numerous changes in its production personnel before Harold Prince agreed to present the work under George Abbott's direction.

Even with a fine cast of superb comedians and an unusual score by Stephen Sondheim, *Forum* failed to excite out-of-town critics and audiences. During the stop at the National Theatre in Washington, Jerome Robbins was called in to resuscitate the expiring production. One of the few changes he recommended was that the opening number, an airy, vaudeville-inspired soft-shoe called "Love Is in the Air," be replaced by a livelier piece more in keeping with the raucous and bawdy spirit of the play. Sondheim first responded

"Tragedy tomorrow, comedy tonight!": Zero Mostel as Pseudolus.

with a song called "Invocation," which went in the right direction, but he then produced the ultimate solution: "Comedy Tonight," with Mostel as the *prologus* of ancient drama, introducing the members of the cast. The number was inserted during the New York previews and was instrumental in transforming a certain disaster into a certain hit.

The remainder of Sondheim's score is equally meritorious, though its attributes were largely ignored by opening night critics. As he later observed, the songs "were the direct antithesis of the Rodgers and Hammerstein school," functioning as respites from the action rather than forwarding plot and developing character.

In 1972 Shevelove directed a well-received West Coast revival that eventually settled on Broadway for 156 performances. Heading the cast was Phil Silvers, who won a Tony for his performance in the role originally written with him in mind.

SHE LOVES ME 4/23/63, Eugene O'Neill Theatre; 302 performances. Music, Jerry Bock; lyrics, Sheldon Harnick; book, Joe Masteroff; orchestrations, Don Walker; producers, Harold Prince, Lawrence Kasha, & Philip McKenna; director, Prince; choreographer, Carol Haney; musical director, Harold Hastings. ★ Barbara Cook, Daniel Massey, Barbara Baxley, Jack Cassidy, Ludwig Donath, Nathaniel Frey, Ralph Williams.
*Ice Cream—***Barbara Cook** Conductor, John Berkman. MGM SE-41180C-2, mx SE-41180C2-2; recorded 4/26/63.

She Loves Me credits as its source a gentle 1930s comedy of manners and situations, *Parfumerie* by Hungarian dramatist Miklos Lazlo. The play had previously served as the basis for two memorable MGM films, Ernst Lubitsch's 1940 classic *The Shop around the Corner* starring Margaret Sullavan and James Stewart, and the 1949 Judy Garland–Van Johnson technicolor musical, *In the Good Old Summertime*. Although each adaptation altered the locale and the secondary characters to some degree, the tender wisp of a plot remained the same: two shopclerks spend each workday at odds with one another while unwittingly conducting an anonymous friendship by mail.

The 1963 stage musical began as a project of producers Lawrence Kasha and Philip McKenna, who hired Jerry Bock, Sheldon Harnick, and Joe Masteroff to effect the transformation. Masteroff first adapted the work as a straight comedy without the usual indications for possible song cues, thus encouraging the composer and lyricist to convert as much dialogue as possible into music. With its *mittel europa* atmosphere, sharply etched characters, and a highly sophisticated score containing twenty-three set musical pieces, *She Loves Me* recalls Jerome Kern's "continental" operettas of the 1930s, *The Cat and the Fiddle* and *Music in the Air*.

In early 1962 Harold Prince joined Kasha and McKenna as co-producer and eventually replaced Gower Champion as director shortly before rehearsals began. Originally, Julie Andrews was set to star, but Prince refused to postpone the production for six months while she completed a film assignment. After considering Julie Harris and Dorothy Collins, he gave the role to

Barbara Cook, who scored a great personal success as the spirited but sentimental heroine Amalia Balash, and surrounded her with a tightly knit ensemble of singing actors. The 1930s European ambiance of the libretto and music was beautifully reinforced by the jewel-box intimacy of William and Jean Eckart's pastel interiors and glistening shop windows. The tiny orchestra pit in the Eugene O'Neill Theatre compelled orchestrator Don Walker to substitute an accordion for the traditional grand piano, thus further enhancing the period atmosphere.

Despite its relatively short Broadway run of nine months, *She Loves Me* lives on in memory and in revival as a brilliant exercise in style and musical theater technique in which song, story, and staging formed a beautifully symmetrical whole. Unfortunately, it was produced at a time when the Broadway musical was at its most extravagant and noisy, and the show's intimate scale proved unenticing to theatergoers. Its cast recording included the entire score, on two LPs—a rare luxury for an original cast album. The song "Ice Cream," a delightful soliloquy of romantic discovery designed for the heroine, provided Barbara Cook with another coloratura monologue which compares in spirit if not in execution to her "Glitter and Be Gay" in *Candide*. As she writes another letter to her anonymous "Dear Friend,"

she discovers a growing affection for her former adversary without realizing that he is her unknown correspondent.

FUNNY GIRL 3/26/64, Winter Garden Theatre; 1,348 performances. Music, Jule Styne; lyrics, Bob Merrill; book, Isobel Lennart; orchestrations, Ralph Burns; producer, Ray Stark; directors, Garson Kanin & Jerome Robbins; choreographer, Carol Haney; musical director, Milton Rosenstock. ★ Barbra Streisand, Sydney Chaplin, Kay Medford, Danny Meehan, Jean Stapleton.
People—**Barbra Streisand** Conductor, Milton Rosenstock. Capitol SVAS-2059, mx SVAS1-2059; recorded 3/29/64.

In 1962 Mary Martin obtained a copy of Isobel Lennart's unproduced screenplay based on the early career of Fanny Brice, the celebrated star of vaudeville, musical comedy, and radio. Seeing the role as a complete change of pace from her most recent assignment in *The Sound of Music*, Martin grew excited at the prospect of turning the film script into a Broadway musical. Upon investigation, she learned that the property was owned by Hollywood producer Ray Stark, who was married to Brice's daughter, Frances. Stark was immediately challenged by the idea of presenting his first stage musical. He formed an alliance with David Merrick to develop a production to star Martin and to be directed by Vincent J. Donehue, with music and lyrics by the *Gypsy* team, Jule

Sydney Chaplin, Barbra Streisand, Bob Merrill, and Jule Styne in rehearsal for *Funny Girl*.

Styne and Stephen Sondheim. Shortly after the planning sessions began, Martin lost interest and defected, Jerome Robbins supplanted Donehue as director, and Sondheim was replaced by Bob Merrill. Among the many actresses considered for the lead were Anne Bancroft, Eydie Gorme, Kaye Ballard, and Carol Burnett, all supremely talented performers but lacking the characteristics that would suggest Brice's special combination of broad Jewish comedienne and sophisticated torch singer. Throughout, Styne championed the potential of Barbra Streisand, who had attracted attention as a frumpy secretary in the 1962 musical *I Can Get It for You Wholesale* and as a distinctive club singer. Despite her inexperience as a stage actress, Streisand convinced the members of the production team that she was uniquely suited for the role. As it edged toward rehearsals, the musical underwent a series of title changes from *My Man*, after Brice's signature song, to *A Very Special Person*, and finally to *Funny Girl*.

For a show that eventually became a hit, *Funny Girl* endured an amazingly stormy development. Merrick resigned as co-producer, leaving the neophyte Stark at the helm. Early in the rehearsal period, Robbins left and was replaced by Bob Fosse and then by Garson Kanin (who retained directorial credit in the show's ads), before returning for last minute retouches prior to the Broadway premiere. In search of the proper musical style, Styne and Merrill wrote fifty-six songs, only fifteen of which remained in the final score. Of these, the soaring ballad "People" was nearly cut during rehearsals at Kanin's insistence. Styne's and Merrill's faith in the piece, along with Streisand's hit single record released during tryouts, kept it in the show. Sung by Fanny after her triumph as a Ziegfeld star midway in the first act, the song was proclaimed the most show-stopping Broadway ballad since Rodgers and Hammerstein's "Some Enchanted Evening."

Lacking the style and dramatic integrity of its older cousin *Gypsy*, *Funny Girl* is a fairly predictable show business rise-fall-and-rise saga, tracing Brice's professional success as a performer and her personal heartache as the wife of dashing but doomed gambler Nicky Arnstein. Lennart's script never transforms the ugly duckling into a glamorous bird of paradise; instead, it focuses on Fanny's triumph over her shortcomings in an era when stage success was equated with physical beauty. The true distinctions of the musical rested in its brassy, propulsive score and its impeccable cast, featuring the comic Kay Medford, the handsome Sydney Chaplin, and the extraordinary Barbra Streisand.

HELLO, DOLLY! 1/16/64, St. James Theatre; 2,844 performances. Music & lyrics, Jerry Herman; book, Michael Stewart; orchestrations, Philip J. Lang; producer, David Merrick; Director-choreographer, Gower Champion; musical director, Shepard Coleman. ★ Carol Channing, David Burns, Charles Nelson Reilly, Eileen Brennan, Sondra Lee, Jerry Dodge, Alice Playten.
Hello, Dolly!—**Carol Channing and Company** Conductor, Shepard Coleman. RCA LSOD-1087, mx RPRS-0017; recorded 1/19/64.

The commercial Broadway musical comedy reached its zenith in the popular *Hello, Dolly!*, which confirmed composer Jerry Herman's status as a latter-day Irving Berlin. The impetus for the show came from David Merrick, who envisioned a musical version of Thornton Wilder's play *The Matchmaker* as the perfect vehicle for Ethel Merman to follow her triumph in *Gypsy*. In fact, he asked Herman to create the score specifically with her in mind. Merman, however, wanted a break from a nonstop series of long runs and declined the part. Merrick then directed Herman and librettist Michael Stewart to tailor the adaptation, called *Dolly: A Damned Exasperating Woman*, for the talents of Carol Channing, who had been without a bona fide Broadway hit since 1948's *Gentlemen Prefer Blondes*.

When a lukewarm reception greeted the musical's 1963 world premiere in Detroit, Merrick seriously considered closing it on the road and dismissing the experience as a total loss. But with skillful overhauling by Herman, Stewart, and director-choreographer Gower Champion, and with help from songwriters Charles Strouse and Lee Adams, who conceptualized the first act finale, "Before the Parade Passes By," and

Dolly's triumphant return to Harmonia Gardens.

Bob Merrill, author of the second act opener, "Elegance," the show solved its seemingly insoluble problems and opened on Broadway to general hat-tossing by critics and audiences alike.

A year after the New York premiere, Channing left to head a successful national tour. Her successors included Ginger Rogers, Betty Grable, Pearl Bailey (in an all-black version), Martha Raye, Phyllis Diller, and finally Ethel Merman. For the Merman edition, the songs "Love Look in My Window" and "World Take Me Back," from Herman's first draft of the score, were reinstated. An acclaimed London and international company was headed by Mary Martin. Boosted by a hit record of the title song by Louis Armstrong, *Hello, Dolly!* remained a Broadway fixture for over seven years.

Michael Stewart's libretto focuses on the resourceful widow Dolly Gallagher Levi and her elaborate machinations to ensnare curmudgeonly shopkeeper Horace Vandergelder, a Yonkers "half-millionaire." On the road to matrimony, Dolly encourages romances between Vandergelder's two clerks and two Manhattan milliners and also engineers the elopement of Vandergelder's whining niece, Ermengarde, with her juvenile suitor. Oliver Smith's settings framed the farce in high style, depicting turn-of-the-century New York in flats splashed with vivid primary colors and backdrops resembling amber-hued stereopticon slides. The celebrated title song occurs early in act 2 and conveys Dolly's joyous return to the Harmonia Gardens, a favorite haunt during the days of her first marriage. As staged by Gower Champion, the number began with Dolly's elegant descent down the red-carpeted, balustraded stairs of the restaurant and concluded with the company wrapped around the orchestra on a runway surrounded by a glowing row of footlights. To more than one observer, the effect recalled the musical theater of another era. In the words of New York Herald Tribune critic Walter Kerr, the song's effect was one of the "most exhilaratingly straight-forward, head-on, old-fashioned, rabble-rousing numbers since Harrigan and Hart rolled down the curtain."

FIDDLER ON THE ROOF 9/22/64, Imperial Theatre; 3,242 performances. Music, Jerry Bock; lyrics, Sheldon Harnick; book, Joseph Stein; orchestrations, Don Walker; producer, Harold Prince; director-choreographer, Jerome Robbins; musical director, Milton Greene. ★ Zero Mostel, Maria Karnilova, Beatrice Arthur, Austin Pendleton, Joanna Merlin, Bert Convy, Julia Migenes. *Sunrise, Sunset*—**Zero Mostel, Maria Karnilova, and Company** Conductor, Milton Greene. RCA Victor LSO-1093, mx RPRS-6682; recorded 9/27/64.

In many ways *Fiddler on the Roof* represented the end of an era, one last glorious flowering before the American musical theater entered an artistic interregnum in search of new approaches and musical styles. The show marked Zero Mostel's final musical role and Jerome Robbins's last effort to date as a Broadway director-choreographer before devoting himself entirely to the ballet world.

Fiddler came about in 1960 simply because Jerry Bock, Sheldon Harnick, and librettist Joseph Stein wanted to write a show together. After considering several works by the famous Yiddish writer Sholem Aleichem, they decided on his stories about Tevye, a philosophical Jewish peasant living in turn-of-the-century Russia. Seeking to add universality to the adaptation, Stein hit upon the theme of the collapse of traditions from generation to generation, as illustrated by the old values of Tevye and his wife, Golde, in conflict with the new beliefs of their five daughters. Stein's metaphor of a fiddler on the roof, trying to maintain his balance while he plays, is used to suggest both tradition and its mutability. The image itself is derived from Marc Chagall's painting, "The Green Violinist."

Fiddler's atypicality made the search for a producer difficult. Following countless backers' auditions, Bock, Harnick, and Stein persuaded Harold Prince to sponsor what promised to be a risky venture. A number of actors were considered to play Tevye, including Danny Kaye, Howard Da Silva, Tom Bosley, Alan King, and Danny Thomas. After each proved either unavailable or unsuitable, the part went to Zero Mostel, who turned it into one of the musical theater's few great male roles. The show endured a troubled tryout tour, with the requisite changes including the insertion

In *Fiddler on the Roof*'s final scene, Tevye (Zero Mostel) and Golde (Maria Karnilova) lead their fellow Anatevkans to a new homeland.

of "Do You Love Me?", a comic duet for Tevye and Golde. Although the out-of-town review in *Variety* predicted "only a moderate Broadway success," the New York premiere received almost unanimous critical approval. Besides its seven-year Broadway run, the show has enjoyed comparable successes in London, Paris, Tokyo, Tel Aviv, Johannesburg, Vienna, and Mexico City.

Fiddler's international popularity is due in no small part to the uncompromising excellence of Bock and Harnick's score. None of the songs was intended to be a hit in the Tin Pan Alley mold, although hits are what several of the songs became. The ensemble numbers "Tradition" and "To Life," joyous celebrations of living life to its fullest, manage to suggest period and locale while keeping to an accessible musical mode. "If I Were a Rich Man," with Harnick's delightful phrases of pseudo-Yiddish doggerel, is a superb dramatic monologue. Easily the show's most poignant musical moment is the bittersweet "Sunrise, Sunset," which accompanies the marriage ceremony of Tevye's oldest daughter, Tzeitel. Its minor-key melody and its lyric sentiment of "one season following another, laden with happiness and tears" provide an appropriate coda for the American musical theater's formative years.

★ SINGERS

EDITH "EDIE" ADAMS (Edith Adams Enke; b.1927, Kingston PA) spent five years at the Juilliard School of Music preparing to become a teacher, but then a chance to be a contestant on Arthur Godfrey's "Talent Scouts" radio series catapulted her into the world of show business. Subsequent appearances and club dates led to her first Broadway assignment as Eileen in WONDERFUL TOWN (1953), which won her two Donaldson Awards. Three years later she brought the cartoon character Daisy Mae to life in the musical comedy *Li'l Abner* (1956). She is perhaps best remembered for her TV performances as a foil for her late husband, comedian Ernie Kovacs, and as spokesperson for Muriel cigars.

ANNA MARIA ALBERGHETTI (b.1937, Pesaro, Italy) grew up in a musical household. Her father, a cellist and baritone, sang with the La Scala company and was concertmaster of the Rome Opera orchestra; her mother was a pianist with the Scuola Reggia Musicale on the island of Rhodes. When World War II ended, Anna Maria embarked on a continental recital tour which resulted in her American concert debut at Carnegie Hall. After a nationwide introduction on "The Ed Sullivan Show," she was selected by Gian Carlo Menotti for a leading role in the film version of his opera *The Medium*. Her only Broadway appearance, in CARNIVAL! (1961), won her a Tony Award. In addition to tours of *Carnival!*, she has appeared in summer stock productions of *The Fantasticks, West Side Story,* and *Kismet*.

CRIS (né Christopher) **ALEXANDER** (b.1920, Tulsa OK) studied drama at the Feagin School in Manhattan and had his Broadway initiation as the starry-eyed Chip in ON THE TOWN (1944). In 1953 he played the supporting role of the shy soda jerk in *Wonderful Town,* which reunited him with the *On the Town* creative team. He is equally famous for his skill as a photographer, and in 1970 he combined his two interests by designing the scenic projections for the Richard Rodgers musical *Two by Two*.

JULIE ANDREWS (Julia Elizabeth Wells; b.1935, Walton-on-Thames, England) first won applause as a child prodigy in England, lending her glorious soprano voice to provincial tours and small parts in holiday pantomimes. She made her West End debut at twelve in the revue *Starlight Roof* (1947). Seven years later, she came to Broadway as the cloche-hatted heroine of the British import *The Boy Friend* (1954). In 1956 she achieved the casting coup of the decade when Lerner and Loewe chose her to play Eliza Doolittle in MY FAIR LADY, both on Broadway and in London. She starred as the faithless Guenevere in *Camelot* (1960) before winning new and wider audiences as a film star.

The Astaires

FRED ASTAIRE (Frederick Austerlitz; b.1899, Omaha NE; d.1987, Los Angeles CA) and **ADELE ASTAIRE** (Adele Austerlitz; b.1897, Omaha NE; d.1981, Phoenix AZ) were child performers, trouping in vaudeville in a homemade act billed as "An Electric Toe-dancing Novelty." They entered the legitimate theater as featured dancers in the Ed Wynn musical *Over the Top* (1917). The shows that followed immediately were *Apple Blossoms* (1919), *The Love Letter* (1921), *For Goodness Sake*, and *The Bunch and Judy* (both 1922). Appearances in the New York and London productions of LADY, BE GOOD! (1924) and *Funny Face* (1927) established them as international celebrities. Vincent Youmans's *Smiles* (1930) gave them a rare failure, but their reputations soared to new heights as the stars of THE BAND WAGON (1931). When that show went on its post-Broadway tour, Adele retired from the theater to marry Lord Cavendish. A solo starring role in GAY DIVORCE (1932) gave Fred a final stage success before the start of his remarkable career in musical films.

KENNY (né Kenneth Lawrence) **BAKER** (b.1912, Monrovia CA) enhanced over a dozen movies of the 1930s and 1940s with his high tenor voice and juvenile appeal. He spent his earliest years in the entertainment industry as the featured vocalist on the Jack Benny radio show. In 1943 he made his only Broadway appearance in ONE TOUCH OF VENUS.

KAYE BALLARD (Catherine Gloria Balotta; b.1926, Cleveland OH) decided to become an actress at the age of five, and despite great discouragement from her family and teachers, she entered show business immediately upon graduation from high school in 1944. Soon she was serving apprenticeships as a comedienne with touring burlesque shows and the Spike Jones band, and in 1946 she landed her first theatrical role in a touring edition of the revue *Three to Make Ready*. Following appearances in the national company of *Top Banana* (1952) and the London production of *Touch and Go* (1953), she won acclaim for her performance as a highly unconventional Helen of Troy in THE GOLDEN APPLE (1954). In 1961 she created the equally memorable role of the Incomparable Rosalie in *Carnival*. Her most recent musical comedy outings include appearances as Molly Goldberg in *Molly* (1973) and as herself in the autobiographical revue *Hey, Ma* (1982).

MARION BELL (b. ca. 1924, St. Louis MO) came to national attention in the MGM film *Ziegfeld Follies* (1946), singing a duet from *La Traviata* with tenor James Melton. In 1947 Lerner and Loewe brought her east to play the Scottish heroine of BRIGADOON. After appearing in the pre-Broadway tryout of the musical *Three Wishes for Jamie* (1952), she devoted the rest of her career to recordings and summer stock appearances.

IRVING BERLIN (see SONGWRITERS)

ISABEL (Margaret) **BIGLEY** (b.1928, New York NY) studied at the Juilliard School of Music and the Royal Academy of Dramatic Art. *Oklahoma!* provided her first opportunity to perform on the musical stage, on Broadway as a chorus replacement and later as Laurey (1947) during the show's long engagement in London. She won the Tony and Theatre World awards for her perform-

ance as Sarah Brown in GUYS AND DOLLS (1950). After playing the leading role in Rodgers and Hammerstein's *Me and Juliet* (1953), she retired from the theater to marry and raise a family.

RAY(mond Wallace) **BOLGER** (b.1904,) Dorchester MA; d. 1987, Cheviot Hills CA) introduced his rubber-limbed comic dancing style to Broadway in the musical comedy *The Merry World* (1926). Following a series of featured spots in the shows *Heads Up* (1929) and *Life Begins at 8:40* (1934) he gained stardom in the Rodgers and Hart extravaganzas *On Your Toes* (1936) and *By Jupiter* (1942). As the giddy Oxford undergrad Charley Wykeham of WHERE'S CHARLEY? (1948) he found a role that would ensure theatrical immortality. His final Broadway efforts were the musicals *All American* (1962) and *Come Summer* (1969). He is perhaps best known as the Scarecrow in the 1939 MGM film *The Wizard of Oz*.

SHIRLEY BOOTH (Thelma Booth Ford; b.1907. New York NY), recognized as one of America's finest dramatic actresses, has frequently displayed her talents in the musical theater. George S. Kaufman's Gilbert and Sullivan–inspired satire *Hollywood Pinafore* (1945) marked her first musical comedy appearance. In the early 1950s she portrayed the brash turn-of-the-century heroines of A TREE GROWS IN BROOKLYN (1951) and *By the Beautiful Sea* (1954). Other musicals in which she has appeared are *Juno* (1959) and *Look to the Lilies* (1970). An Oscar winner for her performance in the film version of her stage hit *Come Back Little Sheba*, she won her widest audiences as TV's *Hazel* in the 1960s.

DAVID BROOKS (Henry David Berger; b.1920, Portland OR) first appeared onstage in leading baritone roles with the Philadelphia Opera Company. Club bookings in Manhattan nightspots and a featured part in the film *Bonnie Lassie* (1943) brought him to the attention of producer John S. Wilson, who cast him as the hero of *Bloomer Girl* (1944). Later in the decade Lerner and Loewe selected him as the leading man of BRIGADOON

Shirley Booth, with Nathaniel Frey (left) and Johnny Johnston, recording the cast album for *A Tree Grows in Brooklyn*.

"Don't let it be forgot":
Richard Burton records
Camelot's title song.

(1947). Brooks sang the role of Macheath in the
1953 world premiere of Marc Blitzstein's transla-
tion of *The Threepenny Opera* at Brandeis
University and in 1962 appeared in Irving Berlin's *Mr. President*. He has also produced and
directed in both theater and television.

ANNE (Wiggins) **BROWN** (b.1915, Baltimore
MD) won wide attention as Bess in the original
1935 Broadway mounting of **PORGY AND BESS**, a
role she subsequently performed in the 1942 New
York revival and European tour (1947/48). She
settled in Norway in 1948, where she continued
to be active as a concert and opera singer and a
vocal instructor.

RICHARD BURTON (Richard Jenkins; b.1925,
Pontyrhydfen, South Wales; d.1984, Celigny,
Switzerland), one of the theater's most brilliant
and erratic stars, first attracted notice in London
and Broadway productions of Christopher Fry's
play *The Lady's Not for Burning* (1951). Among
his most notable appearances on the American
dramatic stage were those in *Time Remembered*
(1957), *Hamlet* (1964), and *Equus* (1980). His
only musical theater role is also perhaps his most
famous one, that of King Arthur in **CAMELOT**,
which he performed in both the original 1960
Broadway production and the 1981 revival. He
starred in a number of films, notably *Who's
Afraid of Virginia Woolf?* (1965) and the Zeffirelli
production of *The Taming of the Shrew* (1967).

YUL BRYNNER (Youl Bryner; b.1915, Sakhalin
Island; d.1985, New York NY) began his peregri-
nations in the world of show business as a singer

in Parisian nightclubs and an acrobat in European
circuses. He journeyed to New York in 1941 as a
member of the British ensemble The Chekhov
Players. His first major role on Broadway came
in 1946 opposite Mary Martin in the play with
music *Lute Song*. At Martin's suggestion, Rodgers and Hammerstein cast him as the volatile
Siamese monarch in **THE KING AND I** (1951). After
twenty years as a film star, he made an inauspi-
cious return to the theater in the musical *Home
Sweet Homer* (1975), then redeemed himself ad-
mirably in a successful revival of *The King and I*
(1976) on Broadway, on a marathon national
tour, and in London.

EDDIE CANTOR (Isidore Itzkowitz; b.1892, New
York NY; d.1964, Hollywood CA) left the tenements of Manhattan's Lower East Side to
perform in amateur shows, work as a singing
waiter in Coney Island eateries, and tour in burlesque prior to winning fame a a member of Gus
Edwards's "Kid Kabaret" vaudeville act. His
frenetic, hand-clapping antics were first presented
on Broadway in Florenz Ziegfeld's *Midnight
Frolic* (1916) and the 1917, 1918, and 1919 editions of the *Follies*. A temporary rift with
Ziegfeld led Cantor to star in the Shubert productions *Broadway Brevities* (1920) and *Make It
Snappy* (1922). He reteamed with Ziegfeld in 1923
with the musical comedy *Kid Boots* and starred
in the 1927 season of the *Follies* and the 1928
musical comedy **WHOOPEE**, his biggest stage
success. He devoted the 1930s chiefly to appearances in splashy Goldwyn movies and radio

spots, then returned to Broadway in 1940 to star as the timid, horse-playing hero of *Banjo Eyes*.

DIAHANN CARROLL (Carol Diahann Johnson; b.1935, Bronx NY) had a promising career as a fashion model while still a teenager. An appearance on a TV talent show, "Chance of a Lifetime," opened the door of the show business world and led to her Broadway debut at nineteen as the ingenue of **HOUSE OF FLOWERS** (1954). Her performance enchanted theatergoers, including Richard Rodgers, who cast her as the leading lady of *No Strings* (1962). Since her Tony-winning performance in that show, she has concentrated on work in film, TV, and recordings.

JACK (né John Elmer) **CARSON** (b.1910, Carmen, Manitoba; d.1963, Encino CA) rose to prominence in the 1940s as the comic lead in numerous Warner Bros. film musicals opposite such stars as Dennis Morgan, Janis Paige, and Doris Day. After his early years as a vaudevillian, his chief stage assignment was in the 1952 Broadway revival of **OF THEE I SING**.

CAROL (Elaine) **CHANNING** (b.1921, Seattle WA), one of the musical theater's foremost comediennes, attained stardom with her first leading role as Lorelei Lee in **GENTLEMEN PREFER BLONDES** (1949). Previously she was Eve Arden's understudy in Cole Porter's *Let's Face It* (1941) and a cast member of the Charles Gaynor revue *Lend an Ear* (1948). In 1954 she succeeded Rosalind Russell in *Wonderful Town*, both in New York and on tour. After personal successes in the short-lived *The Vamp* (1955) and *Show Girl* (1960), she won a Tony for **HELLO, DOLLY!** (1964). In 1974 she returned to the musical theater and Broadway in *Lorelei*, a reworking of *Gentlemen Prefer Blondes*. Most recently she has headlined in national tours of the Jerry Herman revue *Jerry's Girls* (1983) and the comedy *Legends* (1986).

SYDNEY CHAPLIN (b.1926, Los Angeles CA), the son of actors Charlie Chaplin and Lita Gray Chaplin, carried on the family tradition by becoming a co-producer and a performer at Hollywood's Circle Theatre (1947–51). He made his Broadway bow as Judy Holliday's love interest in **BELLS ARE RINGING** (1956) and later starred in two other Jule Styne musicals, *Subways Are for Sleeping* (1961) and *Funny Girl* (1964).

GEORGE M. COHAN (see SONGWRITERS)

BARBARA (Nell) **COOK** (b.1927, Atlanta GA) started singing as a teenager on hometown radio stations. She came to New York in 1948, and after gaining experience in revues at Camp Tamiment in the Poconos and at Manhattan's Blue Angel nightclub, she won her first Broadway role in the charming but ill-fated E. Y. Harburg–Sammy Fain musical *Flahooley* (1951). An engaging performance as Carrie in a City Center

Barbara Cook

revival of *Carousel* launched her on a career as a leading Broadway ingenue. Among her most memorable musicals are *Plain and Fancy* (1955), **CANDIDE** (1956), *The Music Man* (1957) (for which she won a Tony), *The Gay Life* (1961), **SHE LOVES ME** (1963), and *The Grass Harp* (1971). In the 1970s she developed a highly successful club and concert act, then returned to Broadway in 1987, after a nearly twenty-year absence, with her "concert for the theater," a one-woman show that recalled the highlights in her career.

ROBERT COOTE (b.1909, London, England) embarked on a theatrical career in the 1930s with a series of provincial and international tours. In 1934 he performed with an Australian musical comedy stock company, appearing in their production of *Anything Goes*. He debuted on Broadway in Peter Ustinov's comedy *The Love of Four Colonels* (1953). He created the roles of Colonel Pickering in **MY FAIR LADY** (1956) and Pellinore in *Camelot* (1960), returning to the former in the 1976 twentieth anniversary Broadway revival.

EUGENE COWLES (b.1860, Stanstead, Quebec; d.1948, Boston MA) started singing professionally in church choirs in Chicago. In 1898 he joined the prestigious troupe The Bostonians and played leading basso roles in their productions of the operettas *Robin Hood* (1891) and *Prince Ananias* (1894). With the Alice Neilsen Company, he performed as Sandor the gypsy in THE FORTUNE TELLER (1898). Among the other operettas in which he appeared are *Cyrano de Bergerac* (1899), *Babette* (1903), and *The Rose of Algeria* (1909).

JOSEPH COYNE (b.1867, New York NY; d.1941, London, England) appeared at sixteen at New York's Niblo's Gardens in the Kiralfy Brothers' extravaganza *Excelsior*. After a brief stint in vaudeville as half of the team Evans and Coyne, he traveled to London to premiere as Prince Danilo in *The Merry Widow* (1907). Thereafter, his greatest theatrical triumphs occurred in British productions of *The Quaker Girl* (1910) and No! No! NANETTE! (1925).

HOWARD DA SILVA (Howard Silverblatt; b.1909, Cleveland OH; d.1985, Ossining NY) was one of the American theater's most versatile character actors, equally at home with musical and non-musical roles. As a member of the WPA Federal Theater Project, he played Larry Foreman in the original production of THE CRADLE WILL ROCK (1937) and, over a quarter of a century later, directed its celebrated off-Broadway revival in 1964. He is best recalled for creating three roles: the menacing Jud Fry in *Oklahoma!* (1943), the gruff ward heeler Ben Marino in FIORELLO! (1959), and a singing, dancing Ben Franklin in *1776* (1969). Da Silva also co-authored the libretto for the 1965 comedy with music *The Zulu and the Zayda*.

EDITH DAY (b.1896, Minneapolis MN; d.1971, London, England) climbed rapidly to fame as the endearing Irish-American heroine of IRENE (1919). She went on to star in the Broadway casts of Victor Herbert's *Orange Blossoms* (1922) and Vincent Youmans's *Wildflower* (1923). In 1925 she took up permanent residence in London, appearing in West End productions of such American musicals as ROSE-MARIE (1925), *The Desert Song* (1927), *Show Boat* (1928), *Rio Rita* (1930), and *Sunny River* (1943). Her final role was in the London cast of Noel Coward's *Sail Away* (1962).

ALFRED DRAKE (Alfredo Capurro; b.1914, New York NY), one of the most distinguished actors in the musical theater, made his Broadway debut in the operetta *White Horse Inn* (1936) as a member of the chorus and as understudy to its star, William Gaxton. Featured roles in *Babes in Arms* (1937), *The Straw Hat Revue* (1939), *One for the Money* (1939), and *Two for the Show* (1940) brought him to the attention of Rodgers and Hammerstein, who raised him to leading man status as Curly in OKLAHOMA! (1943). He starred in *Sing Out, Sweet Land!* (1944), *Beggar's Holiday* (1946), and a revival of *The Cradle Will Rock* (1947) before his next great success in KISS ME, KATE (1948). In 1953 he won his only Tony Award to date as the wily beggar Hajj in *Kismet*.

Other musicals in which he has appeared include *Kean* (1961), *Gigi* (1973), and the pre-Broadway tryout of Vernon Duke's *Zenda* (1963). He is also an accomplished dramatic actor, librettist, and director.

(Robert) **TODD DUNCAN** (b. 1903, Danville KY) left his post as head of the Music Department at Howard University in Washington, D.C., to be featured as Porgy in the Broadway premiere of PORGY AND BESS (1935). In 1942 he headed the cast of the opera's New York revival and its 1947/48 European tour. Also in the 1940s, he played important roles in *Cabin in the Sky* (1940) and *Lost in the Stars* (1949). Today, he pursues his original vocation as an instructor of vocal technique.

RITA GARDNER (b. 19??, Brooklyn NY) is best remembered for creating the part of Luisa in THE FANTASTICKS (1960). On Broadway, she was featured in ingenue roles in the musicals *A Family Affair* (1962) and *Ben Franklin in Paris* (1964). She was reunited with fellow *Fantasticks* graduate Jerry Orbach in the off-Broadway revival of *The Cradle Will Rock* (1964). In 1987 she developed and performed a well-received one-woman show called *Say It with Music*.

ADOLPH GREEN (see SONGWRITERS)

DICK (né Richard) **GAUTIER** (b.1939, Los Angeles CA) first made his mark as a comedian in numerous West Coast clubs. He has played dozens of parts in dozens of TV series, most notably Hymie the Robot in *Get Smart*, and in feature films. His only Broadway musical role was as the hip-swiveling title character of BYE BYE BIRDIE (1960).

BINNIE HALE (Beatrice Mary Hale-Monro; b.1899, Liverpool, England) debuted on the London stage in *Follow the Crowd* (1916), an adaptation of Irving Berlin's 1915 Broadway musical *Stop! Look! Listen!* In the era between the wars, she became one of Britain's most popular performers, starring in West End productions of Rudolf Friml's *Katinka* (1923), Vincent Youmans's No! No! NANETTE! (1925), and Jerome Kern's *Sally* (1926).

REX (né Reginald Carey) **HARRISON** (b.1908, Huyton, England) acted in a number of London stage comedies and dramas before his first Broadway appearance in the short-lived *Sweet Aloes* (1936). In the 1940s and early 1950s he maintained a productive theater and film career on both continents, appearing onstage in *No Time for Comedy* (1940) and *Bell, Book, and Candle* (1951), on screen in *Blithe Spirit* (1945) and *Anna and the King of Siam* (1949). His effortlessly urbane persona was best served in the role of Henry Higgins in MY FAIR LADY (1956), his only appearance to date in a stage musical. His appearance in its 1964 film version won him an Oscar for best actor.

ROSE HIGNELL (b.1896, Bristol, England) was first seen professionally in the chorus of the D'Oyly Carte Opera Company. She played the role of Polly Peachum in the long-running 1923 London revival of *The Beggar's Opera* and then performed in a number of West End operettas, including *Lilac Time* (1922), *Bitter Sweet* (1929), and *Pacific 1860* (1946). In 1925 she costarred with Harry Welchman in an acclaimed provincial tour of THE STUDENT PRINCE.

RUBY HILL (b. 1922, Danville VA) began her career as a singer, fronting the Noble Sissle band in 1939. She starred on Broadway in the title role of ST. LOUIS WOMAN (1946) and appeared the same season in the comedy *Anna Lucasta*. She has also played in films and was active throughout the 1970s as a club entertainer.

JUDY HOLLIDAY (Judith Tuvim; b. 1921, New York NY; d. 1965, New York NY) experienced her first brush with show business when she landed a job as switchboard operator at Orson Welles's Mercury Theatre. She soon moved onstage as part of a joyously daffy nightclub act called The Revuers, which teamed her with Betty Comden and Adolph Green. Small but important roles led to her big break as replacement for the ailing Jean Arthur during the tryout tour of the comedy *Born Yesterday* (1947). She later starred in the film version, which won her an Oscar. Her old friends Comden and Green gave her a chance at her first musical comedy in BELLS ARE RINGING (1956), and she proved more than equal to the challenge, winning the Tony for best actress. Her final Broadway appearance was in the musical *Hot Spot* (1963).

WALTER HUSTON (Walter Houghston; b. 1884, Toronto, Ontario; d. 1950, Beverly Hills CA) was trained as an architectural engineer but found his true metier in the theatre, bringing his vigorous acting skills to such plays as *Desire Under the Elms* (1924) and *Dodsworth* (1934). Although he sang and danced in vaudeville in the 1910s, his only Broadway musical role was as Pieter Stuyvesant in KNICKERBOCKER HOLIDAY (1938). He also acted in Hollywood films, winning an Oscar in 1948 for his performance in *The Treasure of the Sierra Madre,* under the direction of his son John Huston.

AL JOLSON (Asa Yoelson; b. 1886, Srednike, Lithuania; d. 1950, San Francisco CA), one of the most electrifying entertainers of the century, ran away from his childhood home in Washington, D.C., to enter show business. He toured in various on and offstage capacities with small-time vaudeville and burlesque troupes, eventually winning fame with his blackface performances in Lew Dockstader's Minstrels. With the musical *La Belle Paree* (1911), he began a thirteen-year association with the Shuberts that also included the shows *Vera Violetta* (1911), *The Whirl of Society* (1912), THE HONEYMOON EXPRESS (1913), *Dancing Around* (1914), *Robinson Crusoe, Jr.* (1916), *Sinbad* (1918), *Bombo* (1921), and *Big Boy* (1925). His performance in the first feature-length talking picture, *The Jazz Singer* (1927), resulted in a brilliant, if brief, career in films. Jolson returned to Broadway in the European import *Wonder Bar* (1931) and gave his final musical theater appearance in *Hold On to Your Hats* (1940). His career also encompassed achievements on radio and recordings.

MARIA KARNILOVA (Maria Karnilovich Dovgolenko; b.1920, Hartford CT) danced as a member of the Metropolitan Opera Children's Ballet and, as a young adult, maintained parallel careers as a soloist with various ballet companies and in the ensembles of such musicals as *Stars in Your Eyes* (1939), *Call Me Mister* (1946), *Miss Liberty* (1949), and *Two's Company* (1952). She emerged as a fine comic actress in *Gypsy* (1959)

Judy Holliday sparkles as Ella in
Bells Are Ringing.

and won a Tony Award for her Golde in FIDDLER ON THE ROOF (1964). Other musicals in which she has appeared are *Zorba* (1968), *Gigi* (1973), and *Bring Back Birdie* (1981).

DANNY KAYE (David Daniel Kominsky; b.1913, Brooklyn NY; d.1987, Los Angeles CA) made his Broadway debut with Imogene Coca, Alfred Drake, and a host of other young performers in *The Straw Hat Revue* (1939). Also associated with the show was Sylvia Fine, who became his wife and was instrumental in devising the rapid-fire patter and songs that established him as a major club entertainer. He scored a phenomenal hit in a supporting role in LADY IN THE DARK (1941) and the next season was solo-starred in the Cole Porter wartime musical *Let's Face It!* (1941). In the 1940s and 1950s, his gawky yet graceful comedy talents were confined primarily to films, most notably 1953's *Hans Christian Andersen*, and in the early 1960s he headlined a successful TV series. He returned to the Broadway musical medium in *Two by Two* (1970) after an absence of nearly thirty years.

STUBBY KAYE (b. 1918, New York NY) broke into show business as a contestant on a 1939 radio broadcast of the "Major Bowes Amateur Hour." During the 1940s he sang in stage shows at movie theaters, toured with the USO, and acted as master of ceremonies for the Charlie Barnet and Freddy Martin bands. GUYS AND DOLLS (1950) gave him his first Broadway outing, and has since played a variety of comedy roles in musicals, including *Li'l Abner* (1956), *Good News* (1974 revival), and *Grind* (1985).

LARRY (né Frederick Lawrence) **KERT** (b. 1930, Los Angeles CA) started out as a singer in the choruses of *Tickets, Please* (1952), *John Murray Anderson's Almanac* (1953), and *Ziegfeld Follies* (1956) before winning the leading role of Tony in WEST SIDE STORY (1957). After a brief run in *A Family Affair* (1962) opposite Rita Gardner, he embarked on a new career as replacement for the original leading men in the Broadway productions of *I Can Get It for You Wholesale* (1962), *Cabaret* (1966), and *Company* (1970). His other musicals include *Breakfast at Tiffany's* (1966), *La Strada* (1970), and *Rags* (1986).

BERT LAHR (Bertram Lahrheim; b. 1895, New York NY; d. 1967, New York NY), the screen's beloved Cowardly Lion, went on the stage in 1910 as part of a kiddie vaudeville act. He began as a sentimental balladeer but soon cultivated a skill for the popular low-Dutch comedy. His Broadway debut in *Harry Delmar's Revels* (1927) went almost unnoticed, but one season later he was proclaimed "a new comedy king" as the punch-drunk prize fighter in the musical *Hold Everything!* (1928). His sad-sack demeanor and comic antics enlivened many revues and musicals, including *Flying High* (1930), *Hot-Cha!*

Danny Kaye

(1932), *Life Begins at 8:40* (1934), DUBARRY WAS A LADY (1939), *Seven Lively Arts* (1944), *Two On the Aisle* (1951), and *The Girls Against the Boys* (1959). He revealed gifts as a dramatic actor in the off-Broadway production of *Waiting for Godot* (1956). His final Broadway appearance in the musical *Foxy* (1964) earned him a Tony.

CAROL LAWRENCE (Carol Laraia; b. 1935, Melrose Park IL) debuted as one of the bright young people of Leonard Sillman's *New Faces of 1952*. Small roles in *Shangri-La* and *Ziegfeld Follies* (both 1956) prefaced her rise to leading lady in WEST SIDE STORY (1957). Star billing followed in the musicals *Saratoga* (1959) and *Subways Are for Sleeping* (1961). In 1966 she made her last Broadway appearance to date as Mary Martin's replacement in *I Do! I Do!*

GERTRUDE LAWRENCE (Gertrud Alexandra Dagmar Klasen; b. 1898, London, England; d. 1952, New York NY) started performing for paying audiences as a child, appearing in the famous Italia Conti troupe with, among others, Noel Coward. A professional dancer at twelve, she graduated to featured and then starring roles in a series of bright West End revues produced by Andre Charlot. Her now legendary rendition of "Limehouse Blues" in the American premiere of

Charlot's Revue (1924) led to her first solo starring roles in two musicals by the Gershwins, OH, KAY! (1926) and *Treasure Girl* (1928). Aside from appearances in Lew Leslie's *The International Revue* (1930) and the London musical *Nymph Errant* (1933), she devoted the 1930s to dramatic vehicles. She returned to the musical theater in LADY IN THE DARK (1941) and achieved theatrical immortality in THE KING AND I (1951).

ELLA LOGAN (b. 1913, Glasgow, Scotland; d. 1969, Burlingame CA), known as the diminutive "vocal volcano," was singing for her supper in Glasgow music halls before the age of four. She came to the United States in 1932 and appeared in the Broadway revues *Calling All Stars* (1934), *George White's Scandals* (1939), *Sons O' Fun* (1941) and *Show Time* (1942). She became a star as the feisty heroine of FINIAN'S RAINBOW (1947). Her final stage effort was in the pre-Broadway tryout of the musical *Kelly* (1965). She also sang in a number of 1930s films and in leading nightclubs across the country.

MARY (Virginia) **MARTIN** (b. 1913, Weatherford TX) abandoned a floundering movie career and soared to stardom with her first Broadway role in Cole Porter's LEAVE IT TO ME! (1938). Although her next two musicals, *Nice Goin'* (1938) and *Dancing in the Streets* (1942), folded in tryout engagements, she won acclaim in the 1940s for a rapid succession of varied starring roles in ONE TOUCH OF VENUS (1943), *Lute Song* (1946), Noel Coward's London operetta *Pacific 1860* (1946), the national touring company of *Annie Get Your Gun* (1947), and the landmark SOUTH PACIFIC (1949). In addition to memorable television teamings with Ethel Merman and Noel Coward in the

1950s, she further revealed her versatility in the musicals PETER PAN (1954) and THE SOUND OF MUSIC (1959) and the non-musical plays *Kind Sir* (1953) and *The Skin of Our Teeth* (1955). The 1963 musical *Jennie* proved a misstep, but appearances as Dolly Levi in the 1965 international company of *Hello, Dolly!* and as half the cast (opposite Robert Preston) of *I Do! I Do!* (1966) confirmed her status as "first lady of the American musical theater."

ETHEL MERMAN (Ethel Agnes Zimmerman; b. 1908, Astoria NY; d. 1984, New York NY), the clarion-voiced "queen of musicals," first became Broadway's darling on the opening night of GIRL CRAZY (1930). In the decade and a half that followed, she established herself as a major box office attraction in the shows *George White's Scandals* (1931), *Take a Chance* (1932), ANYTHING GOES (1934), *Red, Hot and Blue!* (1936), *Stars in Your Eyes* (1939), DUBARRY WAS A LADY (1939), *Panama Hattie* (1940), and *Something for the Boys* (1943). ANNIE GET YOUR GUN (1946) gave her ample opportunity to reveal even greater versatility as both singer and actress. She reverted to type as the raucous leading ladies of *Call Me Madam* (1950) and *Happy Hunting* (1956), but her performance in GYPSY (1959) presented her at the pinnacle of her many talents. She made her final Broadway appearance in 1970 as the last actress to star in the original run of *Hello, Dolly!*

HELEN MORGAN (b. 1900, Danville IL; d. 1941, Chicago IL), primarily a club artist famed for her plaintive torch singing, appeared in a number of Broadway musicals. She got her start in the chorus of Jerome Kern's *Sally* (1920) and achieved stardom in two other Kern musicals, SHOW BOAT

Larry Kert and Carol Lawrence perform "Tonight" for the *West Side Story* cast recording.

Helen Morgan

(1927) and *Sweet Adeline* (1929), both of which provided roles that allowed her to transmute her melancholy vocal persona into striking dramatic characterizations. Her other stage appearances include *George White's Scandals* (1925), *Americana* (1926), and the *Ziegfeld Follies* (1931).

ROBERT MORSE (b. 1931, Newton MA) cavorted in countless amateur and stock theatricals prior to his first Broadway undertaking in Thornton Wilder's comedy *The Matchmaker* (1953). The 1958 "comedy about a musical," *Say, Darling,* found him impersonating a fictional Harold Prince, and *Take Me Along* (1959) cast him as the quintessential small town teenager. The long-running **HOW TO SUCCEED IN BUSINESS WITHOUT REALLY TRYING** (1962) brought him stardom and a Tony. After a detour into the world of films and television, he came back to the musical stage in 1972 in the Jule Styne–Bob Merrill show *Sugar.* His most recent Broadway appearance was in the musical *So Long, 174th Street* (1976)

ZERO (né Samuel Joel) **MOSTEL** (b. 1915, Brooklyn NY; d. 1977, New York NY) planned a

future as a painter, but his comic routines at amateur affairs led to a successful booking as a stand-up comedian at the famous nightspot Café Society Downtown. After turns in the revues *Keep 'Em Laughing* (1942) and *Concert Varieties* (1945), he graduated to his first musical comedy role as the villainous Peachum in the Ellington-Latouche *Beggar's Holiday* (1946). Because his political convictions were at odds with the McCarthy-era witch hunts, his career took a nosedive in the early 1950s, but he re-emerged as a fine character actor in the avant-garde plays *Ulysses in Nighttown* (1958) and *Rhinoceros* (1961). He returned to musicals in the 1960s, creating the vastly different roles of Pseudolus in **A FUNNY THING HAPPENED ON THE WAY TO THE FORUM** (1962) and Tevye in **FIDDLER ON THE ROOF** (1964).

WYNN MURRAY (b. 1919, Carbondale PA; d. 1957, Fort Meade MD) heeded the siren call of the theater as a youngster, fleeing her studies at Scranton Conservatory of Music to assume the comic lead in **BABES IN ARMS** (1937). She appeared in eight other Broadway shows, including *The Boys from Syracuse* (1938) and *Hellzapoppin'* (1938). On a USO tour after World War II, she met and married an army man and retired from show business.

KENNETH NELSON (b. 1930, Rocky Mount SC) first came to Broadway as the juvenile lead of the musical *Seventeen* (1951). Following a stint as Henry Aldrich in the television series "The Aldrich Family," he scored hits in a succession of solid off-Broadway endeavors. Among them were the Jerry Herman revue *Nightcap* (1958), **THE FANTASTICKS** (1960), and a dramatic role in *The Boys in the Band* (1967). In 1970 he starred as the clever Sakini in *Lovely Ladies, Kind Gentlemen,* a short-lived musical version of the play *Teahouse of the August Moon.* More recently he has appeared in several West End musicals, including the 1971 revival of *Show Boat.*

HAROLD NICHOLAS (b. 1928, New York NY), afong with his brother Fayard, was recognized as a child prodigy of acrobatic show dancing. After starting out in vaudeville houses in Philadelphia, by 1932 they were regular attractions in the floor shows at Harlem's Cotton Club. The team first danced on Broadway in the *Ziegfeld Follies of 1936* and had featured spots in *Babes in Arms* (1937). In 1946 Harold sang, danced, and acted the male lead in **ST. LOUIS WOMAN**, and Fayard performed a supporting role. The Nicholas Brothers were frequently seen in films of the 1930s and 1940s, including *Kid Millions* (1933), *Stormy Weather* (1942), and *The Pirate* (1948).

BETTY OAKES (b. 19??, Chicago IL) played the romantic lead in the 1951 Broadway revival of *Where's Charley?* opposite Ray Bolger. The following season her lovely soprano voice was heard to advantage in yet another Broadway revival, the twentieth anniversary production of OF THEE I SING (1952). She succeeded Jo Sullivan during the original Broadway run of *The Most Happy Fella* and more recently has appeared in a number of comedies and dramas on and off Broadway.

DEREK OLDHAM (b. 1892, Accrington, England; d. 1968, Haylin Island, England) was a major figure on the early twentieth-century British lyric stage. His first important role was in the initial West End production of Straus's *The Chocolate Soldier* (1914). In the 1920s and 1930s he performed the leads in the English editions of ROSE MARIE, *The Vagabond King*, and *Naughty Marietta*. After 1946 he concentrated on a career as a lecture-recitalist, with occasional forays into TV and films.

JERRY (né Jerome) **ORBACH** (b. 1935, the Bronx NY) had his earliest theatrical experiences off-Broadway, first as a replacement in the role of Macheath in the long-running revival of *The Threepenny Opera* and then as the original El Gallo in the even longer-running THE FANTASTICKS (1960). He made an impressive Broadway debut as the brooding romantic lead of *Carnival!* (1960) and performed in a series of revivals of classic American musicals, including the off-Broadway revival of *The Cradle Will Rock* (1964) and the Lincoln Center presentations of *Carousel* (1965) and ANNIE GET YOUR GUN (1966). The Bacharach-David-Simon musical *Promises, Promises* (1968) brought him his first Tony Award. His most recent performance was as the beleaguered producer Julian Marsh in David Merrick's spectacular stage version of *42nd Street* (1980).

EZIO (Fortunato) **PINZA** (b. 1892, Rome, Italy; d. 1957, Stamford CT) sang with several Italian opera companies, including three years at La Scala, before making his American debut at the Metropolitan in New York. He remained at the Met for twenty-two seasons (1926–1948), earning laurels in the title roles of *Don Giovanni* and *Boris Godunov*, and as Mephistopheles in *Faust*. In 1949 he left grand opera for the musical theater, rising to matinee idol status as Emile de Becque in SOUTH PACIFIC. His only other Broadway role was that of Cesar in *Fanny* (1954).

ROBERT PRESTON Meservey; b. 1918, Newton Highlands MA; d. 1987, Santa Barbara CA) enjoyed a long career as dramatic actor before he became one of the musical theater's foremost leading men. He began his acting career at sixteen, touring with a West Coast Shakespearean company. He first gained national attention through his efforts in dozens of Paramount films of the 1930s and 1940s. His Broadway debut came in 1951 when he replaced José Ferrer in a revival of the Hecht-MacArthur comedy *Twentieth Century*, but stage stardom eluded him until his Olympian turn as THE MUSIC MAN (1957). Al-

though he never achieved a hit of its caliber again, he went on to appear in other musicals, including *We Take the Town* (1962), *Ben Franklin in Paris* (1964), *I Do! I Do!* (1966), *Mack and Mabel* (1974), and *The Prince of Grand Street* (1979).

JOHN (Emmet) **RAITT** (b. 1917, Santa Ana CA) relinquished a promising future in professional athletics to pursue a singing career. A succession of parts in Edwin Lester's Los Angeles Civic Light Opera productions won him both an MGM contract and the lead in the first national company of *Oklahoma!* While on tour, he was tapped by Rodgers and Hammerstein for the role of Billy Bigelow in the original cast of CAROUSEL (1945). Over the next decade, he starred in *Magdalena* (1948), *Three Wishes for Jamie* (1952), and *Carnival in Flanders* (1953) before landing in another hit, THE PAJAMA GAME (1954). In 1965 he donned the carnival barker's togs once again to star in the acclaimed Lincoln Center revival of *Carousel*. Since his most recent Broadway engagement in the country-western musical *A Joyful Noise* (1966), he has devoted his energies to concerts and summer stock tours.

PAUL ROBESON (b. 1898, Princeton NJ; d. 1976, Philadelphia PA) completed his undergraduate studies at Rutgers and earned a law degree at

Paul Robeson as Joe in *Show Boat*.

Columbia before taking up professional acting in 1921 as a replacement in the Broadway cast of *Shuffle Along*. He first won critical attention for his appearances in two plays by Eugene O'Neill, *All God's Children Got Wings* (1924) and *The Emperor Jones* (1925). His greatest triumph in the musical theater was as Joe in the London company, the 1932 Broadway revival, and the 1936 film version of SHOW BOAT. His subsequent New York stage appearances included a highly acclaimed performance as Shakespeare's *Othello* in 1945. Throughout the 1930s and early 1940s he starred in several notable films, including the classic *King Solomon's Mines*. The latter part of his career was devoted to concert engagements which coincided with ardent political activism.

BILL "BOJANGLES" (né William Luther) **ROBINSON** (b. 1878, Richmond VA; d. 1949, New York NY), the "king of the tap dancers," began hoofing in hometown saloons and went on to become one of vaudeville's highest-paid headliners. BLACKBIRDS OF 1928 brought him to Broadway, and later he appeared in the musicals *Brown Buddies* (1930), *The Hot Mikado* (1939), *All in Fun* (1940), and *Memphis Bound* (1945). He also performed in Hollywood films, most notably as Shirley Temple's dancing partner in *The Littlest Rebel* and *The Little Colonel* (both 1935).

LILLIAN RUSSELL (Helen Louise "Nellie" Leonard; b. 1861, Clinton IA; d. 1922, Pittsburgh PA), the doyenne of the turn-of-the-century lyric stage, got her start in the chorus of the first American production of *H.M.S. Pinafore* (1878). Billed as "The English Ballad Singer," she rose to fame in 1883 as soloist at Tony Pastor's Music Hall. For the next two decades, she presided as the *prima donna assoluta* of such varied fare as *The Grand Duchess* (1889), *Girofle-Girofla* (1891), *An American Beauty* (1896), and six seasons in the satirical revues at Weber and Fields' Music Hall, including TWIRLY-WHIRLY (1902).

ROSALIND RUSSELL (b. 1912, Waterbury CT; d. 1976, Los Angeles CA) had a hiatus of over twenty years between her only two appearances in the musical theater. After a fling as a revue artist in the 1930 edition of *The Garrick Gaieties*, she traveled to the West Coast and became one of the screen's most versatile actresses, moving with ease from comedy (*His Girl Friday*) to drama (*Sister Kenny*). In 1953 she recreated her *My Sister Eileen* film role in its musical stage adaptation, WONDERFUL TOWN, for which she won countless awards. Five years later she preserved the role for posterity in a lively CBS television version. Her most famous non-musical role was that of madcap Auntie Mame in the play and film of the same name.

VIVIENNE (Sonia) **SEGAL** (b. 1897, Philadelphia PA) was plucked from student recitals at the Curtis Institute of Music by Sigmund Romberg, who cast her as the lead in his operetta *The Blue Paradise* (1915) only four days before its New York opening. She went on to become one of Broadway's leading sopranos, starring in the shows *Oh, Lady! Lady!* (1918). *The Yankee Princess* (1922), *The Desert Song* (1926), and *The Three Musketeers* (1928). In the early 1930s, she had a brief vogue as a film actress. Later in the decade she returned to the musical theater as an acid-tongued comedienne in three Rodgers and Hart musicals: *I Married An Angel* (1938), PAL JOEY (1940), and *A Connecticut Yankee* (1943 revival). In 1952 she made a final appearance on Broadway, recreating her original role of the predatory Vera Simpson in a triumphant revival of *Pal Joey*.

PHIL SILVERS (Philip Silver; b. 1911, Brooklyn NY; d. 1985, Los Angeles CA), TV's blustering Sergeant Bilko, broke into show business as a child performer in Gus Edwards's kiddie revues (a beginning he shares with Eddie Cantor). Stand-up comedy turns on burlesque circuits helped him travel eventually to Broadway, where he debuted as one of the principals in the musical comedy *Yokel Boy* (1939). Following appearances in films and World War II, he enjoyed acclaim as the comic leads of the musicals *High Button Shoes* (1947), *Top Banana* (1951), which brought him a Tony award, and DO RE MI (1960). In 1972 he won a second Tony for his performance as Pseudolus in a revival of *A Funny Thing Happened on the Way to the Forum*.

NOBLE SISSLE (see SONGWRITERS)

JOHN STEEL (b. 1896, Montclair NJ; d. 1971, New York NY) first sang on Broadway in a 1918 production of the British operetta *Maid of the Mountains*. His full-throated tenor voice proved a valuable accompaniment to the spectacular tableaux in the 1919 and 1920 editions of the ZIEGFELD FOLLIES. He spent the 1922 and '23 seasons in Irving Berlin's *Music Box Revue*, introducing the standard "Lady of the Evening." After an appearance in the 1927 London musical *Castles in the Air*, he abandoned musical comedy for successful engagements in vaudeville and nightclubs.

BARBRA (Joan) **STREISAND** (b. 1942, Brooklyn NY) rose to fame as an unconventional chanteuse in Manhattan cabarets and on Columbia recordings. She entered the world of the New York theater in a one-performance off-Broadway disaster called *Another Evening With Harry Stoones* (1961). The following year, her performance as the put-upon frump Miss Marmelstein in the Harold Rome musical *I Can Get It for You Wholesale* (1962) endeared her to Broadway audiences and critics. She won the coveted leading role in FUNNY GIRL (1964) over a cadre of other contenders and made it irrevocably her own. Since her appearance onstage as Fanny Brice, she has devoted her considerable talents to films and recordings.

BRIAN (né Harry Joseph) **SULLIVAN** (b. 1919, Oakland CA; d. 1969, Geneva, Switzerland) displayed a remarkable singing talent as a schoolboy. While still a teenager he won major tenor roles with West Cost opera companies, including that of Count Almaviva opposite John Charles Thomas's Figaro in *The Barber of Seville*. Following roles in two undistinguished MGM films, he succeeded Charles Fredericks in the 1946 Broadway revival of *Show Boat* and created the part of Sam Kaplan in STREET SCENE (1947). From 1948 to 1964, he was a leading artist with the Metropolitan Opera Company, performing a variety of Wagnerian roles.

JO (née Elizabeth Josephine) **SULLIVAN** (b. 19??, Mound City IL), a bright light in the American musical theater's spectrum of soprano ingenues, braved the Manhattan footlights for the first time in the experimental *Let's Make an Opera* (1951), but her glowing portrayal of Polly Peachum in the popular off-Broadway revival of *The Threepenny Opera* (1954) established her theatrical credentials. She next appeared as the waiflike heroine of THE MOST HAPPY FELLA (1956), winning critical bouquets and eventually marrying the show's author, Frank Loesser, in 1959. After Loesser's death she resumed her career, singing

Jo Sullivan and Robert Weede in a tender moment at the recording sessions for *The Most Happy Fella*'s cast album.

in clubs across the country and starring in an affectionate Broadway tribute to her late husband called *Perfectly Frank* (1980).

TAMARA (Drasin; b. 1907, Poltava, Russia; d. 1943, Lisbon, Portugal) lent her exotic persona and rich contralto voice to such now-forgotten Broadway musicals as *The New Yorkers* (1927) and *Free For All* (1931) before winning fame as the White Russian heroine of ROBERTA (1933). Although her next musical, *Right This Way* (1938), was a failure, the two songs she introduced were hits: "I'll Be Seeing You" and "I Can Dream, Can't I?" Her final stage appearance was as the female lead of Cole Porter's *Leave It to Me! (1938)*.

GWEN (née Gwyneth Evelyn) **VERDON** (b. 1926, Culver City CA) apprenticed as an assistant to choreographer Jack Cole and danced anonymously in the choruses of *Bonanza Bound* (1947), *Magdalena* (1949), and *Alive and Kicking* (1950). She became an "overnight sensation" and won the first of her four Tony Awards as the saucy Claudine in Cole Porter's *Can-Can* (1953). Two seasons later her witty performance as Lola in DAMN YANKEES (1955) raised her to the status of a musical comedy luminary. Her Chaplinesque agility, cooing vocals, and fine acting skills were put to excellent use in a variety of roles on Broadway, including a musical Anna Christie in *New Girl in Town* (1957), an amateur Cockney sleuth in *Redhead* (1959), and the gamine taxi dancer in *Sweet Charity* (1966). Her most recent musical role was the "jazz-slayer" Roxie Hart in Kander and Ebb's *Chicago* (1975).

NANCY WALKER (Anna Myrtle Swoyer; b. 1921, Philadelphia PA) revealed her comic gifts as a child, touring with her parents in vaudeville act. She scored a hit in her first Broadway outing as the indefatigable Blind Date in the musical *Best Foot Forward* (1941). Following a stint in Hollywood as MGM's resident juvenile comedienne, she returned to the theater as the wacky taxi driver Brunhilde Esterhazy in *On the Town* (1944). Among the subsequent musicals in which she has starred are *Barefoot Boy with Cheek* (1947), *Look, Ma, I'm Dancin'* (1948), *Along Fifth Avenue* (1949), *Phoenix '55* (1955), *Copper and Brass* (1957), and *The Girls against the Boys* (1959). Since co-starring opposite Phil Silvers in DO RE MI (1960), she has confined her energies to TV appearances and directing.

ETHEL WATERS (b. 1896, Chester PA; d. 1977, Chatsworth CA) went from the job of chambermaid to that of singer after winning an amateur talent contest in a Philadelphia cabaret. Throughout the 1910s and early 1920s, she was "Sweet Mama Stringbean," the blues-singing star of the T.O.B.A. vaudeville circuit and recording artist for Black Swan records. Appearances at Manhattan's Plantation Club paved the way for her

Ethel Waters

Broadway debut in *Africana* (1927). In the 1930s she was prominently cast in the revues *Blackbirds of 1930, Rhapsody in Black* (1931), *As Thousands Cheer* 1933), and *At Home Abroad* (1935). Concurrently, she was equally successful as a performer in the lavish Cotton Club floor shows. Her finest musical comedy role was the lead in CABIN IN THE SKY (1940). She appeared to great advantage in several stage dramas, most notably *Member of the Wedding* (1951), and films.

SUSAN (Elizabeth) **WATSON** (b. 1938, Tulsa OK) won her first ovations as a member of the London company of *West Side Story*. Upon her return to the States, she performed in the original one-act workshop version of *The Fantasticks* at Barnard College. Her Broadway debut as the teenage ingenue of BYE BYE BIRDIE (1960) led to important parts as the ingenues in *Carnival!* (1961), *Ben Franklin in Paris* (1964), *A Joyful Noise* (1966), and *Celebration* (1969). In 1971 she played the title role in the all-star Broadway revival of *No, No, Nanette*.

CLIFTON WEBB (Webb Parmelee Hollenbeck; b. 1894, Indianapolis IN; d. 1966, Beverly Hills CA) was launched on a theatrical career by his domineering, stagestruck mother. As an adolescent he demonstrated his precocious versatility by switching briefly to a singing career, earning a contract with the Boston Opera Company. *The Purple Road* (1913) provided his initiation into Broadway musical comedy. Soon he established a reputation as one of the theater's most debonair song and dance men, appearing in the legendary shows *Sunny* (1925), *The Little Show* (1929),

Three's a Crowd (1930), *Flying Colors* (1932), and AS THOUSANDS CHEER (1933). His final musical comedy role was in Cole Porter's *You Never Know* (1938). In the 1940s he revealed an exceptional talent as a farceur and a dramatic actor on stage and in films.

ROBERT WEEDE (b. 1903, Baltimore MD; d. 1972, Walnut Creek CA) attended the Eastman School of Music and appeared in the major opera houses of the world in the title role of *Rigoletto* and as Tonio in *Pagliacci*. He switched to the popular musical theater in 1956 as the ebullient hero of THE MOST HAPPY FELLA. He also played the leads in the Broadway musicals *Milk and Honey* (1961) and *Cry for Us All* (1970).

HARRY WELCHMAN (b. 1886, Barnstaple, England; d. 1966, London, England) played a number of supporting and leading roles in English musicals before his only New York assignment as Rassendyl in Romberg's *Princess Flavia* (1925). Returning to England a year later, he became a major operetta star through his appearances in British productions of THE STUDENT PRINCE, *The Desert Song,* and *The New Moon*. His final West End musical comedy performance was in John Osborne's *The World of Paul Slickey* (1959).

ANNA WHEATON (b. 1896, New York NY; d. 1961, Pasadena CA) made her stage debut at the age of eight in a production of *Peter Pan* with Maude Adams. She sang and danced in several important musical comedies of the 1910s and 1920s, most notably as the soubrette in OH, BOY! (1917). Before her marriage and retirement from the theater in the mid-twenties, she played the featured role of Lucille Early in the pre-Broadway tryout of *No! No! Nanette!* (1925).

DOOLEY WILSON (b. 1894, Tyler TX; d. 1953, Los Angeles CA) earned a reputation as "the best singing drummer of his time" during international tours with his band between 1919 and 1930. He came to the theater in the mid-thirties, joining up with pioneering black stock companies in Chicago and Harlem. He appeared on Broadway in *Cabin in the Sky* (1940) and BLOOMER GIRL (1944). He is best remembered for his performance as Sam and his rendition of "As Time Goes By" in the film *Casablanca* (1942).

BRUCE YARNELL (b. 1938, Los Angeles CA; d. 1973, near Los Angeles CA), whose burgeoning career in musical theater and opera was abruptly halted by a fatal airplane accident, made his earliest professional appearances on the West Coast in various TV dramas and series. In the 1960s, he starred in major New York revivals of three great musicals: ANNIE GET YOUR GUN (1966) and *Oklahoma!* (1969) at Lincoln Center and *Carousel* (1966) at the City Center. At the time of his death, he had become an accomplished operatic baritone, singing leading roles with the San Francisco Opera and companies abroad.

★ SONGWRITERS

LEE ADAMS (b. 1924, Mansfield OH), a struggling young writer out of the Columbia School of Journalism, and **CHARLES STROUSE** (b. 1928, New York NY), a graduate of the Eastman School of Music, first teamed as a songwriting duo in 1950. Together they came up through the ranks, writing special material for the shows at the New York resort Green Mansions and the off-Broadway gambols *Shoestring Revue* (1955) and *The Littlest Revue* (1956) before enjoying their initial Broadway success with the songs for BYE BYE BIRDIE (1960). Subsequent Strouse-Adams scores include *All American* (1962), *Golden Boy* (1964), *It's a Bird, It's a Plane, It's Superman* (1966), *Applause* (1970), *I and Albert* (London, 1972), *A Broadway Musical* (1978), and *Bring Back Birdie* (1981). Among the other lyricists with whom Strouse has collaborated are Martin Charnin (*Annie,* 1977), David Rogers (*Charlie and Algernon*, 1980), Alan Jay Lerner (*Dance a Little Closer*, 1983), and Stephen Schwartz (*Rags,* 1986). In 1985 he wrote both the music and lyrics for the off-Broadway revue *Mayor.*

RICHARD ADLER (b. 1921, New York NY) served as a naval officer and composer of radio and television jingles before forming a songwriting partnership in 1950 with **JERRY ROSS** (Jerold Rosenberg; b. 1926, Bronx NY; d. 1955, New York NY), a former child actor with Manhattan's Yiddish Theater. Their fledgling efforts won the favor of Frank Loesser, who became their mentor and publisher. Their Broadway careers began promisingly with the songs for the revue *John Murray Anderson's Almanac* (1953) and then achieved solid success with the consecutive hits THE PAJAMA GAME (1954) and DAMN YANKEES

(1955). After Ross's death Adler went solo, returning to Broadway with both music and lyrics for *Kwamina* (1961) and *Music Is* (1976), but neither show approached the success of his previous endeavors with Ross.

MAXWELL ANDERSON (b. 1888, Atlantic PA; d. 1959, Stamford CT) worked as a newspaper reporter in San Francisco and New York before winning fame as one of America's finest playwrights. Although best known as the author of such dramas as *Winterset* (1935) and the Pulitzer Prize–winning *Both Your Houses* (1932), he collaborated with Kurt Weill on the musicals KNICKERBOCKER HOLIDAY (1938) and *Lost in the Stars* (1949), as well as the uncompleted *Ulysses Africanus* and *Huckleberry Finn.*

HAROLD ARLEN (Hyman Arluck; b. 1905, Buffalo NY; d. 1986, New York NY), acclaimed as "the songwriters' songwriter" by his peers, entered the theater as a performer, singing in vaudeville and playing piano in the pit band of *George White's Scandals* (1928). In 1929, while briefly engaged as a singer and rehearsal pianist for Vincent Youmans's *Great Day,* he converted a piano vamp into "Get Happy," which Ruth Etting introduced in the *9:15 Revue* (1930). During the 1930s he wrote a string of classic songs for Cotton Club revues, Hollywood film musicals, and the Broadway shows *Life Begins At 8:40* (1934), and *Hooray For What?* (1937). His biggest theatrical hits were BLOOMER GIRL (1944) and *Jamaica* (1957). His other stage musicals, ST. LOUIS WOMAN (1946), HOUSE OF FLOWERS (1954), and *Saratoga* (1959) contain exquisite scores in search of workable libretti.

IRVING BERLIN (Israel Baline; b. 1888, Temun, Russia) lays claim to a personal rags-to-riches

Ethel Merman, Richard Rodgers, and Irving Berlin rehearse the *Annie Get Your Gun* score.

saga as eventful and romantic as any musical comedy scenario. Brought to New York City in 1892, he left the tenements of the Lower East Side at the age of eight to make his own way in the world. During a tenure as a singing waiter at a Chinatown restaurant, he wrote the lyrics for "Marie from Sunny Italy," his first published song. He taught himself to compose melodies as well, by picking out tunes on the black keys of the piano, and he achieved fame with both words and music for "Alexander's Ragtime Band" (1911). His earliest efforts for the musical stage were various interpolations into shows with scores written principally by other songwriters. *Watch Your Step* (1914), which fostered a Broadway mania for ragtime, was the first of his seventeen complete theater scores. Following contributions to several editions of the lavish ZIEGFELD FOLLIES and his own patriotic revue *Yip Yip Yaphank* (1918), he joined forces with producer Sam Harris and built the Music Box Theatre, where he presented four seasons of the intimate *Music Box Revues*. During the time of socially conscious musicals in the 1930s, he designed scores for two of the era's more ingenious topical shows, *Face the Music* (1932) and As THOUSANDS CHEER (1933). The 1940s were his most artistically expansive period, with works ranging from the patriotically oriented *Louisiana Purchase* (1940), THIS IS THE ARMY (1942), and *Miss Liberty* (1949) to the brassy slice of Americana ANNIE GET YOUR GUN (1946). The American political scene provided inspiration for his final stage efforts, *Call Me Madam* (1950) and *Mr. President* (1962). Berlin's theatrical songs, like those he wrote for films, reflect both the eras in which they were written and a remarkable timelessness.

LEONARD BERNSTEIN (b. 1918, Lawrence MA) has maintained brilliant careers in both serious and popular music. As a student at Harvard he was onstage pianist for a college production of *The Cradle Will Rock* and became a protégé of its composer, Marc Blitzstein. After graduation he studied conducting at Philadelphia's Curtis Institute and soon became assistant to Serge Koussevitzky. He burst into prominence as a last-minute substitute for Bruno Walter at a 1943 concert of the New York Philharmonic. His first major composition, the ballet *Fancy Free* (1943), teamed him with choreographer Jerome Robbins, and a year later he and Robbins joined with Betty Comden and Adolph Green to create ON THE TOWN (1944). Bernstein's musical theater works in the 1950s reflect a complex and eclectic talent, ranging from the traditional, in the incidental songs for Jean Arthur's *Peter Pan* (1950) and the period musical comedy score for WONDERFUL TOWN (1953), to the unconventional, in the comic operetta CANDIDE (1956) and the jazz-flavored WEST SIDE STORY (1957). In 1976 he collaborated with Alan Jay Lerner on the ambitious *1600 Pennsylvania Avenue*.

An exuberant Leonard Bernstein leads a spirited chorus during a recording session for the *Candide* cast album.

EUBIE (né James Hubert) **BLAKE** (b. 1883, Baltimore MD; d. 1983 New York NY), renowned ragtime composer and pianist, became enthralled with music at the age of six, when his parents bought an organ and arranged for him to study with a local musician. Despite his mother's misgivings, he began to play piano professionally in various Baltimore clubs while still a teenager. In 1915 he met Noble Sissle, and together they joined James Reese Europe's Society Orchestra. After World War I they reteamed to write and perform in a vaudeville act called "The Dixie Duo." Their first Broadway score was for the acclaimed SHUFFLE ALONG , originally produced in 1921, revised and revived in 1928, '33, and '52. Other musicals bearing Blake melodies are *Elsie* (1923) and *Chocolate Dandies* (1924), both written with Noble Sissle; *Blackbirds* (1930) with Andy Razaf; and *Swing It* (1932) with Cecil Mack and Milton Reddie. In 1978 a Broadway revue called *Eubie!* paid tribute to the Blake legacy in a cavalcade of his many songs and rags.

MARC BLITZSTEIN (b. 1905, Philadelphia PA; d. 1964, Martinique, West Indies) was a piano soloist with the Philadelphia Orchestra at fifteen. While studying composition in Europe with Nadia Boulanger and Arnold Schoenberg, he became fascinated with the politically militant musical theater of Kurt Weill and Bertolt Brecht, an influence strongly felt in his "play in music" THE CRADLE WILL ROCK (1937). His other works for the theater, *No for an Answer* (1941), *Regina* (1949), *Reuben, Reuben* (1955), and *Juno* (1959), were ambitious and uncompromising in their design but commercially unprofitable. He is perhaps best remembered for his English adaptation of Weill and Brecht's *The Threepenny Opera,* which enjoyed a long off-Broadway run in the 1950s and early 1960s.

JERRY (né Jerrold Lewis) **BOCK** (b. 1928, New Haven CT) and **SHELDON** (Mayer) **HARNICK** (b. 1924, Chicago IL) first collaborated on the score for the flop *The Body Beautiful* (1958). Previously Bock had teamed with lyricists Larry Holofcener and George David Weiss on the songs for the Sammy Davis, Jr., vehicle *Mr. Wonderful* (1956), and Harnick had penned clever lyrics for such revues as *New Faces of 1952* and *Phoenix '55* (1955). Despite their less-than-promising beginning, the team of Bock and Harnick eventually became one of the theater's most versatile and successful songwriting duos with the shows FIOR-ELLO! (1959), *Tenderloin* (1960), SHE LOVES ME (1963), FIDDLER ON THE ROOF (1964), and *The Apple Tree* (1966). Shortly after their musical *The Rothschilds* (1970) opened on Broadway, Bock abandoned the theater for other pursuits and Harnick paired with other composers, including Richard Rodgers (*Rex*, 1976).

IRVING (né Isidore) **CAESAR** (b. 1895, New York NY) was an employee at Ford Motor Company when his lyric for "Swanee," written with George Gershwin, was introduced in *The Demitasse Revue* (1918). Its success persuaded him to take up songwriting full-time. He continued to contribute interpolations for *The Greenwich Village Follies* and *George White's Scandals* (both 1921) and then graduated to such book musicals as NO! NO! NANETTE! (1925) and *Hit the Deck* (1927). His last Broadway musical was *My Dear Public* (1943), a lamentable effort which he also produced.

TRUMAN CAPOTE (b. 1924, New Orleans LA; d. 1987, Beverly Hills CA) was a prolific author of short stories, novels, and non-fiction. Although adapting his short story HOUSE OF FLOWERS constitutes his single foray into writing for the musical theater (1954), his works *Breakfast at Tiffany's* and *The Grass Harp* were adapted as musicals by other authors.

MARK (Moose) **CHARLAP** (b. 1927, Philadelphia PA; d. 1974, New York NY) came to Broadway after studies at the University of Pennsylvania and a residency in Tin Pan Alley that produced the hits "My Favorite Song" and "English Muffins and Irish Stew." With Carolyn Leigh, he contributed a number of songs to Mary Martin's *Peter Pan* (1954). Other musicals for which he provided scores are *Whoop-Up* (1958) with Norman Gimbel and *Kelly* (1965) with Eddie Lawrence. He also wrote several symphonic compositions.

GEORGE M(ichael) **COHAN** (b. 1878, Providence RI; d. 1942, New York NY) was the modern American musical theater's first omnibus figure: an accomplished dramatist, composer, lyricist, director, producer, actor, and song and

Sheldon Harnick, Jerry Bock, and producer Harold Prince at the Imperial Theatre on the opening night of *Fiddler on the Roof.*

dance man. Born into a family of vaudevillians, he was first presented to the public at three in an act billed as "Master Georgie—Violin Tricks and Tinkling Tunes." He penned vaudeville sketches in his teens and in 1901 wrote, composed, directed, produced, and starred in his first work for the Broadway stage, *The Governor's Son*. For the next three decades he devised and often appeared in a series of musical comedies and plays that endorsed a jaunty, affirmative view of American life and its virtues. Among these were LITTLE JOHNNY JONES (1904), *Forty-Five Minutes from Broadway* and *George Washington, Jr.* (both 1906), *The Little Millionaire* (1916), *Little Nellie Kelly* (1922), and *Billie* (1928). His "Over There" from *The Cohan Revue of 1918* stirred patriotic fervor during World War I. In the 1930s Cohan turned almost exclusively to performance, achieving success in O'Neill's comedy *Ah, Wilderness!* (1935) and as a fictional FDR in Rodgers and Hart's *I'd Rather Be Right* (1937). His life and work provided the source for the 1942 film *Yankee Doodle Dandy* and the 1968 stage musical *George M!*

BETTY COMDEN (b. 1915, New York NY) and ADOLPH GREEN (b. 1915, New York NY), whose exclusive partnership has endured for fifty years, have been kindred spirits since their student days at New York University. They broke into show business along with Judy Holliday as members (and frequent writers) of a satirical nightclub act, the Revuers. When the group disbanded in the early 1940s, Comden and Green joined up with Leonard Bernstein to write the book and lyrics for their first Broadway excursion, ON THE TOWN (1944), in which they also played featured roles. Also with Bernstein, they wrote the songs for WONDERFUL TOWN (1953) and an uncompleted musical version of Thornton Wil-

der's comedy *The Skin of Our Teeth* (ca. 1964). With the 1951 revue *Two on the Aisle*, they began a long and productive collaboration with Jule Styne, which resulted in *Peter Pan* (1954), BELLS ARE RINGING (1956), DO RE MI (1960), *Fade Out—Fade In* (1964), *Hallelujah, Baby!* (1967), and others. They have also teamed with Saul Chaplin (*Bonanza Bound*, 1947), Morton Gould (*Billion Dollar Baby*, 1948), Cy Coleman (*Straws in the Wind*, 1974; *On the Twentieth Century*, 1978), and Lawrence Grossman (*A Doll's Life*, 1982). In 1985 they developed a stage version of their celebrated screenplay for *Singin' in the Rain*. Comden and Green have also maintained their identities as performers, most notably in the 1958 and 1977 productions of their two-person revue, *A Party With Comden and Green*.

HOWARD DIETZ (b. 1896, New York NY; d. 1983, New York NY) maintained parallel careers in the entertainment industry as a writer and an arts administrator. A graduate of Columbia University's School of Journalism, he first published his comic rhymes in college and city newspapers. After a stint in the navy during World War I, he took a job as an advertising agent at a Manhattan firm. His promotional tactics for client Samuel Goldwyn eventually secured him a position as director of advertising and public relations at MGM Studios. He wrote his earliest professional lyrics for the song "Alibi Baby," interpolated into the 1923 W. C. Fields vehicle *Poppy*, but Dorothy Donnelly, the show's official lyricist, refused to allow his name on the song sheets and programs. Dietz received full credit on his next two shows, *Kind Sir* (1924) with Jerome Kern and *Merry-Go-Round* (1927) with Jay Gorney and Henry Souvaine, but failed to establish a lasting collaboration. In 1929 he began an enduring partnership with Arthur Schwartz that resulted in the

Adolph Green and Betty Comden

scores for twelve musicals. Among the most notable are *The Little Show* (1929), *Three's a Crowd* (1930), **THE BAND WAGON** (1931), *Revenge with Music* (1934), *At Home Abroad* (1935), *Inside U.S.A.* (1948), *The Gay Life* (1961), and *Jennie* (1963). Dietz also teamed with Jimmy McHugh on the revue *Keep Off the Grass* (1940) and Vernon Duke on the musicals *Jackpot* and *Sadie Thompson* (both 1944).

WALTER DONALDSON (b. 1893, Brooklyn NY; d. 1947, Santa Monica CA) was a self-taught composer and musician, despite the fact that his mother was an accomplished pianist. He trod the familiar route of song-plugger to songwriter and composed the music for a number of pop hits of the 1920s and 1930s, including "My Blue Heaven" and "Little White Lies." His two excursions into the theater resulted in the scores for the flop *Sweetheart Time* (1926, with Ballard MacDonald) and the smash **WHOOPEE** (1928, with Gus Kahn).

DOROTHY DONNELLY (b. 1880, New York NY; d. 1928, New York NY) starred in the American premiere of Shaw's *Candida* and created the role of the notorious Madame X. Her first libretto was for the 1916 operetta *Flora Bella*. In 1921 she began a collaboration with Sigmund Romberg which produced the memorable operettas *Blossom Time* (1921), **THE STUDENT PRINCE IN HEIDELBERG** (1924), and *My Maryland* (1927). She also teamed with composers Stephen Jones (*Poppy*, 1923) and William Kernell (*Hello, Lola*, 1926).

VERNON DUKE (Vladmir Dukelsky; b. 1903, Parafianovo, Russia; d. 1969, Santa Monica CA) revealed a musical precocity at the age of eight when he composed a full ballet score. Five years later he began studies with Reinhold Glière at the Kiev Conservatory but was forced to flee Russia during the 1917 revolution. He arrived in America in 1921 and soon became a protégé of George Gershwin, who encouraged him to anglicize his name and to devote his talents to popular music. Duke's first theater songs were heard in the British musicals *Yvonne* (1926), *The Yellow Mask* (1928), and *Open Your Eyes* (1930). *Walk a Little Faster*, the 1932 revue that introduced "April in Paris," brought his work to Broadway audiences. He contributed to the 1934 and '36 editions of the *Ziegfeld Follies* and in 1940 wrote the score for his best-known musical, **CABIN IN THE SKY**. His later works for the musical stage, *Banjo Eyes* (1941), *The Lady Comes Across* (1942), *Dancing in the Streets* (1943), *Jackpot*, *Sadie Thompson* (both 1944), *Sweet Bye and Bye* (1946), *Two's Company* (1952), *The Littlest Revue* (1956), *The Pink Jungle* (1959), and *Zenda* (1963), were plagued with insurmountable production problems. Besides his popular songs and theater scores, he composed many concert works under his real name.

DOROTHY FIELDS (b. 1905, Allenhurst NJ; d. 1974, New York NY), daughter of knockabout dialect comedian Lew Fields (see *Twirly-Whirly*), grew up surrounded by the colorful personages who inhabited the New York theater world. Her father's strong opposition to her ambitions as an actress persuaded her to enter show business as a lyricist. Teaming up with composer Jimmy McHugh in 1926, she devised the rhymes for several editions of Cotton Club revues and moved on to Broadway as co-author of the score for **BLACKBIRDS OF 1928**. With McHugh she also contributed to the musicals *Hello, Daddy* (1928) starring her father, *Lew Leslie's International Revue* (1930), and *Singin' the Blues* (1931). Throughout most of the 1930s she wrote songs for Hollywood films, then came back to Broadway at the end of the decade to collaborate with Arthur Schwartz on the songs for the musical comedy *Stars in Your Eyes* (1939). In the 1940s, in addition to frequent lyric-writing assignments, she teamed with her brother, Herbert, on the scripts for *Let's Face It* (1941), *Something for the Boys* (1943), *Mexican Hayride* (1944), *Up in Central Park* (1944), *Annie Get Your Gun* (1946), *Arms and the Girl* (1950), *By the Beautiful Sea* (1954), and *Redhead* (1959). She composed her finest set of lyrics in 1951 for **A TREE GROWS IN BROOKLYN**. Her final works, *Sweet Charity* (1966) and *Seesaw* (1973), were written with composer Cy Coleman.

RUDOLF FRIML (b. 1879, Prague, Bohemia; d. 1972, Hollywood CA) had his first composition published when he was ten. He studied with Antonín Dvořák at the Prague Conservatory and came to the United States in 1906 as accompanist for violinist Jan Kubelik. His light compositions for salon orchestras brought him to the attention of producer Arthur Hammerstein, who hired him to replace Victor Herbert as composer of the operetta *The Firefly* (1912). Of the nineteen works that followed, Friml's greatest artistic and commercial successes were *Katinka* (1915), **ROSE-MARIE** (1924), *The Vagabond King* (1925), and *The Three Musketeers* (1928). After the failure of his operetta *Music Hath Charms* (1934), he embarked on a new career as a popular concert artist and composer of film scores.

GEORGE GERSHWIN (Jacob Gershvin; b. 1898, Brooklyn NY; d. 1937, Hollywood CA), and his brother **IRA GERSHWIN** (Israel Gershvin; b. 1896, New York NY; d. 1983, Beverly Hills CA) grew up in a household centered around the family's highly prized upright piano. George quickly taught himself to play, and after brief studies of the classics, he pursued an interest in popular music and dropped out of school at fifteen to become a song-plugger at the Jerome H. Remick Co. Impatient with the firm's indifference toward his compositional aspirations, he left to tour as accompanist for vaudeville luminary Nora Bayes and to act as rehearsal pianist for Victor Her-

Broadway comes to Hollywood: Jerome Kern, Dorothy Fields, and George Gershwin at the Coconut Grove, 1936.

bert's *Miss 1917* (1917). A year later he wrote his first complete Broadway score for *La La Lucille* (1918) with Arthur Jackson and B. G. DeSylva. Concurrently, Ira's fascination with literature and his keen wit directed him toward a career as a lyricist. Using the pseudonym Arthur Francis (after his brother Arthur and his sister Frances) he first worked with George on "The Real American Folk Song," whch was interpolated into the 1918 Nora Bayes musical *Ladies First*. Three years later the Fred and Adele Astaire vehicle **Lady, Be Good!** (1924) was the first complete Broadway score to bear the credit line "music and lyrics by George and Ira Gershwin." Throughout the jazz age and into the depression, the brothers created a canon of highly eclectic theater works, including *Tip Toes* (1925), **Oh, Kay!** (1926), *Funny Face* (1927), *Strike Up the Band* (1927 and 1930 versions), **Girl Crazy** (1930), **Of Thee I Sing** (1931), *Let 'Em Eat Cake* (1933), and **Porgy and Bess** (1935, with DuBose Heyward). During the same period, George proved himself as an orchestral composer with *Rhapsody in Blue* and *An American in Paris* while Ira contributed lyrics to the revues *Life Begins at 8:40* (1934, with Harold Arlen and E.Y. Harburg) and the *Ziegfeld Follies* (1936, with Vernon Duke). After George's death in 1937, Ira wrote the lyrics for the stage musicals **Lady in the Dark** (1940, with Kurt Weill), *The Firebrand of Florence* (1945, again with Weill), and *Park Avenue* (1946, with Arthur Schwartz). Together and with others, the Gershwins also wrote songs for Hollywood films.

ADOLPH GREEN (see **BETTY COMDEN**)

OSCAR (Greeley Clendenning) **HAMMERSTEIN II** (b. 1895, New York NY; d. 1960, Doylestown PA), the American musical theater's foremost lyricist-librettist, was born into a prominent theatrical family of producers and theater owners. Impelled by his parents to pursue a law degree, Hammerstein could not deny his family heritage and began writing and performing in varsity shows while a student at Columbia University. A collaboration with his mentor Otto Harbach on the books and lyrics for *Wildflower* (1923, with Vincent Youmans and Herbert Stothart) and **Rose-Marie** (1924, with Rudolf Friml and Stothart) brought him to the attention of Broadway habitués. In 1925 he formed a long and prosperous partnership with Jerome Kern which revamped the state of the musical theater with such works as **Show Boat** (1927), *Sweet Adeline* (1929), and *Music in the Air* (1932). Concurrently, Hammerstein wrote the libretti for the swashbuckling Broadway operettas *Song of the Flame* (1925, with Harbach, Stothart, and the Gersh-

Oscar Hammerstein II

wins), *The Desert Song* (1926, with Harbach and Sigmund Romberg), and *The New Moon* (1928, with Frank Mandel and Romberg). After a serious career slump in the late 1930s and early 1940s, he teamed with Richard Rodgers to create a new sensibility for American operetta in the classic shows OKLAHOMA! (1943), CAROUSEL (1945), *Allegro* (1947), SOUTH PACIFIC (1949), THE KING AND I (1951), and THE SOUND OF MUSIC (1960).

OTTO HARBACH (Otto Abels Hauerbach; b. 1873, Salt Lake City UT; d. 1963, New York NY), a seminal figure in the development of the modern theater lyric and libretto, trained originally to be an English teacher. While pursuing a doctorate at Columbia University, he teamed with composer Karl Hoschna to write the pre-World War I stage hits *Three Twins* (1908) and *Madame Sherry* (1910). *The Firefly* (1912) was the first of ten scores Harbach penned in collaboration with Rudolf Friml, an association that reached its summit in ROSE-MARIE (1924). Harbach also achieved major works in partnership with Jerome Kern (*The Cat and the Fiddle*, 1931; ROBERTA, 1933), Sigmund Romberg (*The Desert Song*, 1926), Vincent Youmans (*Wildflower*, 1923; *No! No! Nanette!*, 1925), and Louis Hirsch (*Going Up*, 1917). In 1920 he became a mentor of and collaborator with Oscar Hammerstein II, beginning with *Jimmie* (1920, with Herbert Stothart) and ending with *Good Boy* (1928, with Bert Kalmar and Harry Ruby).

E(dgar) Y(ipsel) HARBURG (Isidore Hochberg; b. 1898, New York NY; d. 1981, Los Angeles CA) hoped to become an actor, but his parents' fear that he would be compelled to perform on Jewish holidays led him to turn to his interest in writing. After graduation from New York City College in 1918, Harburg spent the next decade as the proprietor of an electric appliance business. He returned to writing in earnest in 1929, composing songs with Jay Gorney for the revue *Earl Carroll's Sketchbook*. The 1930s brought a variety of stage assignments, including the lyrics for *New Americana* (1932) with Gorney, *Life Begins at 8:40* (1934) with Harold Arlen and Ira Gershwin, and *Hooray for What?* (1937) with Arlen. Harburg's whimsical outlook and social concerns found expression in his lyrics for the commercial successes BLOOMER GIRL (1944) and *Jamaica* (1957), both with Harold Arlen, FINIAN'S RAINBOW (1947), with Burton Lane, and the fascinating failure *Flahooley* (1951), with Sammy Fain. Devastated by the blacklisting tactics of the McCarthy era, he worked on only two more Broadway musicals: *The Happiest Girl in the World* (1961), an uneasy amalgam of Offenbach and Aristophanes, and *Darling of the Day* (1968), a charming but unappreciated Edwardian period piece written with Jule Styne.

SHELDON HARNICK (see **JERRY BOCK**)

LORENZ (Milton) **HART** (b. 1895, New York NY; d. 1943, New York NY) displayed a puckish wit from the age of six, when he began to concoct satiric verses for family celebrations. Strongly influenced by the lyrics of W. S. Gilbert and P. G. Wodehouse, Hart had his professional beginnings as a translator of German operetta libretti for the Shubert brothers. His search for the perfect collaborator ended in 1919 when he was introduced to a sixteen-year-old would-be composer named Richard Rodgers. Contributions to varsity shows at Columbia University, amateur theatricals, and occasional interpolations into scores by other songwriters prefaced their first success, the songs for the 1925 Theatre Guild revue, *The Garrick Gaieties*. Hart and Rodgers forged a unique and vigorous presence in the

E. Y. Harburg and Harold Arlen

Broadway musical theater, with Rodgers's lilting melodies tempering Hart's wistfully sardonic verses. Among their most notable works are *Dearest Enemy* (1925), *A Connecticut Yankee* (1927), *On Your Toes* (1936), BABES IN ARMS, *I'd Rather Be Right* (both 1937), *I Married An Angel, The Boys from Syracuse* (both 1938), PAL JOEY (1940), and *By Jupiter* (1942). Hart's persistent neurosis and alcoholism led to serious rifts in the partnership. Shortly after attending the opening of a 1943 Broadway revival of *A Connecticut Yankee*, he succumbed to pneumonia.

VICTOR HERBERT (b. 1859, Dublin, Ireland; d. 1924, New York NY), the progenitor of American operetta, was trained as a cellist at the Stuttgart and Vienna conservatories. He came to the United States in 1879 to join the orchestra of the Metropolitan Opera Company, where his wife was a leading soprano. He then served as bandmaster of the 22nd Regimental Band and conductor of the Pittsburgh Symphony. *Prince Ananias* (1894), the first of his forty-three theater scores, was commissioned and produced by the Boston Ideal Opera Company (The Bostonians). His most significant operettas include THE FORTUNE TELLER (1898), *Babes in Toyland* (1903), *Mlle. Modiste* (1905), *The Red Mill* (1906), *Naughty Marietta* (1910), and *Sweethearts* (1913). Herbert's favorite among his own works was *Eileen* (1917), set in his native Ireland. His final operetta. *The Dream Girl* (1924), was produced shortly after his death.

JERRY (né Gerald) **HERMAN** (b. 1933, New York NY), whose music and lyrics promote the grand traditions of the musical comedy, taught himself as a child to play piano by ear. He studied briefly at the Parsons School of Design but switched muses and pursued a degree in drama at the University of Miami. His songs for the off-Broadway revues *I Feel Wonderful* (1954), *Nightcap* (1958), and *Parade* (1960), sparked the interest of Broadway producer Gerard Oestreicher, who hired him to write the Israeli-flavored score of *Milk and Honey* (1961). In the mid-1960s he composed two of Broadway's biggest hits, HELLO, DOLLY! (1964) and *Mame* (1966). Following the quick demise of his next show, *Dear World* (1969), he suffered a temporary career slump, turning out appealing scores for the otherwise ill-conceived and commercially unsuccessful *Mack and Mabel* (1974) and *The Grand Tour* (1979). In 1980 his contributions to the modest British import *A Day in Hollywood/A Night in the Ukraine* were instrumental in its favorable American reception, and three years later he reclaimed his position in the vanguard of Broadway songwriters with the music and lyrics for the marathon hit *La Cage aux Folles* (1983).

DUBOSE HEYWARD (b. 1885, Charleston SC; d. 1940, Tryon NC) drew on his childhood memories of life in the wharf districts of Charleston to create a number of fictional works about southern blacks. He adapted his 1925 novel *Porgy* into first a stage drama (1927) and then, with Ira Gershwin, a libretto for the folk opera PORGY AND BESS (1935).

LANGSTON HUGHES (b. 1902, Joplin MO; d. 1967, New York NY) began his writing career in the 1930s as a columnist for the *Chicago Defender* and the *New York Post*. His stature in the 1940s as an eminent American poet led to a collaboration with Kurt Weill on the score for STREET SCENE (1947). He also wrote the scripts and lyrics for the musicals *Simply Heavenly* (1957, with David Martin) and *Tambourines to Glory* (1963, with Jobe Huntley), as well as the drama *Shakespeare in Harlem* (1958).

TOM (né Thomas) **JONES** (b. 1928, Littleton TX) and **HARVEY** (Lester) **SCHMIDT** (b. 1929, Dallas TX) began writing songs together as undergraduates at the University of Texas. Following stretches in the army, during which they maintained their collaboration by mail, they moved to New York and contributed songs to the off-Broadway *Upstairs at the Downstairs* revues produced by Julius Monk. THE FANTASTICKS (1960), their first professionally produced full-length musical, still holds the world record for the longest run. Their scores for *110 in the Shade* (1963) and *I Do! I Do!* (1966) have enjoyed equally favorable, though more modest, successes. In 1966 Jones and Schmidt established the Portfolio Workshop, an off-Broadway space for the development of experimental musicals. Of the shows created there, *Celebration* (1969) transferred to Broadway for a limited engagement. They attempted a return to Broadway in 1981 with *Colette*, which closed in tryouts, and their musical version of Thornton Wilder's *Our Town*, renamed *Grover's Corners*, began a national tour of regional theaters in 1987. In addition to his work as a composer, Harvey Schmidt has recorded albums of piano music and designs the witty cover art of Ben Bagley's "Revisited" series of recordings. Jones has worked as both an actor and a director.

GUS KAHN (b. 1886, Coblenz, Germany; d. 1941, Beverly Hills CA) won fame with his first published song, the 1907 hit "I Wish I Had a Girl." With composer Egbert Van Alstyne he turned out a series of pre–World War I standards, including "Memories" and "Pretty Baby." In the 1920s his partnership with Walter Donaldson produced the Tin Pan Alley classics "My Buddy" and "Yes Sir, That's My Baby" and the score for WHOOPEE (1928). Kahn also contributed lyrics to the musicals *Holka Polka* (1925) with Will Ortman, *Kitty's Kisses* (1926) with Con Conrad, *Rainbow* (1928) with Vincent Youmans, and *Show Girl* (1929) with the Gershwins.

JEROME (David) **KERN** (b. 1885, New York NY; d. 1945, New York NY), "the father of the modern American musical theater," developed his love for music through the Bohemian folk songs taught him by his mother. He studied theory and orchestration at the New York College of Music, then went to London, where some of his earliest songs were interpolated into the West End musicals produced by American impresario Charles Frohman. Returning to the States in 1904, Kern became an assistant at the T. B. Harms publishing firm. As rehearsal pianist for the new musical shows published by Harms, he seized every opportunity to audition his own melodies and succeeded in placing his groundbreaking ballad "They Didn't Believe Me" in the 1914 British import *The Girl from Utah*. Displeased with the conventional musical theater, Kern set out to reform it according to his own philosophical vision. His first efforts were revealed in the initimate Princess Theatre musicals *Nobody Home* (1915), *Very Good Eddie* (1915), **OH, BOY!** (1917), and *Oh, Lady! Lady!* (1918), and their immediate descendants, *Leave It to Jane* (1917) and *Sitting Pretty* (1924). He created the songs for *Sally* (1920) and *Sunny* (1925), two lavish star vehicles for Marilyn Miller, before bringing his aims to complete fruition in the classic score for **SHOW BOAT** (1927) with Oscar Hammerstein II. In the 1930s he spent much of his time in Hollywood writing screen musicals, coming back to Broadway periodically with *The Cat and the Fiddle* (1931), **ROBERTA** (1933) and *Very Warm for May* (1939). In 1945 Kern returned to New York to begin discussions for a new musical based on the life of Annie Oakley, but before work could begin, he died suddenly of a cerebral hemorrhage.

BURTON LANE (né Levy; b. 1912, New York NY) was initially a professional song-plugger. His earliest compositions were included in the revues *Three's a Crowd* (1930) and the *Earl Carroll Vanities* (1931). Although best known as the composer of **FINIAN'S RAINBOW** (1947), he has also written the melodious scores for *Hold On to Your Hats* (1940), *On a Clear Day You Can See Forever* (1965), and *Carmelina* (1979).

CAROLYN LEIGH (b. 1926, Bronx NY; d. 1985, New York NY) penned the lyrics for the 1950s pop hits "Young at Heart" and "For All We Know." The songs for Mary Martin's **PETER PAN** (1954), written with Mark Charlap, marked her entry into the musical theater, and with Cy Coleman she wrote the scores for the musical comedies *Wildcat* (1960) and *Little Me* (1962). In 1967 she conceived the story and wrote the lyrics for *How Now, Dow Jones*, a musical send-up of Wall Street. Her sudden death cut short a collaboration with Marvin Hamlisch on a musical version of the film comedy *Smile*.

JOHN (Treville) **LATOUCHE** (b. 1917, Richmond VA; d. 1956, Calais VT) became seriously interested in writing for the theater while an undergraduate at Columbia University, where he authored numerous lyrics and sketches for the annual varsity shows. His fledgling professional efforts were heard in the Harold Rome revue *Pins and Needles* (1937), and the following year his "Ballad of Uncle Sam" (later, "Ballad for Americans"), for the revue *Sing for Your Supper* (1939), was acclaimed as "the long-awaited American epic." **CABIN IN THE SKY** (1940) gave him his first opportunity to write lyrics for a Broadway book musical and he subsequently contributed to *Banjo Eyes* (1941), *The Lady Comes Across* (1942), *Rhapsody* (1944), *Polonaise* (1945), *Beggar's Holiday* (1946), *Ballet Ballads* (1948), **THE GOLDEN APPLE** (1954), and *The Vamp* (1955). His sudden death left unfinished his lyrics for *Candide* (1956).

ALAN JAY LERNER (b. 1918, New York NY; d. 1986, New York NY) was born not only with a silver spoon in his mouth but also with a golden touch for creating graceful, witty lyrics and libretti. The son of a wealthy retailer, he discarded thoughts of entering the family business as a teenager and began writing in earnest for the annual Hasty Pudding shows at Harvard. A fateful meeting with Frederick Loewe at the Lamb's Club in 1942 resulted in one of the musical thea-

Alan Jay Lerner and Frederick Loewe

ter's great partnerships. After false starts with the fast flops *The Life of the Party* (1942) and *What's Up?* (1943), they hit their stride with the musicals *The Day Before Spring* (1945), BRIGADOON (1947), *Paint Your Wagon* (1951), MY FAIR LADY (1956), and CAMELOT (1960). The first of several temporary rifts in the partnership allowed Lerner to team with Kurt Weill on the score for *Love Life* (1948). They reunited briefly in the mid-1970s for two disappointing works, a stage adaptation of their celebrated film musical *Gigi* (1973) and a film musical based on Saint-Exupéry's *The Little Prince* (1974). Lerner's career never quite recovered from the dissolution of his professional union with Loewe, though there were fleeting moments of his former brilliance in the musicals *On a Clear Day You Can See Forever* (1965) with Burton Lane, *Coco* (1969) with André Previn, *Lolita, My Love* (1971) with John Barry, *1600 Pennsylvania Avenue* (1976) with Leonard Bernstein, *Carmelina* (1979) with Lane, and *Dance a Little Closer* (1981) with Charles Strouse.

FRANK (né Francis Henry) **LOESSER** (b. 1910, New York NY; d. 1969, New York NY) first made a name for himself as a lyricist for the movies, paired with such composers as Alfred Newman, Hoagy Carmichael, Burton Lane, and Jule Styne. During World War II he had his first opportunities to write both words and music for the all-soldier shows he developed as a member of the U. S. Army's Special Services Division. His Broadway debut as the lyricist for 1936's *The Illustrator's Show* (with Irving Actman) went all but unnoticed, but his score for WHERE'S CHARLEY? (1948) launched him on a long and prosperous career that produced GUYS AND DOLLS (1950), THE MOST HAPPY FELLA (1956), *Greenwillow* (1960), and the Pulitzer Prize winner, HOW TO SUCCEED IN BUSINESS WITHOUT REALLY TRYING (1961). *Pleasures and Palaces* (1965), his last musical produced during his lifetime, closed during its pre-Broadway tryouts in Detroit. His final theatrical work, *Señor Discretion*, was produced posthumously in New York in 1985 under the supervision of his widow, Jo Sullivan Loesser. One of the most dynamic and creative figures in the twentieth-century entertainment industry, Loesser was also a first-rate librettist, producer, publisher, and talent scout, fostering the careers of songwriters Meredith Willson, Richard Adler, and Jerry Ross and producer Ben Bagley.

FREDERICK LOEWE (b. 1901, Berlin, Germany; d. 1988, Palm Springs CA) was introduced to the musical theater by his father, tenor Edmund Loewe, who was the world's first Danilo in the 1905 Vienna premiere of *The Merry Widow*. At fifteen Frederick was accomplished in the realms of both serious and light music, a concert pianist and the composer of the continental hit song "Katrina." He came to America in 1924, eager to

pursue an international career in music. After temporary detours as a prospector, a cowpoke, and a bantam-weight prizefighter, he won theatrical attention with the songs for the operetta *Great Lady* (1938), written with lyricist Earle Crooker. In 1942 a chance encounter with Alan Jay Lerner at the Lamb's Club led to a long and productive, though often stormy, partnership (see **ALAN JAY LERNER**).

(Thomas) **JOSEPH McCARTHY** (b. 1885, Maiden MA; d. 1943, New York NY) quit high school at sixteen to become a shop clerk and sing occasionally in cafes. His experiments with lyric-writing brought him to the attention of George Krey, a Boston music publisher who engaged him as a song-plugger. After writing the words for two songs and succeeding in getting them published, he came to New York to work for the firm of Leo Feist, Inc. He soon became intrigued with the musical theater and contributed interpolations to the shows THE HONEYMOON EXPRESS (1913) and *Ziegfeld Follies of 1919*. His greatest Broadway hits, IRENE (1919), *Kid Boots* (1923), and *Rio Rita* (1927), were written with Harry Tierney.

JIMMY (né James Francis) **McHUGH** (b. 1894, Boston MA; d. 1969, Beverly Hills CA) pursued a number of different occupations before becoming a song-plugger for the Boston office of Irving Berlin's publishing company. By 1921 McHugh had moved to Mills Music Company in New York City, where he remained a partner and staff composer until 1930. An introduction to fellow employee Dorothy Fields resulted in an eight-year exclusive partnership which produced songs for Cotton Club revues, Hollywood films, and the Broadway musicals BLACKBIRDS OF 1928, *Hello, Daddy* (1928), *Lew Leslie's International Revue* (1930), and *Singin' the Blues* (1931). With other lyricists he contributed to the scores of *The Streets of Paris* (1939, with Al Dubin), *Keep Off the Grass* (1940, with Howard Dietz and Dubin), and *As the Girls Go* (1948, with Harold Adamson). His final theatrical effort, a 1957 musical version of the 1940s comedy *Strip for Action* written with Harold Adamson, was an out-of-town casualty.

JOHNNY MERCER (b. 1909, Savannah GA; d. 1976, Los Angeles CA), like his friend and frequent collaborator Harold Arlen, broke into show business as a performer, acting in Broadway plays and singing with the Paul Whiteman and Benny Goodman bands. He penned his earliest theater lyrics for the revues *Garrick Gaieties* (1930) and *New Americana* (1932) before heading west and becoming one of Hollywood's top songwriters. Throughout his career he periodically returned to Broadway, either as lyricist for composers Hoagy Carmichael (*Walk with Music*, 1940), Harold Arlen (ST. LOUIS WOMAN, 1946; *Sar-*

atoga, 1959), Robert Emmett Dolan (*Texas, Little Darlin'*, 1949; *Foxy*, 1964) and Gene de Paul (*Li'l Abner*, 1956) or setting words to his own melodies (*Top Banana*, 1951). His final stage work was the British musical *The Good Companions* (1974), written with André Previn.

BOB MERRILL (Henry Lavan; b. 1926, Atlantic City NJ) worked as a child actor, a film director, a casting agent, and a TV producer before churning out the words and music for such catchy fare as "If I Knew You Were Coming, I'd Have Baked a Cake" and "How Much Is That Doggie in the Window?" He turned to plays by Eugene O'Neill (*Anna Christie; Ah, Wilderness*) for his first Broadway efforts (*New Girl in Town*, 1957; *Take Me Along*, 1959) and then achieved his most artistically satisfying work to date, CARNIVAL! (1961). The subsequent musicals for which he wrote both music and lyrics (*Breakfast at Tiffany's*, 1966; *Henry, Sweet Henry*, 1967; *The Prince of Grand Street*, 1979) failed to match the success of his earlier shows. As a lyricist, he has teamed with Jule Styne on the scores for FUNNY GIRL (1964), *Prettybelle* (1971), and *Sugar* (1972).

JAMES V. MONACO (b. 1885, Fornia, Italy; d. 1945, Beverly Hills CA) came to the United States in 1891. By the time he was seventeen he had become a full-time musician, playing piano in various New York cabarets. During his tenure in Tin Pan Alley, he authored the hit "Row, Row, Row." His theater compositions consisted of various interpolations into the scores of *Hanky Panky* (1912), *Ziegfeld Follies of 1912*, THE HONEYMOON EXPRESS (1913), and *Afgar* (1920). In the 1930s and 1940s, he wrote the music for many of the screen musicals emanating from Paramount and Twentieth-Century-Fox studios.

JEROME MOROSS (b. 1913, Brooklyn NY; d. 1983, Miami FL) first won public favor with his musical excursion into Americana, the ballet *Frankie and Johnny*. In 1948 he collaborated with John Latouche on *Ballet Ballads*, an experimental blend of story, song, and dance which received considerable critical acclaim. He and Latouche paired again in 1954 to produce the unconventional THE GOLDEN APPLE. Moross was also active in Hollywood films as an orchestrator and a composer.

OGDEN NASH (b. 1902, Rye NY; d. 1971, Baltimore MD), the master of whimsical verse, worked as a teacher and a Wall Street bond salesman before winning fame with his clever puns and distorted rhymes. Although his first efforts as a theater lyricist resulted in the score (with Kurt Weill) for the popular ONE TOUCH OF VENUS (1943), his subsequent musicals (*Sweet Bye and Bye*, 1946; *Two's Company*, 1952; *The Littlest Revue*, 1956) were all commercial failures. In 1971 his works were turned into an off-Broadway "revusical" called *Nash at Nine*.

Cole Porter listens to a playback from the *Kiss Me, Kate* original cast recording.

COLE (Albert) **PORTER** (b. 1891, Peru IN; d. 1964, Santa Monica CA) was raised in the lap of luxury, thanks to his maternal grandfather's lumber industry wealth. Aside from precocious juvenilia, his earliest compositions were ditties written for varsity shows while he was a Yale undergraduate. A disastrous Broadway debut in 1916 with the score for *See America First* impelled him to make a hasty retreat to France, where his studies with Vincent D'Indy at the Paris Conservatoire belied a public persona of elegant idleness. In 1928 producer E. Ray Goetz persuaded him to give Broadway another try by writing the songs for the "musicomedy" *Paris*. As a musical comedy craftsman, Porter came into his own in the 1930s with the sophisticated music and lyrics for *The New Yorkers* (1930), GAY DIVORCE (1932), ANYTHING GOES (1934), *Jubilee* (1935), *Red, Hot, and Blue* (1936), LEAVE IT TO ME! (1938), and DuBARRY WAS A LADY (1939). In 1937 a riding accident left him with crippling injuries that he endured throughout the rest of his life. In the early 1940s his work was, for the most part, artistically undistinguished, although *Panama Hattie* (1940), *Let's Face It!* (1941), *Something for the Boys* (1943), and *Mexican Hayride* (1944) were commercially successful. Just when his techniques seemed out of date, he came up with the score for KISS ME, KATE (1948), the finest of his long career. His 1950s shows *Out of This World* (1950), *Can-Can* (1953), and *Silk Stockings* (1955) produced the hit songs "From This Moment On," "I Love Paris," and "All of You."

LEO ROBIN (b. 1900, Pittsburgh PA) adopted songwriting as his livelihood after studying law and working as a newspaperman. Although his best work was done for movie musicals of the 1930s and 1940s, he contributed lyrics to the stage musicals *Hit the Deck* (1927, with Vincent Youmans), GENTLEMEN PREFER BLONDES (1949, with Jule Styne), and *The Girl in Pink Tights* (1954, with Sigmund Romberg and Don Walker).

RICHARD (Charles) **RODGERS** (b. 1902, Hammels Station, Long Island NY; d. 1979, New York NY), the dean of American show music composers, was influenced at an early age by his parents' affection for the operettas of Lehar and Herbert. At Columbia University he became the first freshman to compose the music for the annual varsity show. The collegiate romp, *Fly With Me* (1920), also marked the beginning of a twenty-four-year collaboration with the talented, unpredictable Lorenz Hart. Five years later they rose to prominence with their songs for the surprise hit *The Garrick Gaieties* (1925). With Hart, Rodgers went on to produce scores for twenty-eight more musical comedies, including *Dearest Enemy* (1925), *A Connecticut Yankee* (1927), *On Your Toes* (1936), BABES IN ARMS (1937), *I'd Rather Be Right* (1937), *I Married An Angel* (1938), *The Boys from Syracuse* (1938), PAL JOEY (1940), and *By Jupiter* (1942). In 1943 Rodgers embarked on a new partnership with Oscar Hammerstein II that forwarded a new kind of American operetta in the classic musicals OKLAHOMA! (1943), CAROUSEL (1945), SOUTH PACIFIC (1949), THE KING AND I (1951), and THE SOUND OF MUSIC (1959) and the lesser works *Allegro* (1947), *Me and Juliet* (1953), *Pipe Dream* (1955), and *Flower Drum Song* (1958). After Hammerstein's death in 1960, Rodgers set his own lyrics to music for *No Strings* (1962) and then teamed with other lyricists on *Do I Hear a Waltz?* (1965, with Stephen Sondheim), *Two by Two* (1970, with Martin Charnin), *Rex* (1976, with Sheldon Harnick), and *I Remember Mama* (1979, with Charnin and Raymond Jessel). In addition to his accomplishments as a composer, author, and producer, Rodgers worked to preserve the legacy of the American musical theater by establishing, in the 1960s, the Music Theatre of Lincoln Center series and the Rodgers and Hammerstein Archive of Recorded Sound at New York Public Library.

SIGMUND ROMBERG (b. 1887, Nagy Kaniza, Hungary; d. 1951, New York NY), a prime exponent of American operetta, began his musical studies in Hungary. Sent to Vienna to study engineering, Romberg developed an interest in the musical theater traditions of von Suppe and Strauss and planned to be a professional musician. In the hope that a long trip might lead him to a more practical career choice, his parents sent him to America in 1911. There his early ragtime piano pieces brought him to the attention of the Shubert brothers, who hired him as a staff composer. Over the next several years, he churned out functional but largely undistinguished specialty material for several editions of *The Passing Show* revues and such musical comedies as *The Whirl of the World* (1914) and *Dancing Around* (1915), all written with lyricist Harold Atteridge. His first successful operettas were *The Blue Paradise* (1915) with Herbert Reynolds and *Maytime* (1917) with Rida Johnson Young, both adapted from European sources. Romberg proved the master of the genre with THE STUDENT PRINCE IN HEIDELBERG (1924) with Dorothy Donnelly, *The Desert Song* (1926) with Otto Harbach and Oscar Hammerstein II, and *The New Moon* (1928) with Hammerstein. Beset by consistent failure in the 1930s, he switched coasts and composed songs for a number of the better movie musicals of the decade. His last Broadway hit was *Up in Central Park* (1945) with Dorothy Fields, and his final work (posthumously staged), *The Girl in Pink Tights* (1954) with Don Walker and Leo Robin, purported to recount the creation of *The Black Crook* (1866), the first long-running American musical.

HAROLD (Jacob) **ROME** (b. 1908, Hartford CT) earned a degree in architecture from Yale, but, unable to find a job in his field, he returned to his first love, composing music and lyrics. While writing shows for a summer resort in the Adirondacks, he came to the attention of the International Ladies Garment Workers' Union, who hired him to devise the songs for their revue PINS AND NEEDLES (1937). He continued specializing in "songs with social significance" in the scores for *Sing Out the News* (1938), *Let Freedom Sing* (1942), and *Call Me Mister* (1946). His first score for a Broadway book musical was *Wish You Were Here* (1952), followed by the music and lyrics for the David Merrick–produced FANNY (1954), *Destry Rides Again* (1959), and *I Can Get It for You Wholesale* (1962). His most recent Broadway efforts were the incidental songs for the comedy *The Zulu and the Zayda* (1965) and the English lyrics for the French revue *La Grosse Valise* (1966). In 1970 he tackled the challenge of designing a musical version of *Gone with the Wind*, which ran in Tokyo as *Scarlett* and in London and Los Angeles with its original name.

JERRY ROSS (see **RICHARD ADLER**)

HARVEY SCHMIDT (see **TOM JONES**)

Arthur Schwartz and Howard Dietz

NOBLE (Lee) SISSLE (b. 1889, Indianapolis IN; d. 1975, Tampa FL), best known as lyricist and original cast member of SHUFFLE ALONG (1921), began his show business career as a singer with Edward Thomas's Male Quartet and Hann's Jubilee Singers. He met Eubie Blake in 1915 when both were members of a Baltimore band. They later joined James Reese Europe's Society Orchestra, and during World War I, Sissle toured with Europe's regimental band. In 1919 he and Blake wrote and performed a popular vaudeville act which toured on the Keith circuit. In 1924 they followed the success of *Shuffle Along* with *The Chocolate Dandies*, in which Sissle also played a leading role.

HARRY B(ache) SMITH (b. 1860, Buffalo NY; d. 1936, Atlantic City NJ), author of 123 musical plays, remains the most prolific Broadway librettist-lyricist on record. During his career of nearly fifty years, he collaborated with over thirty major composers, including Victor Herbert, Reginald DeKoven, John Stromberg, John Philip Sousa, Jerome Kern, and Sigmund Romberg. His greatest successes were *Robin Hood* (1891), THE FORTUNE TELLER (1898), *The Girl from Utah* (1914), *Watch Your Step* (1914), and *Countess Maritza* (1926).

ROBERT B(ache) SMITH (b. 1875, Chicago IL; d. 1951, New York NY), younger brother of Harry B. Smith, also was a prominent librettist-lyricist of the late nineteenth- and early twentieth-century musical theater. TWIRLY-WHIRLY (1902), written with composer John Stromberg, was his first Broadway outing. He collaborated with his brother on the scripts for *The Spring Maid* (1910), *Gypsy Love* (1911), *Sweethearts* (1913), and others.

ARTHUR SCHWARTZ (b. 1900, Brooklyn NY; d. 1984, Kintnersville PA) wrote some of his earliest songs in partnership with Lorenz Hart when both worked as counselors at a Maine boys' camp in the early 1920s. A self-taught pianist, Schwartz longed for a career writing show music but bowed to his father's wishes and earned a law degree in 1924 from New York University. After four years as a lawyer, he became a full-time composer with the songs for *The Little Show* (1929), written with his frequent collaborator, Howard Dietz. Throughout the 1930s and 1940s, Schwartz and Dietz proved themselves the masters of the revue genre, creating the memorable scores for *Three's a Crowd* (1930), THE BAND WAGON (1931), *Flying Colors* (1932), *At Home Abroad* (1935), and *Inside U. S. A.* (1948). Schwartz also composed the music for nine book musicals, including three with Howard Dietz, *Revenge with Music* (1934), *The Gay Life* (1961), *Jennie* (1963); three with Dorothy Fields, *Stars in Your Eyes* (1939), A TREE GROWS IN BROOKLYN (1951), *By the Beautiful Sea* (1954); and one with Ira Gershwin, *Park Avenue* (1946). All, however, are impaired to varying degrees by faulty scripts.

STEPHEN (Joshua) SONDHEIM (b. 1930, New York NY) had his first brush with the musical theater as a youth, learning the basics of lyric-writing and dramatic construction from his neighbor Oscar Hammerstein II. Upon graduation from Williams College with a degree in music, he was awarded a two-year fellowship which allowed studies with avant-garde composer Milton Babbitt. A stint as a scriptwriter for the 1950s TV series "Topper" preceded his Broadway debut as lyricist for a pair of landmark musicals: WEST SIDE STORY (1957, with Leonard Bernstein) and GYPSY (1959, with Jule Styne). Briefly, he also succeeded his mentor Hammerstein as Richard Rodgers's lyricist on the short-lived *Do I Hear a Waltz?* (1965). A FUNNY THING HAPPENED ON THE WAY TO THE FORUM (1962) was the first produced musical for which he wrote both music and lyrics. His next show, *Anyone Can Whistle* (1964), was a commercial disaster but has become a cult favorite because of its many innovations in form and content. In 1970 Sondheim embarked on a collaboration with producer-director Harold

Prince, which brought a new maturity to the musical theater with *Company* (1970), *Follies* (1971), *A Little Night Music* (1973), *Pacific Overtures* (1976), and *Sweeney Todd* (1979). The partnership turned sour with 1983's *Merrily We Roll Along* and Sondheim paired with writer-director James Lapine on the Pulitzer-winning *Sunday in the Park with George* (1984) and *Into the Woods* (1987).

JOHN STROMBERG (b. 1853, New York NY; d. 1902, New York NY) served an apprenticeship as an arranger for Witmark music publishers prior to the 1865 publication of his first song, "My Best Girl's a Corker." With *The Art of Maryland* (1896) he began a six-year affiliation with Weber and Fields as staff composer for their satirical extravaganzas. At the time of his suicide, he had written four songs for Weber and Fields's TWIRLY-WHIRLY (1902).

CHARLES STROUSE (see **LEE ADAMS**)

JULE STYNE (Julius Kerwin Stein; b. 1905, London, England), one of the theater's most prolific composers, trained to be a concert pianist and was something of a prodigy in his adopted hometown of Chicago. His fascination with American popular music led to jobs as a bandleader, a vocal coach for Shirley Temple and Alice Faye at Twentieth-Century-Fox Studios, and an Oscar-winning Hollywood songwriter. Following an out-of-town disaster called *Glad to See You* (1944), he began an enduring residency on Broadway with the score (in collaboration with Sammy Cahn) for *High Button Shoes* (1947). At the end of the decade, he turned out a string of hits with Leo Robin for GENTLEMEN PREFER BLONDES (1949). His finest work, GYPSY (1959) with Stephen Sondheim, provided a narrative that perfectly matched his talent for creating music that typifies the brashness and sentimentality of show business. Among the other lyricists with whom he has collaborated on theater scores are Betty Comden and Adolph Green (*Two On the Aisle*, 1951; *Peter Pan*, 1954; BELLS ARE RINGING, 1956; *Say, Darling*, 1958; Do RE MI, 1960; *Subways Are for Sleeping*, 1961; *Fade Out—Fade In*, 1964; *Hallelujah, Baby!*, 1967; and *Lorelei*, 1973), Bob Merrill (*Funny Girl*, 1964; *Prettybelle*, 1971; and *Sugar*, 1975), E. Y. Harburg (*Darling of the Day*, 1968), Herb Gardner (*One Night Stand*, 1980) and Susan Birkenhead (*Treasure Island*, 1985).

HARRY (Austin) **TIERNEY** (b. 1890, Perth Amboy NJ; d. 1965, New York NY) made his professional bow as a concert pianist but soon discovered that his talent for writing popular songs was more marketable. He broke into the theater by the time-honored method of interpolating songs into various revues, including several editions of the *Ziegfeld Follies*. In 1919 he produced the score for the intimate, memorable IRENE, and in the 1920s he provided the music for the Ziegfeld extravaganzas *Kid Boots* (1923) and *Rio Rita* (1927). Other musicals bearing his melodies are *The Broadway Whirl* (1921), *Up She Goes*, *Glory* (both 1922), and *Cross My Heart* (1928).

KURT (Julian) **WEILL** (b. 1900, Dessau, Germany; d. 1950, New York NY) studied composition with Humperdinck and Busoni in Berlin and wrote his first opera, the jazz-tinged *Royal Palace*, at twenty-four. With poet-playwright Bertolt Brecht, he developed a politically oriented music theater in 1920s Berlin that included *The Threepenny Opera* (1928), *Happy End* (1929), and *Mahagonny* (1930). Forced by the threat of the Nazi regime to leave Germany in 1933, Weill and his wife, actress-singer Lotte Lenya, eventually settled in the United States in

Backstage at *Lady in the Dark*: conductor Maurice Abravanel, Kurt Weill, and Ira Gershwin.

1935. His first American theater piece, the anti-war musical drama *Johnny Johnson* (1936, with Paul Green), recalled the atonal sounds and dour political commentary of his Berlin *oeuvre*, but beginning with the songs for **KNICKERBOCKER HOLIDAY** (1938, with Maxwell Anderson), he moved stylistically toward the musical mainstream. In the early 1940s Weill produced the sophisticated scores for **LADY IN THE DARK** (1940, with Ira Gershwin), **ONE TOUCH OF VENUS** (1943, with Ogden Nash), and *The Firebrand of Florence* (1945, with Ira Gershwin). Later in the decade he returned to a musical theater of operatic and socio-political ambitions with **STREET SCENE** (1947, with Langston Hughes) and *Lost in the Stars* (1949). At the time of his death, he and Maxwell Anderson had completed five songs for a projected musical version of *Huckleberry Finn*. Ironically, his greatest success in the American musical theater was the posthumous 1954 off-Broadway production of *The Threepenny Opera* which ran for 2,707 performances.

RICHARD WILBUR (b. 1921, New York NY) was educated at Amherst and in the early 1950s established himself as one of the leading voices in contemporary American poetry. He won the Prix de Rome in 1954 for his verse and is known as the foremost English translator of Molière's plays. His single foray into the musical theater was in providing many of the lyrics for **CANDIDE** (1956).

MEREDITH WILLSON (Robert Meredith Reiniger; b. 1902, Mason City IA; d. 1984, Santa Monica CA) made a belated but auspicious Broadway debut at the age of fifty-three as the composer, lyricist, and co-librettist of **THE MUSIC MAN** (1957). A music man himself, he had his professional beginnings as flutist with John Philip Sousa's Band and the New York Philharmonic Orchestra. In the 1930s he launched a notable career as a musician and personality on various NBC radio broadcasts. His compositions during the 1940s and early 1950s ranged from symphonic works to the popular song "May the Good Lord Bless and Keep You." Following *The Music Man*, Willson contributed songs to two more Broadway musicals, *The Unsinkable Molly Brown* (1960) and *Here's Love* (1963). His final stage musical, *1491* (1969), expired during its West Coast tryouts.

P(elham) G(renville) WODEHOUSE (b. 1881, Guildford, England; d. 1975, Southampton NY) planned a future as a financier but soon discovered his metier in writing humorous fiction and verse. His lyrics were first set to music by Jerome Kern in a number of West End musicals produced by Charles Frohman. The success of Wodehouse's *Psmith* novels brought him to the United States, where he secured a job as drama critic for *Vanity Fair* magazine. While covering the premiere of the musical *Very Good Eddie* (1915), he was reunited with Kern, who invited him to collaborate on future projects. Joined by librettist Guy Bolton, Kern and Wodehouse revolutionized the American musical theater with the Princess Theatre shows *Nobody Home* (1915), **OH, BOY!** (1917), and *Oh, Lady! Lady!* (1918). In addition, the trio wrote the progenitor of the collegiate musical comedy *Leave It to Jane* (1917). Wodehouse and Bolton also co-authored the book for *Oh, Kay!* (1926) and the original script for *Anything Goes* (1934).

VINCENT (Millie) YOUMANS (b. 1898, New York NY; d. 1946, Denver CO), the son of a rich Manhattan milliner, started piano lessons at age four. After a tour of duty in the navy during World War I, he took a job at Harms, Inc., where fellow song-plugger George Gershwin found him a spot as Victor Herbert's rehearsal pianist. Although his first complete theater score was for the out-of-town casualty *A Night Out* (1920), his next opus, *Two Little Girls in Blue* (1921, with Ira Gershwin), established him among Broadway's most promising newcomers. The giddy, effervescent tunes he wrote for the musical comedies *Wildflower* (1923, with Oscar Hammerstein II, Otto Harbach, and Herbert Stothart), **NO! NO! NANETTE!** (1925, with Otto Harbach and Irving Caesar), *Oh, Please!* (1926, with Anne Caldwell), and *Hit the Deck* (1927, with Clifford Grey and Leo Robin) revelled in the hedonistic spirit and rhythm of the jazz age. His scores for the ambitious musicals *Rainbow* (1928, with Hammerstein and Gus Kahn), *Great Day!* (1929, with Edward Eliscu and Billy Rose), and *Through the Years* (1932, with Edward Heyman) displayed his respect for the accomplishments of *Show Boat* (1927) without emulating any of its artistic homogeneity. Youman's first return to the lighter atmosphere of musical comedy resulted in a failure, *Smiles* (1930, with Harold Adamson, Clifford Grey, and Ring Lardner), but his songs for *Take a Chance* (1932, with B. G. DeSylva) provided a final Broadway triumph.

★ BIBLIOGRAPHY

Musical Theater Histories

Baral, Robert. *Revue*. New York: Fleet, 1962.
Bordman, Gerald. *American Musical Theater: A Chronicle*. New York: Oxford University Press, 1978.
———.*American Operetta*. New York: Oxford University Press, 1981.
———.*American Musical Comedy*. New York: Oxford University Press, 1982.
———.*American Musical Revue*. New York: Oxford University Press, 1985.
Burton, Jack. *The Blue Book of Broadway Musicals*. Watkins Glen, N.Y.: Century House, 1969.
Engel, Lehman. *The American Musical Theater: A Consideration*. New York: CBS Legacy, 1967.
Ewen, David. *New Complete Book of the American Musical Theater*. New York: Henry Holt, 1976.
Gottfried, Martin. *Broadway Musicals*. New York: Harry M. Abrams, 1979.
Green, Stanley. *Broadway Musicals Show By Show*. Milwaukee: Hal Leonard Books, 1985.
———.*The Encyclopedia of the American Musical Theatre*. New York: Dodd, Mead, 1970.
———.*Ring Bells! Sing Songs!: Broadway Musicals of the 1930s*. New Rochelle, N.Y.: Arlington House, 1971.
———.*The World of Musical Comedy*, revised and expanded edition. New York: A. S. Barnes, 1980.
Jackson, Arthur. *The Best Musicals From Show Boat to A Chorus Line*. New York: Crown Publishers, 1977.
Mates, Julian. *The American Musical Stage Before 1800*. New Brunswick, N. J.: Rutgers University Press, 1962.
———.*America's Musical Stage*. Westport, CT: Greenwood Press, 1985.
Mordden, Ethan. *Better Foot Forward: The History of the American Musical Theatre*. New York: Grossman Publishers, 1976.
———.*Broadway Babies: The People Who Made the American Musical*. New York: Oxford University Press, 1983.
Smith, Cecil, and Glenn Litton. *Musical Comedy in America*. New York: Theatre Arts Books, 1981.
Traubner, Richard. *Operetta*. New York: Doubleday, 1981.

Discographies

Hummel, David. *The Collector's Guide to the American Musical Theatre*, vols. 1 & 2. Metuchen, N.J.: The Scarecrow Press, 1984.
Raymond, Jack. *Show Music on Record*. New York: Frederick Ungar, 1981.
Rust, Brian A. L., and Allen Debus. *The Complete Entertainment Discography*. Middlesex, England, 1977.
———. *London Musical Shows on Record*. London: British Institute of Recorded Sound, 1958.

DWIGHT BLOCKER BOWERS, a graduate of Hiram College and the University of Connecticut, is a performing arts historian at the Smithsonian's National Museum of American History. He produces and directs an ongoing series of programs that explore American theater music and, in 1988, was co-curator of the museum's Irving Berlin centennial celebration. With James R. Morris and J. R. Taylor, he co-authored the Smithsonian Collection's highly acclaimed seven-record set, *American Popular Song: Six Decades of Songwriters and Singers.*

PHOTO CREDITS

Grateful acknowledgement is made to the following archives and individuals for the use of photographs:

ASCAP—13, 45, 118, 119

CBS—70, 75, 81, 101, 102, 107, 111, 114, 123

Culver Pictures—9

Friedman-Abeles—86, 90, 91, 99

Stanley Green Collection—16, 21, 24, 28, 30, 34, 39, 46, 47, 50, 67, 69, 95, 97, 115, 125, 126

International Ladies' Garment Workers' Union Records, Labor-Management Documentation Center, M. P. Catherwood Library, Cornell University—35

Mrs. Danny Kaye—106

Library of Congress—8

Library of Congress Federal Theatre Project Collection at George Mason University, Fairfax VA—36

Museum of the City of New York—11, 100, 108, 112

National Portrait Gallery, Smithsonian Institution—52

New York Public Library at Lincoln Center; Astor, Lenox, and Tilden Foundations—3, 10, 25, 27, 29, 32, 103, 121

Rodgers and Hammerstein Archive, New York Public Library—61, 113

Theatre Arts Collections, Harry Ransom Research Center, University of Texas at Austin—facing 1, 19, 23, 37, 40, 41, 42, 43, 51, 53, 55, 56, 58, 59, 60, 62, 63, 65, 68, 71, 72, 76, 77, 79, 80, 83, 84, 87, 88, 92, 94, 105, 116

INDEX

Shows

Songs